Happy As a Big Sunflower
Adventures in the West, 1876–1880

Rolf Johnson

Edited and with an introduction by Richard E. Jensen

University of Nebraska Press
Lincoln and London
In association with the Nebraska State Historical Society

∞

Library of Congress Cataloging-in-Publication Data
Johnson, Rolf, 1856–1922
  Happy as a big sunflower : adventures in the West, 1876–1880 ; edited
and with an introduction by Richard E. Jensen.
  p. cm.
"A Bison original."
Includes bibliographical references and index.
ISBN 0-8032-7614-1 (alk. paper)
 1. Johnson, Rolf, 1856–1922—Diaries. 2. Pioneers—Nebraska—Phelps County—Diaries.
3. Swedish Americans—Nebraska—Phelps County—Diaries. 4. Frontier and pioneer
life—Nebraska—Phelps County. 5. Phelps County (Neb.)—Biography. 6. Phelps County
(Neb.)—Social life and customs—19th century. 7. Pioneers—West (U.S.)—Diaries. 8.
Frontier and pioneer life—West (U.S.) 9. West (U.S.)—Biography. 10. West
(U.S.)—Social life and customs—19th century. I. Jensen, Richard E. II. Title.

F672.P5 J64 2000
978.2'392031'092—dc21
[B]

00-036381

This book is dedicated to the memory of R. Bruce Chamberlin, grandson of Rolf Johnson. Mr. Chamberlin donated the Johnson diaries to the Phelps County (Nebraska) Historical Society in 1974 to assure their continued preservation. The diaries are housed in the Society's Nebraska Prairie Museum at Holdrege, Nebraska. The publication of the diaries is with the permission of Mr. Chamberlin and the Phelps County Historical Society.

Contents

Illustrations

Acknowledgments

A number of people have contributed to this publication in significant ways. The late R. Bruce Chamberlin deserves special recognition for assuring the continued preservation of his grandfather's diaries. Thanks are also due to Mr. Chamberlin and the Phelps County Historical Society, custodian of the diaries, for allowing publication. Mr. Chamberlin was born in Curtis, Nebraska, in 1916. He received a degree in chemical engineering from the University of Colorado. Most of his adult life was spent in California and after his retirement, he actively pursued a lifelong interest in history. For ten years he was a volunteer history tour guide at the Oakland Museum of California. Membership in the Sierra Club and the Nature Conservancy were only two of his other many and varied interests. He died on October 18, 1997. Grace C. Johnson of Orleans, Nebraska, and Harry D. Dahlstrom of Holdrege offered insights into Phelps County pioneer days. Ms. Johnson provided the Johnson family photographs reproduced here. Several Nebraska State Historical Society employees made substantial contributions. James E. Potter made the initial transcripts of the diaries and both he and R. Eli Paul read initial drafts of this offering. Their comments noticeably improved the merit of the book. Dell Darling produced legible maps from very crude drafts. Patricia Gaster prepared the index, and Debra Brownson produced the layout.

Introduction

Rolf Johnson began writing his diary on December 31, 1875, when he was nineteen years old and living with his parents near Henderson Grove, Illinois. Ten weeks later the Johnson family left the state and relocated in Phelps County, Nebraska. For the next three years Rolf recorded his experiences on the farming frontier. While it seems he kept the diary for his own amusement and perhaps as a mnemonic device, he has left us with an honest and vivid description of the realities of pioneer life. During the first two years in Phelps County Rolf was preoccupied with the endless tasks facing immigrants in an undeveloped land. During this period he wrote about the difficulties in building sod houses, plowing the prairie, digging wells, and many other challenges the newcomers had to face. He described the roaring prairie fires that swept away some settlers' homes and the grasshopper plague that destroyed the crops and impoverished his parents and many of their neighbors. As these challenges were overcome and Rolf became more accustomed to his new surroundings, his thoughts turned to other subjects. He began to write more about local politics, parties, and informal gatherings, and the diary becomes an account of social life in a frontier community. His innocent relationships with several young women are paramount and are described with shy candor. In the summer of 1879 he unexpectedly announced his "intention of going west for a season." It was the beginning of an odyssey that would take him to the Black Hills of Dakota, south into the Colorado Rockies, and on to New Mexico. During this period the diary becomes a travelogue, but with a strong emphasis on his many new friends and acquaintances. His journal ends abruptly in Cubero, New Mexico, on November 26, 1880.[1]

Rolf was the eldest son of John and Karen Svenson Johnson. His parents were married on April 11, 1854, in Nebbeboda, a province on the southern tip of Sweden; one month later they immigrated to the

United States.[2] The Johnsons' reason for leaving their native land is not known, but many people migrated because of worsening economic conditions, while others found the State Church of Sweden, which was nominally Lutheran, to be too oppressive. A major exodus began in 1852, and by the end of 1854 approximately 9,600 people left the country, nearly all of them going to the United States. The Johnsons may also have been swayed by an emigrant guide published in Chicago in 1853 by Rev. Erland Carlsson. The guide enumerated the many advantages of coming to the United States and was widely distributed in Sweden.[3]

Like many emigrating Swedes the young couple chose Chicago as their first home in the new country. Then in 1867 they moved to Altona in northwestern Illinois, in the heart of a predominately Swedish district.[4] The first group of Swedes arrived in this general area in 1846 and founded Bishop Hill. In the spring of 1870 the Johnsons moved a few miles to Henderson Grove, a small Swedish settlement founded in 1849.[5] The Johnsons bought a farm nearby, but the timing was not especially advantageous. The lack of rainfall in 1873 severely damaged crops across the state, and the drought of 1874 was considered the worst in Illinois history. The financial panic of 1873, which plunged the nation into what was possibly the country's deepest depression, worsened the plight of farmers everywhere.[6] By the winter of 1875–76 it was necessary for John to leave his family of six children on the farm and go to work in a coal mine in the nearby village of Soperville.

On January 22 the Johnsons met Leander Hallgren and Victor Rylander, land agents for the Union Pacific Railroad. The agents came to Henderson Grove hoping to assemble a group of people who would move to Phelps County, Nebraska. The county had been formed in 1873 and encompassed about 530 square miles, but had an estimated population of only 110.[7] The Union Pacific wanted more settlers along the rail line to provide the company with additional business, and the railroad also owned land it hoped to sell to the colonists.

The Union Pacific had received title to thousands of acres of land on July 1, 1862, when President Abraham Lincoln signed the Pacific Railroad Act. The company received the odd numbered sections of government land in a band twenty miles wide on either side of the right of way west of the Missouri River. Railroad holdings in Phelps County totaled approximately 128,000 acres, and the land was being offered for sale at $2.50 an acre. The grant was intended to help defray construction costs of the railroad line.

Settlers who had money could also purchase government land. The Preemption Act of September 4, 1841, allowed the sale of up to 160 acres, one quarter of a square mile, of surveyed or unsurveyed government land to adult males or widows. A buyer had to make improvements, but did have twelve months before the final payment came due. When the Johnsons went west, government land in Phelps County could be purchased for $2.50 per acre.

Probably the best reason for moving to Phelps County was the possibility of acquiring up to half a square mile (320 acres) of virtually free land under the Homestead and the Timber Culture Acts. The Homestead Act, which took effect on January 1, 1863, made it possible for a settler to receive the title, or "prove up," on 160 acres of government land after living on it for five years and making certain improvements. There was a $10 filing fee. The other option for free land was provided by the Timber Culture Act of 1873. Tree culture was a very popular idea among politicians, promoters, and others who did not have to do the work. As early as 1857 officials of Nebraska Territory suggested combining tree culture with a free homestead law. It was Nebraska's Senator Phineas W. Hitchcock who introduced the timber culture bill in the U.S. Congress, which became law on March 3, 1873. It called for planting forty acres of trees on a quarter section and cultivating them for eight years before a patent could be issued.[8] Farmers complained that planting and caring for 12,000 seedlings was an unreasonable burden and on March 13, 1874, the act was amended and the number of acres of trees reduced to ten. After eight years the title was given if there were 675 living trees per acre. A claimant did not have to live on the land, and this led to abuses of the law. A speculator might make a timber claim and hold it in the hope the value of the land would increase. If a buyer were found, the speculator would receive an agreed upon amount of money and then relinquish his claim. The newcomer could then file for a homestead, timber claim, or buy the land outright from the government.[9]

Most Phelps County settlers considered a timber claim to be the easiest initial step in acquiring land. Ninety-six percent of the timber claims were on plots that had never been claimed previously, but of these approximately 70 percent were canceled by the original filers. In

Phelps County, timber claims accounted for less than 14 percent of all claims for which titles were eventually granted. Claimants either re-filed under the Homestead Act or surrendered the claim and moved elsewhere. Later claimants could file for a timber claim, but more often the acreages were converted to homesteads. While timber claims were frequently changed to homesteads, the reverse was almost never done.[10]

Hallgren and Rylander undoubtedly mentioned these methods of acquiring land when they talked to prospective clients in Henderson Grove. It is equally likely they would have stressed the personal advancement and financial security one could gain through growing with a new state, while at the same time mentioning the high cost of land in Illinois that limited upward mobility. They probably also assured their listeners that Nebraska was no longer in the heart of the Great American Desert, and suitable only for nomadic hunters. In the 1870s climatologists noticed sporadic increases in precipitation in the West. Real estate agents and other promoters exaggerated these findings and claimed that plowing the prairie caused the increase in rainfall. They declared the desert to be a burgeoning Garden of Eden and many people believed them.[11]

Although the land agents certainly dwelt upon the advantages of Phelps County, they would have minimized the hardships a settler would face. There were some real and some imagined disadvantages that a prospective settler had to consider carefully. Many easterners were convinced that Indians posed a serious threat to the lives of Nebraska settlers. Before the Johnsons left Illinois, John's sister and her husband told exaggerated stories about Indian raids that Rolf said "was enough to make one's hair stand on end." In the mid-1870s there were a number of significant confrontations in the West between Indians and whites. Although these conflicts did not directly effect Phelps County, the gory reports in the press kept some settlers on edge. Rolf told of one incident when a distant herd of antelope was mistaken for Indians and the white community panicked, fearing an Indian attack was imminent.

Settlers soon learned they had to face more immediate problems than the far-off Indian wars. In 1874 and 1875 grasshoppers, or Rocky Mountain locusts, swarmed over much of the state and left many farmers destitute. As a result Gov. Robert W. Furnas formed the Nebraska Relief and Aid Society on September 18, 1874, to provide some assistance to the impoverished farmers.[12] Newspapers in the West admitted there was a problem, but tried to present the most promising picture possible. The *Platte Valley Independent*, a newspaper in Grand Island, published a lengthy interview with Charles V. Riley, Missouri's state entomologist, who claimed there would not be any locusts in 1876; his explanation was convoluted and not very convincing. Kearney's *Central Nebraska Press* assured its readers that a solution would be found, but did not explain what it was although the paper promised, "the land will not be abandoned to the locust."[13]

Unfortunately many farmers had to abandon the land. Hall County was especially devastated, resulting in a general exodus, although there may have been other contributing factors. In 1877 the *Grand Island Times* published seven columns of very small print listing land to be sold for back taxes. The parcels totaled an estimated 80,000 acres or just over 20 percent of the county that was either deserted or the residents had avoided the tax collector.[14]

When the insects returned again in 1876, it was an especially severe blow to the new settlers in Phelps County. Rolf was looking for work in eastern Nebraska when the devastation occurred, but he saw the aftermath and wrote, "Crops were all destroyed and cornstalks eaten clear to the roots" by the grasshoppers. A Phelps County settler who witnessed the invasion was working on a homestead only a few miles from John Johnson's farm. On August 5 he noticed "a thin brownish colored cloud or haze" over the horizon to the north. It was the enormous swarm of grasshoppers that descended on the county.[15] A farmer in Red Willow County, Nebraska, also vividly recalled the infestation:

> I had about 100 acres of corn, and in two hours after they [the hoppers] commenced to light I believe they would average a depth of four inches all over the ground, and as much hanging to the stalks of the corn as could find holding places. A person who has never seen them, you can't make them understand it. I had a nice crop there in 1876, at ten o'clock in the morning and at four o'clock in the afternoon there was absolutely nothing left on the place. I had an acre of onions, and every place there had been an onion there was a hole in the ground.[16]

Another obstacle that delayed settlement in some parts of the state was the lack of surface water. The only surface water in Phelps County was the Platte River in the north and Spring Creek and perhaps one or two other small streams near the southern boundary. Hauling water from these steams was not practical, so experienced wellmen were hired to dig wells, removing dirt from the shaft one bucket at a time. Rolf spent several days hoisting the buckets from a well that was dug to a depth of 110 feet before water was reached. By the mid-1870s mechanical augers were being marketed to drill wells. They were less dangerous than digging by hand, but the machines were more expensive than most people could afford.[17] After the Johnsons had been in Phelps County for two years, Rolf mentioned that his father hired a man to "drill" a well, perhaps a reference to an auger. Well-drilling machinery was used by at least one Phelps County pioneer. Andreas Olson, who arrived in 1876, described the process:

> The wellmaking machinery consisted of a large cast iron auger, about 12 inches in diameter, suspended in a three post derrick about 30 feet high. The auger was turned by two men, who pushed on two short and heavy levers, that hooked on the 4 by 4 inch beams, on which it hung. In going round it was necessary for the men to continually look away to the horizon in order not be become dizzy and ill.[18]

Windmills were another aid in solving the water problem. By the 1870s they were being manufactured on a large scale in the United States. People on the Plains were also experimenting with homemade mills.[19]

Fencing was not a particular concern to the early settlers because there was so much vacant land. After a few years the number of immigrants increased dramatically and fencing become vitally important. By 1874 barbed wire was being marketed in the United States, and advertisements for the product began appearing in central Nebraska newspapers at least by the summer of 1877. Philip C. Funk erected a barbed wire fence in Phelps County in the fall of 1879 and claimed it was the first in the county, but it may not have been.[20] In his entry for November 28, 1878, Rolf mentioned a "wire fence" around a pasture.

There were other factors a prospective Phelps County settler had to consider. In 1876 getting crops to a market was a major undertaking.

The closest railroad was on the north side of the Platte River, and the nearest bridge was south of Kearney. This meant a trip of more than thirty miles from the center of the county to the railroad.

At this same time the state was emerging from an era of political turmoil; however, the newcomers could not have known that the worst problems were past. Gov. David Butler had been impeached and removed from office in 1871 and a new state constitution was rejected, causing deep political rifts. Perhaps the most obvious negative political consideration was the state's staggering debt.[21]

The Johnsons pondered the move to Nebraska for three days before they made the decision to relocate. They were joined by eight other families and six bachelors, totaling nearly forty people. Most, if not all of them, were Swedes from the Henderson Grove area. They left on March 6, 1876, and others would follow in the weeks to come.[22]

The emigrants may have found some comfort in knowing they would not be the first Swedes from the Henderson Grove vicinity to go west. In 1868 Anders W. Dahlsten, a pastor at Galesburg, Illinois, organized the Galesburg Colonization Committee. This association aided emigrants in establishing a number of Swedish colonies in Kansas. In 1871 a committee from Altona explored the potential in Nebraska for a Swedish settlement and the next year a colony was founded at Stromsburg.[23] In the spring of 1875 F. A. Bieyon, a U.P.R.R. land agent, convinced a group from the Wataga area, only about five miles east of Henderson Grove, to emigrate. This group included brothers Olaf and Matthies Hedlund, who took adjoining timber claims near the center of Phelps County on December 4, 1875. Olaf Hedlund would become one of the leaders of the county's Swedish colony.[24] Swedes from other areas of the United States also preceded the Johnsons. In 1875 about twenty Swedes founded Svea in adjoining Kearney County. Swedish settlements around Mead, Swedeburg, and Malmo in east central Nebraska also predated the Phelps County colony. There was also a Swedish section of Omaha centered on a Swedish Lutheran Church organized in 1868.[25]

The area being touted by Hallgren and Rylander was not totally uninhabited. In the late 1850s two road ranches were established near the Platte River to serve emigrants traveling by stagecoach or covered wagon on the Overland Trail to the Far West. Plum Creek Station was near the mouth of the creek in the northwest corner of Phelps County.

Garden Station was about six miles from the county's eastern border or seventeen miles west of Fort Kearny.[26] It is unlikely that more than four or five families ever lived at Plum Creek and at Garden. Owners of the outposts kept a supply of goods desired or sometimes desperately needed by the travelers. Horses, mules, and oxen were offered in exchange for trail-weary trail animals and some ranches boasted a blacksmith shop. Early ranches depended heavily on the travelers who passed their little commercial centers in the spring. Somewhat later, most became stagecoach stations, providing fresh horses and offering meals for the passengers. Both of the Phelps County ranches benefited briefly when the Pony Express carried mail to the West Coast.

When the Union Pacific Railroad laid tracks along the north side of the Platte River in the fall of 1866 the ranches became obsolete. Many people left and the post office at Plum Creek was discontinued on March 16, 1868, but the area was not completely abandoned.[27] The first homesteads were filed in the northeast corner of Phelps County on August 13, 1872, by Henry V. Hoagland and Albert Flood. Caleb James Dilworth homesteaded at the Plum Creek ranche in 1873, but there is evidence he lived in the area prior to that time. William Knaggs settled at or near Garden Station in 1872 and operated a cattle ranch. There were other residents at this early date along the Platte River and also in the southern part of the county, where settlers were moving northward along streams that flowed into the Republican River.[28]

A total of 109 homesteads and timber claims had been filed in Phelps County by the end of 1875, just prior to the Johnsons' arrival. Thirty-eight of the claimants were probably Swedish. Because the land records do not list national origin it was necessary to count only those entries with Swedish-sounding names. This method has undoubtedly resulted in some degree of error, but because of the caution used in determining which were Swedish names the error would count fewer rather than more Swedes. Forty settlers were clustered in two townships (T5N and T6N R17W) in the southeast corner of the county. Twenty-six or two-thirds of this group had Swedish-sounding names. This concentration was probably the northern frontier of a Swedish settlement started in 1871 along the Republican River due south of the townships. Another forty claims were scattered along the north edge of the county within four miles of the Platte River. A few of these people had probably been there since the Overland Trail days and some, like the Dilworths, were cattle ranchers. Only four of this group had Swedish names. The remaining twenty-nine claimants, including eight Swedes, were scattered across the county.[29]

When the Johnsons and their friends arrived, Rolf noted specifically that they were "going out to found a Swedish settlement." This tendency among Swedes to form ethnic enclaves has been noticed by scholars of immigration and settlement, and events in Phelps County certainly support this observation.[30] The influx of settlers in 1876 and 1877 more than doubled the number of claims for Phelps County land and more than 70 percent of the newcomers were Swedes, the highest percentage of any group to come to the county.[31]

It is evident these Swedish settlers were staking a claim to a large portion of the county and in doing so radically changed the existing settlement pattern. They eschewed the strip along the Platte River and instead chose to settle in a band that Rolf referred to as "The Divide," a term that remains in the present-day lexicon. This is a relatively level tableland about eight miles wide beginning near the northwest corner of the county and extending across the county to the southeast. This plain is bounded on the northeast and southwest by more rugged terrain dropping into the flood plains of the Platte and Republican rivers. Nearly all of the Swedes who came to the county prior to the Johnsons' arrival located on the southeast end of the divide, but the remainder of it was virtually unoccupied in 1876. Because the divide was good farmland and a few Swedish settlers were already established on the southeast end, the divide was an ideal location for what Rolf came to refer to as "our settlement." This designation was certainly appropriate. Ninety percent of the settlers on the divide were Swedes by the end of 1879. Most of the non-Swedes there were concentrated at the southeast end, but even some of these seem to have had a Swedish connection. One of these settlers counted as a non-Swede was Anders J. Smith.

Nearly all of the Swedes who came in 1876–77 chose a homestead or timber claim on an unoccupied section of land. While this is one way to distance one's self from neighbors, it is likely the Swedes had a more purposeful goal. This stratagem allowed the Swedes to gain as much control over "our settlement" as possible, and the adjacent vacant quarters were taken almost exclusively by Swedes in the years that followed.

This selection of land was quite different from the choices made by other ethnic groups. Mennonite settlers of this same era in Nebraska preferred to take their 160-acre claims in narrow strips one-fourth mile wide and one mile long rather than the usual square measuring one-half mile on each side. The Mennonites also preferred to stay close together and took adjacent claims. Their settlements have been described as "crowded as close together as the alternating homestead lands permitted." Early Danish emigrants in Howard County, Nebraska, took the usual square claim, but they too crowded as close together as possible.[32]

It seems the early Swedish settlers were not concerned about losing the unclaimed parcels to non-Swedes. Comments in Rolf's diary and the dates that John Johnson filed for his preemption show that for several months they lived on land for which they had no legal claim. Although they were technically squatters, they made many improvements that increased the value of the parcel. Anyone could have filed a claim at the government land office and the Johnsons could have been evicted. There are several hints in Rolf's diaries that squatting was not an uncommon practice both by Swedes and non-Swedes. On April 15, 1876, Rolf wrote that settlers had occupied Spring Creek for "nearly its entire length." By the end of 1876 land records show that only twenty people had claimed government land along the fifteen-mile course of the stream.[33]

Howard Ruede, a young homesteader in northern Kansas in 1877, described how extra land was held in his neighborhood. A settler would legally claim a quarter section, but might use an adjacent quarter for pasturage or some other purpose or simply to reserve it for future purchase. If a newcomer showed interest in the extra quarter he would be told the land was "held by my brother-in-law, who is coming here from Iowa soon to live on it." This probably worked in most cases because it would have been easier for the newcomer to move on than to travel twenty or thirty miles to the nearest land office to challenge the earlier settler's mendacity.[34]

The preemption act was another option for temporarily holding the land because it allowed a settler to live on the land for a year before making payment. If at the end of the year the settler did not have the money to purchase the land, the preemption could be changed to a homestead or timber claim. John Johnson used this option. It is not known how many settlers filed for a preemption, but buying government land was not popular in the early days of Phelps County settlement. Only nine parcels had been purchased by 1880 and when all of the government land was in private hands, there was a total of only 128 purchases. It seems the Swedish settlers either were more frugal or were simply poorer than their non-Swedish neighbors, who accounted for nearly 90 percent of the purchases.[35]

Swedes in Phelps County were better at receiving the title to land than settlers in the state as a whole. The population of township T7N R18W in Phelps County was almost entirely Swedish and here 69 percent of the first filers received title to the land. A township in Harlan County was being settled at about the same time, but entirely by non-Swedes. In the Harlan township 54 percent of the original claimants proved up. This is somewhat better than statewide, where only half of the original claimants remained on the land and received their titles.[36]

In addition to their attempt to monopolize the land, the 1876–77 Swedes also turned their attention to politics. Phelps County was organized in the spring of 1873 and Williamsburg was chosen as the county seat although, as one early historian pointed out, "the place never grew to the dignity of a town." The first election was held on April 3 and seven of the eight elected officials lived along the Platte River. Rolf referred to this group as the "Phelps County Ring" and he and the other Swedes were determined to seize control of the county's political affairs. The Swedes opposed the ring because the incumbents had plunged the county into debt totaling nearly $25,000 with little to show for it.[37] The debt was a convenient political weapon with which to attack the ring, but even had there not been a debt it seems certain from the tone of Rolf's diary that there would have been an all-Swedish slate of candidates. After the Swedish party gained control they showed no more fiscal restraint than had the old county ring. By 1879 the deficit was approaching $36,000, but an overwhelming majority of the voters refused to vote bonds to pay the debt. Four years later a bond issue was passed by a slim margin.[38]

In the fall of 1876 the Swedes nominated their slate of candidates, but they had only modest success in the initial effort to unseat the old guard. Although Rolf blamed their loss on the unethical practices by the ring, the real cause was innocent mishandling of election returns by the Swedes themselves. As the number of Swedes grew so did their political successes. A major victory occurred in November 1879, when the county seat was moved from Williamsburg to the appropriately named Phelps Center, a location much more convenient to the Swedes on the divide.[39]

The Johnsons were probably unaware of the ring or the county debt when they first saw the Nebraska Plains from the windows of a Union Pacific train on March 7, 1876. Rolf did not seem to comprehend the vastness of the country until four days later, when he traveled by wagon to the center of Phelps County. When Rolf neared the future site of Phelps Center he saw "nothing but miles and miles of level prairie" blackened by a recent fire. This open grassland was dotted with "hundreds of thousands of bleaching buffalo skeletons," but the animals and the Pawnees who once hunted them had disappeared. There were four timber claims in the area, but the only evidence would have been mounds of dirt piled up by the absentee settlers to mark the claims' boundaries. The nearest homestead on the divide was ten miles to the southeast, where Kate Olson had filed a claim the previous December.[40]

The emptiness of the divide would have been a sharp contrast to the rolling woodlands of Illinois where Rolf was reared. Despite the marked differences, it seems he adjusted quickly to his new environment, although some pangs of homesickness were evident during his first Christmas in Phelps County. Generally, he took the hardships of pioneering life in stride, although he described some of the adversities as "not quite as pleasant as being out buggy riding with a girl."

Although Rolf did not complain about pioneer life, another Swedish eyewitness at about this same time viewed the life more critically. Pastor C. J. Nyvall was affiliated with the Swedish Mission Friends and was accompanying a group of about sixty Swedish immigrants who were planning to settle "in the vicinity" of Kearney. Nyvall described his perception of a pioneer's life:

> When one gets to know through firsthand contacts what pioneer life in America is like, one wonders how people can endure it. It seemed to me, however, as if some have become so accustomed to living in these hovels that they are not very eager to improve their circumstances. It even happens sometimes that when a settler has finally succeeded in acquiring a comfortable home he sells out, if he

gets a good price, and moves farther west to begin all over again. Even though the settlers may have plenty of food, may own several fine horses and other livestock, and perhaps from sixty to eighty acres of cultivated fields, they themselves live, as already mentioned, in wretched wooden sheds, in sod houses, or in dugouts. The settler's wife usually has fine clothing, hats, etc., while the man is ragged. Interior comforts are not pretentious. A visitor is happy if he is given a place in the same bed as the family. One may sleep comfortably enough on the floor of a sod house but in wooden houses, where the wind penetrates the walls, one cannot do so because of the cold. The furniture usually consists of one large bed, a table, three or four chairs, and a chest of drawers. Preachers who would serve the Lord in America by seeking out the scattered immigrants must be prepared for severe privations.[41]

The Johnsons were more fortunate than many early Nebraska settlers because they had some financial assets. Before leaving Illinois they sold a farm and some hogs and cattle, but unfortunately Rolf did not give any details. He was able to buy two used guns for $16 without a comment or complaint about the price. Shortly after the Johnsons arrived in Nebraska, John purchased a wagon, a yoke of oxen, a sow, twelve hens, and some corn costing a total of $192. This was a substantial outlay of cash at a time when a common laborer in Phelps County could earn only $20 a month. The Johnsons had been in Nebraska for only about two weeks when John applied for a preemption on a quarter section of land near the center of the county. This also suggests the family had some cash in reserve because they could not reasonably expect to make enough profit during the first year on the claim to pay the required $400.

It appears some of the Johnsons' neighbors were quite affluent. John M. Dahlstrom was able to purchase railroad land and then build the first frame residence on the divide.[42] At the same time the Johnsons were better off than some of their other neighbors. When Andrew Brunzell and his wife, Annie, arrived in 1877, they were so poor they could not afford to buy draft animals. Rolf and his friends joined in breaking the sod on Brunzell's homestead four miles south of Johnson's claim.

In even worse financial straits was Howard Ruede, a twenty-three-year-old typesetter with total assets of about $50, who homesteaded near Osborne, Kansas, in 1877. Ruede's letters to friends and relatives back in Pennsylvania span about a year and a half and describe some of the same kinds of experiences discussed by Rolf. The similarity ends there. Ruede felt he could not afford a stove so he built a fireplace out of sod, but it leaked smoke badly. Rolf never mentioned a stove, but their sod house had a wooden floor over a cellar so a stove would have been mandatory. Ruede wanted a revolver, but thought ammunition was too expensive, while Rolf could blaze away at meadowlarks just to test his shotgun. Ruede bemoaned his ragged clothes while Rolf chided himself for losing $5 to a swindler just before buying a new suit. Ruede did not complain about his situation, but his lack of tools and draft animals, his insect-infested sod house, and a starvation diet are a startling contrast to the Johnsons' experiences.[43]

The Johnsons had been in the county for less than a year before their savings were nearly gone. Grasshoppers destroyed virtually all of the crops in Phelps County during the Johnsons' first summer there, and whatever assets they had were probably needed just to survive. Rolf merely mentions in passing that during the first winter in the county many settlers, including himself and his brothers, were forced to "make their living" by collecting buffalo bones strewed across the prairie and selling them in Kearney for six dollars a ton. The collectors probably earned only pennies a day at this task, but there was no other way to earn money during the winter months. John Johnson did not have the cash to pay for his preemption and had to let it lapse. Later he filed for a homestead on the same quarter section and for a timber claim on an adjacent quarter.[44]

Rolf also filed a preemption on a quarter section adjacent to his father's homestead in the spring of 1878. Rolf never mentioned how he expected to pay for the land and there is nothing to suggest that he lived there, but he did make improvements of some kind. A year later he sold the claim to Aaron Blomquist for $100. Unfortunately Rolf does not offer the slightest hint concerning his reason for selling the land. Perhaps he just needed some money. Two weeks later on May 5, 1879, he went to the land office and filed for a homestead on a quarter section about two miles to the northeast. Blomquist accompanied him and filed for a homestead on Rolf's old preemption.[45]

Rolf was twenty-three years old when he filed for the homestead, an age when most men would be thinking seriously about marriage, a family, and the future. His prospects for the future were certainly promising. People in the community liked and trusted him, having hired him to teach school and elected him to minor political positions. Rolf's ability to laugh at himself was undoubtedly an asset. He tells of one incident when he was invited to dinner and the hostess had baked a pan of rolls, covered them with a cloth, and placed them on a chair to cool. Rolf mistook the covered rolls for a cushion and sat on the chair crushing the rolls to the "great delight" of everyone except his hostess. It is also evident from his diary that Rolf made friends easily and rarely criticized the actions of others despite the obvious disreputable character of some of his associates. Rolf's outgoing personality, good looks, and at least a modicum of financial security combined to make him a very eligible bachelor. At least one young woman, Clara Mathilda "Thilda" Danielson, would have been happy to marry him. When they attended Rolf's sister's wedding, Thilda suggested they join the bride and groom in a double ceremony, but Rolf confided in his diary that he was "not quite prepared to leave the state of single blessedness for that of double misery."

A month after filing for his homestead Rolf announced his "intention of going west for a season." It was not unusual for him to set out on an expedition for a few weeks. Rolf had spent part of the two previous summers harvesting grain for farmers in the eastern part of the state and one fall on a buffalo hunt near the Colorado border. These jaunts had a specific purpose, but when Rolf left in 1879, it seems he had no plan at all in mind. He drifted into Sidney, where he met a bullwhacker who needed an extra hand to haul freight as far as the South Platte River. Rolf agreed to go, and other chance meetings took him on to the Black Hills and then south through Colorado and into New Mexico. Here the diary ends abruptly on November 26, 1880.

Rolf ended his wanderings near the end of 1882 and returned to Phelps County, but his prospects were somewhat diminished. Not only had his homestead application been canceled, but all of the best land was by then in private hands.[46] Many of his old friends had moved away or were married, including Thilda. She had found a new beau, N. P. Holm, married him less than five months after Rolf left for the West, and settled on a homestead about six miles northeast of Phelps Center.[47]

After his return Rolf may have lived with his parents while he reestablished himself in the area. On November 19, 1883, he was appointed postmaster at Phelps Center, but he held the position for only three months. The next summer he filed a timber claim on land located about four miles northeast of his father's homestead.[48] By this time he was courting Ellen Brunsberg, a twenty-two-year-old woman who had emigrated from Sweden with her parents in 1882 and settled in the county. On September 1, 1884, they were married by a judge in a quiet ceremony at her parents' home. Their first child, Lilly, was born the following March. At this time the family was living in Phelps County, probably on the timber claim, but in the state census of 1885 Rolf gave his occupation as a notary public.[49] Two years later he canceled the timber claim, and the couple moved to Gothenburg in Dawson County, where Rolf worked as a bookkeeper for E. G. West, owner of the Gothenburg Elevator.[50]

In the summer of 1892 Leander Hallgren, the land agent who convinced Rolf's father to come to Nebraska, had a similar position with a Texas land company. He and fellow agent Jonas Adling were in Gothenburg and convinced Rolf and several others from the surrounding area to go on a "prospecting trip" to the Lone Star State. Although Rolf decided against moving to Texas, he felt the company offered opportunities and became a land agent himself. The opening may have been created when Hallgren died in Kearney in July 1892.[51] The following February Rolf led a group of prospective settlers from Gothenburg to the vicinity of El Campo, Texas, about seventy miles southwest of Houston.[52] Rolf quit the land agent business and opened his own store in Gothenburg about 1896. He advertised himself as a "dealer in hardware, tinware, stoves, barb wire, etc." and assured his customers his tinware was the best quality and "would never rust." Perhaps his store was not profitable because by 1900 he was again employed as a bookkeeper. Rolf next turned to politics and was elected county assessor, but in 1912 he was soundly defeated.[53]

Rolf and Ellen faced some personal tragedies during their life together. Six children were born to the couple, but only Blanche and sons Rolle and Rurie survived to adulthood. There is also a hint of financial burdens. At the turn of the century they were living in Gothenburg in a house they owned, but ten years later they had moved to a rented house. Then Rolf's health began to decline, and early in

September 1920 he and his daughter, who was by then Mrs. Bruce Chamberlin, went to Denver to find suitable living quarters. Mrs. Johnson followed a short time later. Rolf's condition did not improve, and he died of "heart trouble" on January 27, 1922. His body was taken to Phelps County and buried in the Moses Hill Cemetery, where Rolf had witnessed the first interment in the graveyard forty-six years earlier.[54]

Note on the Diaries

Excerpts from Rolf Johnson's diaries have been published previously. In November 1939 the editor of the *Holdrege Daily Citizen* learned of the existence of the diaries and received permission from the Johnson family to publish portions "in so far as it pertains to Phelps County." Excerpts from the diaries appeared each week throughout the winter. The editor deleted several entries, perhaps thinking they might be offensive or embarrassing to Phelps County residents. The *Holdrege Daily Citizen* reissued the Phelps County portion of the diaries during the summer of 1976. Excerpts concerning Rolf's wanderings through South Dakota, Wyoming, and New Mexico were published in the *1954 Brand Book*, the journal of the Denver Posse of the Westerners. The journals are in four identical books, suggesting they were purchased at the same time. They are six-by nine-inch marbleboard-covered and bound books with numbered pages. There are faint horizontal lines as well as double and single vertical lines near the right and left margins that would make them convenient ledger books, such as a bookkeeper or store owner might use.

The books are in excellent condition, which would not be likely if they had been carried on a buffalo hunt or a wagon trip to Deadwood. There are only subtle changes in the handwriting, suggesting the copies were made over a period of time, but the changes are not so great as one might expect of someone writing over a six year period under very different circumstances. This uniformity suggests the diaries were copied from the original notebooks and raises a question concerning the amount of editing that may have been done. Unfortunately we will probably never know if sections were added or deleted, nor do we know whether Rolf, or someone else, transcribed the diaries.

Rolf offers no reasons for keeping a diary. Some diarists write from an overblown estimation of their own importance, but such a rationale would not fit Rolf's personality. It is more likely he kept a diary for his own entertainment, but he has left us with a sprightly eyewitness account of Nebraska pioneer life.

The diaries, totaling 625 pages, contain very few errors. Occasionally Rolf, or whoever transcribed the diaries, omitted a word and these have been added in brackets. Misspelled common words have been silently corrected rather then inserting the intrusive [*sic*]. Sometimes Rolf misspelled personal names or place names and these have also been silently corrected when the correct spelling was known or could be determined from other sources. An example would be his inconsistent spelling of "Center/Centre" when referring to the locality of Phelps Center. His practice of combining certain words, such as "goodlooking" and "sixshooter," and dividing others, such as "down town" and "to day" has not been altered. Rolf's spelling of Spanish place names and other less commonly used words was quite accurate, hinting he may have consulted maps and other sources.

The diaries reflect Rolf's preference for simple, declarative sentences, but occasionally he used an incomplete sentence and more frequently wrote "run on" sentences. The editor has added punctuation as necessary to aid the reader. Each page in the diaries begins with a carefully printed heading of a few words summarizing the major topic of the page. These have been omitted in this work because the headings would appear after every few lines, usually in mid-sentence, and would create an annoying distraction to the story Rolf is telling. The editor has devised and added the chapter titles.

It was impossible to more fully identify many of the people Rolf knew in Phelps County, or met during his travels, particularly persons whom he mentioned only by their nicknames. Many of the Phelps County settlers can be found in the U.S. Land Office tract books, which record their homesteads, preemptions, and timber claims. Unless additional biographical information was available, however, these individuals have not warranted mention in the notes.

CHAPTER 1

Illinois Homeland

North Prairie, Mercer Co., Ills.
Friday, Dec. 31, 1875
Yesterday I was present at the wedding of Hakan Johnson, a cousin of
my father, to Miss Selia Swenson. The affair took place at the resi-
dence of Mr. Warner in the town of Alexis, formerly called "Bobtown."
The Rev. Mr. Workman officiated. Among the guests were Peter S.
Nelson of Knox County; Swan Rembeck of Galesburg (Hakan's
brother); Sam Ericson of Woodhull (Selia's cousin); Peter Sandberg of
Alexis; Gust. J. Peterson and Charlie Stromquist of North Prairie; Mrs.
Workman, Mr. and Mrs. Warner, myself, and several persons not
known to me. After the ceremony we partook of a splendid supper;
we then adjourned to the residence of Mrs. Christa Olson of North
Prairie, some four miles distant, where we had a big time, plenty of
music, cake and apples, and a keg of beer, and danced and enjoyed
ourselves until 2 o'clock this morning.[1]

The guests being in excess of the sleeping accommodations we natu-
rally were a little crowded and Swain Anderson, Charlie Stromquist,
Sam Ericson, and I got into one bed. This proved too much for the
bed, the bottom dropping out and letting us down on the floor.

Most of the guests left to day and the newly wedded couple went to
spend the honeymoon at Swen Jacobson's, a relative of the bride.

Mrs. Olson, with whom I am stopping, is a wealthy widow with five
good looking daughters, their ages ranging from 10 to 19, as follows:
Christine, 19; Annie 17; Bertie, 15: Elsie, 12; and Susie aged ten years. The
house is consequently a rendezvous for the young bloods of the vicinity.

Saturday, January 1, 1876
Heavy gale, doing damage to fences, barns, and so forth. "Cross-Eyed
John," Mat Jacobson, and Vinton Connor were callers and we had a
pleasant time.

Sunday, Jan. 2, '76
Lot of visitors, among them, "Big Gus" of Henderson Grove.

Jan. 5
This [morning?] while trying to milk a cow with sore teats, Charley Stromquist and Swain Anderson got so out of humor, they relieved their feelings by having a fight. I was bottle holder for both of them. I decided the fight a draw.

Jan. 10
Have been staying at Mrs. Olson's all the time since my last entry. Made one or two trips to Alexis with Hakan and one to North Henderson with Christine.

We are invited to a house warming at Absalom Peckinpaugh's this evening.

Jan. 11
Last night I participated in a house warming in Peckinpaugh's new house. We had music, apples, candy, and nuts. We danced and amused ourselves in various ways and were pleasantly entertained.

Those present were the Peckinpaughs, Absalom, John, Jasper, Lewis and Mary (The latter a pretty girl of 14 or 15); Byron Morford of North Henderson, Amos Goff, Gust Peterson, Charley Stromquist, all the Olson girls and myself.

The fun went on until the "wee sma' hours," and then we went home. Had a cold to day and toothache and was badly teased by the girls about Mary P. so I feel rather cross.

Jan. 12
This afternoon a party of gay young folks arrived at Mrs. Olson's on a visit. They were John, Mat, and Hannah Holcomb, and Henry Matson of Altona, and Betsey and Thilda Rasmusson of Paxton. The girls are very goodlooking, Miss Holcomb in particular, who is a lovely blonde with a graceful figure.

Jan. 13
We had a high old time last night, dancing, singing, cards, and games. This morning was a repetition of last night's revel. The guests departed

after dinner, and we felt comparatively lonesome, particularly Stromquist, who was mashed on Thilda Rasmusson. Our girls have nicknamed him "Charlie the Lovesick."

Sun. Jan. 16
Hakan Johnson and his bride have gone into housekeeping about half a mile from here and this morning I called on them and found they were getting on first rate. This afternoon I was playing dominos at Mrs. Olson['s] with Mat Jacobson, Pete Brown, and the girls.

Henderson Grove, Knox Co. Ills. Jan. 20
This morning, Hakan, Selia, and I started with a team for my house in Henderson Grove. The roads were very rough so we drove slow and arrived at 3 o'clock P.M. At our house I found Thilda Bergland, who was visiting my sister Hilda.

Jan. 22
This evening in company with my parents, I went to church to hear Rev. Jacob Danielson of Lockport (formerly of this place) preach. We also met Mr. Victor Rylander and Leander Hallgren, U.P.R.R. land agents, who are organizing a colony for the settlement of Phelps County, Nebraska.[2]

Among the colonists are many of our friends and I think we will go too.

Sun. Jan. 23
Wrote letters to cousin Ida Lundberg of Sweden and Uncle Nelse Nebbelin of Iowa.

Jan. 24
Went over to Hall Hitt's to see Frank and Tilfert Stewart. Staid several hours playing cards and shooting at targets.

Jan. 25
We had many visitors. Mr. and Mrs. Peter S. Nelson, Swan Rembeck, Rev. J. Danielson, Mr. and Mrs. Johannes Anderson, Robert Peterson, Carl Carlson, and Chas. M. W. Johnson. The weather is very mild and has been so all winter. The roads are fearful muddy.

We have concluded to immigrate to Nebraska the coming spring.

Jan. 29

Yesterday I went over to Olof Bergland's to see my young friends, Peter and Thilda Bergland. They are twins and 17 years old, and Thilda, a bewitching blonde, used to be my girl. Selma Jacobson was there too and we spent a very pleasant evening and I stayed all night. Went home this morning.

Sun. Jan. 30

Spent a pleasant evening with Pete and Thilda Bergland and August Nelson, who called on me and my sister Hilda.

Jan. 31

Went over to Soperville to see my father who is engineer at Becker & Atwood's coalbank and boards at Charley Nelson ['s].[3]

February 1st

This is my brother George's birthday, he is eight years old and 3 feet 8 inches in height.

Feb. 3

Went to Galesburg this morning in company with Chicago Nelson and his daughter Emma, a fat flirt of sweet sixteen. On the way we caught up with Vendla Stenfelt, alias Ella Stone, who was walking to town. I got out of the buggy and walked with her a piece.

She is the daughter [of] Fridolf Stenfelt and despite her youth (she is barely 16) she has a pretty bad reputation. A few years ago, she ran away from home and several hundred men scoured the woods in search of her and she was finally captured at Saluda by One-eyed Johnson.[4]

I rode back from town with Hall Hitt. Weather quite cold.

Altona, Ill., Feb. 6

Yesterday Thilda Bergland, sister Hilda, and I started for Altona. We walked to Wataga, passing through the dilapidated town of Henderson. At Wataga we took the train and went to Altona, where my uncle, Louis Nebbelin, lives. We took Aunt Nebbelin by surprise and she hardly knew us as it is about 6 years since we saw each other. After a little chat with Aunt, I took Thilda out into the country a couple of miles to the house of her relative, Swan Nelson, whom she came to visit. There I left her and went back to uncle's.

Uncle, aunt, and my cousins were very glad to see us. In the evening I went with uncle up town and saw several old friends, Nelse Nelson, John Fredericks, Mr. Ferguson, my old teacher Miss Kate Sawyer, and others.

Last night we sat up very late discussing the past, present and future.

Staid in the house most all day with my cousins of whom I have four, Swen, John, Alfred, William, and Charles Edward, their ages ranging from 12 to 1 years.

Feb. 7

This morning Hilda and I took an affectionate leave of our relatives and went out into the country to Nelson's, where we had agreed to call for Thilda Bergland.

Nelson has a fine house and farm and half a dozen interesting daughters. We stopped to dinner and then Hannah Nelson took us in the buggy to Oneida driving a spirited team of horses.

At Oneida we said goodby to Hannah and went by rail to Galesburg. Here we parted from Thilda, who went to see her uncle Henry Bergland, while Hilda and I went to uncle Nels Hawkinson's cosy cottage on East Grove Street. Uncle Nels and Aunt Elna tried to persuade us not to go to Nebraska and drew such dark pictures of the perils and hardships of frontier life, of grasshopper plagues and Indian raids, that it was enough to make one's hair stand on end.[5]

This evening we played dominos with cousin Josie, who is a pretty, graceful girl of sixteen.

Feb. 8

Came from Galesburg home in company with August Bragg.[6]

Feb. 9

Went to Soperville to see father and got a letter from uncle Nels Nebbelin of Centerville, Iowa.

Feb. 11

In shutting up our pigs I fell down in a mud puddle and just then I saw Thilda Bergland coming through the woods and I scooted up to the house and had barely got some clean clothes on when Thilda came in.

Febr. 13
The Stewart boys and I went hunting to day. We shot 8 quails, 1 rabbit, and 2 doves.

Feb. 15
Participated in a spelling match at the Pleasant Grove School house this evening. When I arrived the house was full and two rows of spellers were up. Sadie Watters chose me on her side. Mollie Holmes pronounced the words. I went down on the word "stretch," which surprised me as well as everyone else.

At recess we amused ourselves in various ways.

After recess, Will Yarde and Charlie Vestel "choosed up." On Will's side were: Pete Bergland, Buck Sperry, Thilda Bergland, Albert Miller, Ike Watters, Mary Beatty, Frank Stewart, "Pet" Stewart, Ed Dusenberry, Put Willey, Ella Hilligoss, and Charley Holmes. On Charlie's side were: Ikey Yade, Sadie Watters, Clara Lawson, Jim Trout, Hattie Hitt, Will Watters, Elsey Watters, Jim Dusenberry, Sissie Stewart, Tilfert Stewart, Sallie Lawson and myself. Miss Holmes gave out the words lively and one after another the spellers went. I was next [to] the last man to go down leaving Jim Trout up as champion speller.

North Prairie, Feb. 17
Pete Bergland and I went on foot to North Prairie to visit Hakan Johnson and the Olsons. We passed through Shanghai, a dilapidated one horse town, about noon and arrived at Hakan's place about 2 P.M.

At Hakan's we found Sam Ericson's brother Eric. We stopped till after supper, when we went over to Mrs. Olson's. We found John and Charley Peckinpaugh and Olof Holcomb from West Point, Iowa, there and all the girls at home. A very pleasant evening.

Febr. 19
Yesterday we divided our time between Mrs. Olson and Hakan Johnson. Pete Bergland got along swimingly with the girls. They call him "saltpeter." Last night we had a good time with the girls, dancing, flirting, and carousing.

Mrs. Olson tried to dissuade me from going to Nebraska. She wants me to stay with her next summer, and jocosely remarked she would give me eighty acres of land and my choice of the girls if I would stay.

This morning, as we sat engaged in conversation with the girls, Old Swen Jacobson drove up with a team and buggy. Finding he was going to Galesburg and would pass near our houses, he offered us a ride which we accepted with thanks. So we took a last farewell of Mrs. Olson and the girls, promised to write to them and were off. On the way I stopped at Hakan Johnson['s] to kiss Selia goodby and we were off for home.

Sun. Feb. 20
Went to Church to hear Rev. J. Danielson preach. In the afternoon went over to Bergland's to have some fun. Found the Larson boys John, Lewis, Aug., and Martin and August Johnson there with Selma Jacobson and Pete and Thilda. Towards evening all the boys went away but Pete. The old folks went to prayer meeting so Pete and Thilda, Selma and I had a gay time all to ourselves.

Feb. 21
Stopped last night at Bergland's, got home this morning after breakfast.

Feb. 22
This afternoon Mr. Ullquist and "Shoemaker" Anderson came with a team to get the hogs Ullquist had bought of father. The first hog we put in the wagon jumped over the dashboard on to the horses, who became frightened and ran away. My brothers Emil and Justus were on the wagon. Emil was shaken off first and one wheel went over his leg. The horses pulled out into a field full of stumps where Justus was thrown out, punching a big hole in the ground with his head. Fortunately neither of them were much hurt. Ullquist finally got hold of the lines and brought the horses to a standstill after they had dragged him on his belly in the mud several rods. When we went to look for the hog we found it down in the pasture with our dog Terry holding on to its ear like grim death.

Febr. 25
Went to Galesburg in company with August Bragg and Charlie Rosenburg.

Febr. 26
Last night I attended a dance at John Hogan's. Old George

Moneymaker scraped the violin. It came near being a stag dance, there being about twenty boys and only five girls, Thilda Bergland, Eve Atkins, Mida Hagan, and Sallie and Christine Lawson. We did very well, however, and had a good time. Called at Bergland's this morning.

Feb. 28
Frank and Tilfert Stewart spent the evening with me and Hilda playing the "game of author's."

Feb. 29
Father has sold out his farm and cattle to his cousin, Peter S. Nelson, and we are getting ready to start for the west. I have bought a small rifle of Nelson for $10 and a light shotgun of Lewis Johnson for $6 so as to be prepared for emergencies.

March 4
Yesterday two teams loaded with our furniture and chattels went to Galesburg for shipment to Nebraska.

Last night I attended a dance at John Hogan's. A row was started by Lew Larson and George Jackson and the affair broke up about midnight midst revolver shots and yells. I fired some half a dozen shots. Nobody was hurt as far as I could find out.

Sun. March 5
We left Henderson Grove to day and went to Nelson's, where we stopped to dinner after which we went on to Galesburg and stopped at Nels Hawkinson's.

I felt kind of sad to leave my forest home that has sheltered me nearly six years, but I guess this feeling will soon wear off midst the excitement of new scenes and life on the plains.

CHAPTER 2

The Trip to Nebraska

Mon. March 6 [1876]

I am twenty years old to day and it is curious we should leave my native state on my birthday perhaps never to return.

At noon to day we got on board the C. B. & Q. train bound east and went to Rock Island crossing, where we changed cars for the west and got on board the C. R. I. & P. train, which took us through a wooded country watered by Green and Rock rivers. Passed through the large towns of Geneseo and Moline, and arrived at Rock Island before dusk. There I had my first glimpse of the "father of waters," the mighty Mississippi, which we crossed on a fine bridge and struck the Iowa shore at Davenport, a picturesque city built among the wooded bluffs. It was named in honor of Col. Davenport, who was murdered by the Illinois banditti many years ago.[1]

The train has stopped in Davenport for supper and now while every one is busy eating I will write down the names of the Nebraska immigrants [on] this train:

> John Johnson & family of Henderson Grove, Ills.
> A. P. Anderson and wife, Galesburg, "
> Fridolf W. Stenfelt & family, Henderson Grove, "
> Andrew Olson, Princeton "
> John S. Salgren & family, Princeton, "
> August Carlson & fam., Princeton, "
> Mr. & Mrs. Hakanson, " "
> Charles Nelson & fam., Henderson Grove "
> Chas. W. Johnson & fam. " " "
> Carl Carlson, " " "
> Mr. & Mrs. Johannes Anderson " " "
> Anton Peterson " " "
> Frank Julius Carlson Boge, " " "

Alexander Danielson, Lockport   "

Sam Ericson, Woodhull[2]   "

Kearney, Nebraska, March 7

I slept in the emigrant car last night, but awoke as we were crossing the bridge over the Des Moines river and got a moonlight glimpse of Des Moines, the capital of Iowa.

Passed through a hilly and wooded country to Council Bluffs. The forests on the line of the railway presented a magnificent appearance being covered with hoar frost.

Council Bluffs is a fine city built on a flat between the river and a ridge of high bare bluffs from which the town takes its name.[3]

The train stopped here long enough to let us take a look at a couple of buffalo which were confined in a pen near the depot.

While crossing the Missouri river on a fine bridge we were entertained by a blind musician named Sam Chase, who sang several songs and played the violin with great skill.[4]

We stopped two hours in Omaha, the largest city in Nebraska, built on the wooded bluff on the west shore of the Missouri. Leaving Omaha we soon crossed the Elkhorn and found ourselves on the plains, which stretched away to the horizon, a treeless waste covered with brown and russet wild grass. Occasionally we would pass a farm house or a "dug-out," the latter a simple excavation in the earth covered with a mud roof. Passed through several towns of which Fremont, Columbus, and Grand Island were the largest.[5]

Occasionally a stream with a fringe of trees along the banks broke the monotony of the scene. Pawnee Indians in all the glory of red blankets, moccasins and dirt stared at us from the platforms at some of the stations and at the crossing of Loup river we saw a whole village of wigwams, with bucks, squaws, papooses, ponies and dogs. And at one place we saw a gang of four wolves trotting leisurely over the prairie. We caught occasional glimpses of the Platte, a broad shallow stream with low banks, glittering like silver in the sunlight.[6]

We arrived at our destination, Kearney, about two hours after dark, where we were met by Mr. Chas. A. Brant, a blacksmith of Kearney and an old friend of my folks, whom they had not seen for over 20 years. He insisted that we must make his house our house during our stay in town. We accepted his kind offer, and are now domiciled in his house. His family consists of his wife and son, Peter, a young man about my own age.

March 8

This morning Pete Brant took me out to see the town, which is an enterprising place claiming 1,500 inhabitants. It contains a good many stores, churches, school house, banks, & c., many of them of brick and quite pretentious. The town has two rail roads, the U. P. & B. & M. R. and a U. P. round house is located here.[7]

Kearney used to be a notoriously hard town. Large herds of cattle from Texas were driven up here for shipment and the herders or cowboys used to ride about the streets shooting, yelling, and raising hell generally; sometimes they would even ride horse back into the saloons and amuse themselves by shooting the bottles off the shelves. Collisions between the herders and citizens were of frequent occurrence and bloody battles have been fought on the streets. Pete Brant was an eye witness of some of them and gave me an account of the killing of Ed Smith, a cowboy, by Marshal Dick Stimpson and the shooting of Milton Collins by Jordon P. Smith, a herder, last year. I was already conversant with the main facts through the papers.[8]

In the afternoon Pete and I went down to the Platte, about half a mile from town. A number of flat, sandy islands covered with rank grass and willows divided the river into half a dozen channels, each spanned by a wooden bridge. The bridge over the main channel is about a mile long, and wide enough for trains to pass each other.[9]

Kearney, March 10

This evening Frank Hallgren and John M. Dahlstrom of Kearney Co., called. Dahlstrom has sold his place in Kearney, Co., and bought a section of land in the center of Phelps Co., where he intends to locate. He is going to take some lumber out there tomorrow and wants me to drive one of his teams, which I agreed to do.[10]

CHAPTER 3

Phelps County, Nebraska

Williamsburg, Phelps Co. Neb., Mch. 11 [1876]
This morning we started for "Phelps Center" (as the site of the new colony is called) with four loads of lumber. Besides Dahlstrom and I there were two loads of lumber for the erection of an emigrant house in Phelps Center, by Rylander and Hallgren. These teams were driven by Frank Hallgren and Charley Nelson.[1]

After crossing the Platte we turned west and drove up the valley some twenty miles when we came to Williamsburg, the county seat of Phelps Co., containing 4 houses, a school house, courthouse (an unpretentious frame building) and two dwelling houses. One of the latter, belonging to A. S. Baldwin, has been opened as a temporary hotel by a Dane named Albert Hansen and his wife, and here we put up for the night. We found but one other guest and he was an important personage; General Caleb J. Dilworth, District Attorney and Commissioner of Phelps County. The other house in town is occupied by ex-Sheriff John F. Shafer.[2]

This has been a very cold day, the wind sweeping from the north across the valley with terrific force. I had to walk most of the time to keep my feet warm.

Sun. March 12
This morning we drove out some seven or eight miles south to where Dahlstrom had two carpenters at work building a house. We found them living in the cellar, over part of which they had made a roof, and fixed a fireplace in the wall and when we came up [they] were cooking coffee and graham bread.[3] They invited us to "pitch in" for our dinner which we did.

As far as the eye could reach in any direction, not a sign of human habitation was visible (except about 3 miles south east where Rylander and Hallgren are building an emigrant house and digging a well for the accommodation of the colonists). Nothing but miles and miles of level prairie burnt black by the prairie fire. Hundreds of thousands of bleaching buffalo skeletons are scattered over the plains showing what a terrible slaughter of these animals has been going. In Kearney I saw mountains of buffalo bones along the railroad track, where they had been hauled for shipment east.[4]

Dahlstrom and I unloaded our wagons and went back to Williamsburg, where we found Leander Hallgren with a party of land hunters from the east.

This evening most of the party have been playing dominos, while I have been reading a Danish book I borrowed of Mrs. Hansen.

March 13
Weather mild and pleasant. Drove in to Kearney this forenoon. A large outfit of men, wagons, and mules from St. Joe, Mo. under the leadership of Tom Davis, bound for the Black Hills, camped here to day. They are well armed and do not fear the Indians.[5] I spent a portion of the afternoon in their camp.

Father has bought a yoke of oxen and a wagon of Mr. Brant for one hundred and twenty five dollars.

March 14
This morning a long caravan of wagons drawn by horses, mules, and oxen, and loaded with household utensils and farming implements pulled out of Kearney, crossed the river and wended its way westward. It was the emigrants, the "pioneers of the plains," going out to found a Swedish settlement in Phelps County. The women and children were packed like sardines in one wagon and hurried on ahead. The weather was intensely cold and I had to walk to keep warm. I drove our oxen, a pair of wild, half-broken Texas steers called Jerry and Bryan. I had a big load and a small team not much used to steady pulling, so I was the last one to reach Williamsburg, where I arrived about 9 o'clock P.M.

The oxen got so tired at last they actually laid down every hundred yards or so and it took me about 2 hours to drive the last mile. Father drove one of Dahlstrom's teams so he was ahead.

When I got to Williamsburg I found the emigrants crowded into John Shafer's little house, which he had kindly opened to them.

March 15

Last night over 30 persons slept on the floor in Shafer's house. This morning the weather being very cold it was concluded to have the women and children at Williamsburg until the weather moderates. Most of the men went on to Phelps Center with the loaded wagons. Mr. & Mrs. A. P. Anderson and our family moved into the hotel, where we are comparatively comfortable. I have passed the time reading one of Baldwin's books, "The Gold Hunters in Europe or The Dead Alive" by W. W. Thomes. Charley Nelson's already large family was further increased by the arrival to day of a little "bug eater," name at present unknown. He was born in Shafer's house and is the first child of Swede descent born in Phelps County.[6]

A blinding storm of wind and snow is raging this afternoon so it is impossible to see 100 feet.

March 16

Slept on the floor of the hotel last night and was so cold I could not sleep. Cold but not stormy weather.

March 17

Yesterday I made the acquaintance of George Steward, a young fellow living about a mile from here, and at his invitation I went with him home and staid all night. Spent the evening playing cards.

Dahlstrom and I with two teams drove out to his house in Kearney Co., about 30 miles S. E. of Williamsburg, over the trackless prairies. Saw an antelope at a distance of 400 yards.

I was introduced to Mrs. Dahlstrom, and to Mr. & Mrs. Rothsten and Fred Holmquist who are living in Dahlstrom's house.

Sun. March 19

I am still a[t] Dahlstrom's in Kearney Co. A snow storm is now raging the like of which I have never seen before. The snow is flying about with blinding force and it is about as much as a man's life is worth to go out to the well after a bucket of water.

March 21

Dahlstrom and I drove to Phelps Center. We had some difficulty in crossing the "draws" (as the sloughs and gullies on the prairie are called) as they had drifted full of snow while the level prairie is bare. On arriving at Phelps Center we found my folks and Stenfelt's family occupying Dahlstrom's cellar, they having moved up from Williamsburg last Saturday. Dahlstrom's house not being finished so they moved into the cellar, and had an awful hard time to keep from freezing during the recent storm as they had little or no wood. Dahlstrom's house is on Section 23, Town 7, Range 19. Father, while in Kearney, entered two quarters of government land in Section 24, Town 7, Range 19, in all half a section (320 acres) half of it being preemption and half timber claim.[7]

March 22
Last night "Turkey Creek Johnson," a Swede, and Hans Hanson, a Norwegian from Turkey Creek, Harlan Co. Neb., came here to dig a well for Dahlstrom so we were rather crowded last night. 18 persons to eat and sleep in a place 14 by 20, which was full of furniture besides.[8]

The rest of the emigrants are staying in the Emigrant House. Despite all these hardships, which are very discouraging, I have heard no murmur nor words of complaint. Verily the pioneers of Phelps Center are of the stuff of which heroes are made.

Here we are, the weather is very inclement; the nearest town nearly 30 miles away; no wood for fuel; no hay for the stock; no water except to melt snow. It is enough to try the patience of Job! I am glad to see everybody so cheerful and hopeful.

March 24
This being mother['s] birthday, Mr. and Mrs. A. P. Anderson came over from the Emigrant House on a visit. The weather is now warm and pleasant and the snow bank around the house commenced to melt and the water ran into the cellar in torrents threatening to set everything afloat. By hard work we managed to stem the tide.

March 25
Father and I went to Wm. Lee's near Williamsburg after a load of hay.[9] On the way home we were overtaken by a snowstorm and nearly lost our way. We got stuck with our load in a big draw a couple of miles

from home and in trying to get out, the oxen broke the wagon tongue and we had to leave the load and go home.

March 28
Yesterday we had a fearful snow storm. We had to bring the wood down into the cellar and saw and split it there. Last evening we had to bring the horses into the house for fear they'd perish outside and they kept stamping overhead all night so we could not sleep, fearing they would come through the floor.

We commenced to dig a well for Dahlstrom today. Johnson does the digging while Hans and I do the hoisting.

We get our water at present from a buffalo wallow filled with snow water about 10 rods from the house.

April 1
Did not feel inclined to play any April fool jokes. A snow storm has been raging all day and we have been crowded into the dark cellar like so many rats in a hole.

Sun. April 2
Fine weather again with about 6 inches of snow on the ground.

Tried my new shotgun today on a meadow lark with flattering success. Could see nothing else to shoot at.

April 5
Returned this evening from helping Dahlstrom move from Kearney Co. I am terribly tired. Dahlstrom, A. P. Anderson, Charley Nelson, Andrew Olson, Aleck Danielson, Frank Hallgren, and Stenfelt all had loads. We went out there yesterday and left there this morning. Weather was fine and the ground being soft from the melted snow we very frequently got stuck with the loads, but by the united efforts of the men brought them out all right. Charley Nelson in particular performed prodigies of strength and was a host in himself.

April 6
Grouse are plenty and some around the place every morning. Hans has shot several with my gun.

My youngest brother, Robert, is one year old to day.

April 7

Hans Hanson and I shot two grouse this morning.

While out driving this afternoon our dog, Terry, got kicked by one of the oxen, Jerry, and fell under the wheels and was run over but not much hurt.

April 8

Dahlstrom, Emil, Justus, and I have been down on one of the islands on the Platte after two loads of willows and poles. We had some trouble crossing the channel, came near getting stuck in the quicksand. Saw 6 antelope and innumerable grouse, ducks, and geese.

Sun. April 9

Father and sister Hilda attended the funeral of Mrs. Hakanson, an old lady who died in Williamsburg a couple of days ago of consumption. She was the mother of Aug. Carlson and was buried on his claim about 2 miles north of here.

April 12

I have had the toothache without intermission for 24 hours. It nearly drives me crazy.

April 14

Stenfelt and I went down to Williamsburg and bought a load of hay of old Jim Steward. Stopped there to dinner and had fricasseed grouse. Hay is worth $4 per ton.

April 15

Father and I have been down to Spring Creek after a load of elm poles, which we brought of old Sam Moser for $1.50.[10]

Spring Creek, in the south western corner of this county, is different from all other creeks I have ever seen being nothing more or less than a deep canyon with precipitous wall[s] filled with trees in the midst of which flows a small stream which empties into the Republican river, some 15 miles below. It is settled nearly its entire length, the settlers mostly living in "dugouts" which is partly a cave and partly built of logs and mud. They are perched here and there on the steep banks and hidden away in crevices like so many swallows nests.[11]

Sun. April 16
Divine services were conducted in Dahlstrom's house by Mr. Salgren. All of the settlers attended.

April 17
Finished Dahlstrom's well so now we have an abundance of cold, clear water. It is 110 feet deep.

We are very busy these days building sod houses and stables and hauling hay for the stock and material for building.

April 20
Father went down to Turkey Creek yesterday and got back to day. He bought a cow, a sow, a dozen of hens, and some corn costing in all sixty-seven dollars.

April 21
J. P. Landquist, who boards at Dahlstrom's, helped father and I put a roof on our house to day.

April 25
Saw four antelopes.

Removed from Dahlstrom's cellar to our new house, which is about a quarter of a mile from Dahlstrom's. I will attempt to describe how it was built:

First we broke sod with a breaking plow; this we cut off into bricks which were 2 feet long, 12 inches wide and four inches thick; of this we built the walls of the house. In the center of the house is a big crotch; in this and on the end walls rests the ridge pole; next come the rafters, about 1 1/2 feet apart, which are simply round poles of elm, ash, and cottonwood with the bark on. On top of this is a layer of willows; on top of them a thin layer of sod and over all about six inches of dirt. We have a cellar and board floor though it is something unusual in a sod house.

The house is 16 x 21 feet inside and the walls are two feet thick. Its gables stand north and south. On the west side is a door and half a window, on the east a half window and on the south a whole window. These houses are very comfortable being cool in summer and warm in winter.[12]

April 28
Went over to Dahlstrom's to hear Rev. J. Peterson of Des Moines, Iowa, preach. He was an able, earnest speaker, and looks very much like the portraits of Henry Ward Beecher.[13]

April 29
Went down to the Platte after a load of wood. When I got back and was trying to unhitch the ox chain the oxen started to run away. I was knocked down, run over, and kicked by the oxen and run over by the wagon too. Fortunately I was not much hurt, though mother came running pale as death thinking I would be killed.

Sun. April 30
I am sore all over to day and the imprint of Jerry's hoofs are to be seen on several parts of my body.

May 3
Went down to the Platte after a load of wood. Stopped at Williamsburg to get my mail. The post master is William A. Dilworth, Clerk of Phelps Co., and son of Old Gen. Dilworth.[14]

Sun. May 7
Had a snow storm yesterday, snow all thawed off to day. This evening while I was writing a letter to Uncle Lewis, mother started to go out, and as she opened the door she encountered an antelope on the threshold. Before I could get my gun he was gone. I guess the light streaming through the window attracted it. Antelope are pretty numerous and we see them every day. They are of the variety called "pronghorns."

May 9
I have been with Frank and Leander Hallgren out in the western part of the county surveying. We drove in a buggy and had a fine ride over the plains. While eating lunch at noon an antelope trotted up to within 100 yards of us and stopped. Frank fired at it and missed and it trotted off.

May 10
Have been helping Charley Johnson build his sod house. Building sod houses, especially when the wind blows, is not quite as pleasant as being out buggy riding with a girl. One's nose, eyes, mouth, ears, and hair gets full of loose dirt. Ok! its bad!

May 12
Had a splendid time trying to break prairie with our oxen!

They were unaccustomed to pulling a plow and tried to walk in forty directions at once. Several times they made a beeline for the stable and then there was music by the whole band and we would waltz out on the prairie again.

Sun. May 21
Emil, Justus, and I started to explore a range of sandhills 4 or 5 miles north east of here. We had a pleasant walk over the prairie, which is carpeted with a soft velvety coat of buffalo grass and many varieties of prairie flowers.

From the top of one of the hills we had a fine view of the surrounding country. To the east stretched a thousand hills clothed with green grass; to the north the broad valley of the Platte, with the river like a belt of silver with its emerald isles; to the south and west the vast plain with the settlement lay stretched out like a map before us. We found a relic of prehistoric times on this hill. It was an arrow-head of flint.

May 23
Big storm of wind and rain yesterday and Dahlstrom's, Anderson's and our cattle stampeded. We have been hunting them to day horseback. Couldn't find them. This evening at dusk as I was returning to Dahlstrom's I rode under the clothes line and nearly sawed my head off.

Dahlstrom, Aleck Danielson, J. Anderson, and my father, who were out hunting cattle, did not return this evening.

May 24
The cow hunters came home to day with the cattle. They struck the trail yesterday in a draw east of here, followed it over the sandhills and found the cattle a[t] George Bleakman's on the Platte nine miles

away. They stopped at Bleakman's over night.

An antelope came up within 25 yards of the children who were out in the field. Our dog Terry sprang at it and caught it by the leg. The antelope kicked the dog on the nose, made him let go, and lit out for the sandhills.

May 27
Slew my first rattlesnake with an axe about 40 rods from the house. He was over three feet long and sported seven rattles.[15]

Sun. May 28
We had a number of visitors: Salgren & family; Dahlstrom and family; Mr. & Mrs. J. Anderson, Charley Johnson, and Aleck Danielson.

May 30
Father, Dahlstrom, and I have been over to Johannes Anderson's to help him break his oxen to the plow.

Father is now working for Dahlstrom at $20 per month while I stay at home, break prairie, plant corn & c.

June 3
As Emil and I were returning from a trip to the Platte we saw a large hawk sitting on the prairie. We drove toward it and just as it rose to fly I fired and brought it down with a broken wing. I then dismounted and secured it, though not without a struggle in which I was both clawed and bitten. We brought it home and tied it up to a stake.

June 6
Killed my hawk to day. He was so savage he attacked every one who went near him.

Saw a herd of six antelopes grazing between our house and Dahlstroms.

June 8
Attended a breaking bee at Chas. Nelson's. There were 10 teams and we broke up ten acres.

Sadly in want of rain. The ground is so dry and hard it is almost impossible to plow.

June 9
Emil and I were out in the sandhills. We saw about 30 antelope and had some fun chasing some fawns. They run and cry "ma" like a lamb.

Sun. June 11
Emil and Aleck Danielson caught two antelope fawns in the sandhills yesterday, but did not bring them home.

June 17
J. Anderson, Aleck Danielson, Justus and I have been out on the head of Spring Creek after two loads of wood.

Sun. June 18
Frank Hallgren called on me and we spent a couple of hours pleasantly looking over my books and pictures.

June 19
Emil and I went after a load of wood in a canyon in the sand hills where half a dozen box elders were growing. On the way back a big jackrabbit jumped up and I brought him down with a shot from my gun.

June 21
Johannes Anderson, Aleck Danielson, Aaron W. Johnson, Andrew Olson, and I have been down on Spring Creek after wood. After driving a mile or so on the way back the tire came off one of the hind wheels of my wagon and all the felloes crushed so I had to throw off my load and go home without it. It was late this evening and it was so dark, we had great difficulty in finding our way home.

John P. Bragg of Oneida, Ills. is staying with us. He is out looking at the country with a view to locate. New settlers are coming out every week and our settlement has more than doubled since last spring.

June 23
We have no well so we have a big barrel and a sled and every day I haul a barrel of water from Dahlstrom's.

Made the acquaintance of Clarence Peterson, a young hunter from Harlan Co. He was out hunting to day and shot two antelope, which he divided among the settlers.

Kearney, Neb. June 26

Went into Kearney to get the wheel repaired that was broken on the trip from Spring Creek. I am stopping at Brandt's.

June 29

Got back from Kearney. Wilma Carlson, daughter of August Carlson rode with me out.[16] First time I ever took a girl ox-riding.

July 4

I celebrated the centennial by sowing and harrowing three acres of buckwheat.[17]

Sun. July 9

Frank Hallgren called in company with Swan C. Nelson, who has just come out from Illinois. Swan is a son of Charlie Nelson and like his father is noted for his great strength and muscular development. He is an old friend of mine and I was glad to see him.

July 10

Swan Nelson and I went out antelope hunting. Swan had a Spring-field carbine and I had my squirrel rifle. We fired several shots at antelope without success and spent an hour or so crawling in the grass on our hands and knees to get near what we took to be an antelope reclining in a buffalo wallow but which proved to be a big buffalo skull. This discouraged us and we went home.

To morrow a party of us are going to start for Hastings, a town on the B. & M. R. R. about 60 miles east of here, to work in the harvest.

CHAPTER 4

Summer Rambles
in Eastern Nebraska

Hastings, Adams Co. Neb., July 12 [1876]
Yesterday Swan Nelson, John Salgren, Chas. W. Johnson, Andrew J. Johnson, I, and Andrew Olson with his team left Phelps Center. We drove all day through a thinly settled country, camped last night on the open prairie. Continued our journey this morning and arrived about noon at Juniata, a small town on the railroad. Six miles further on we came to Hastings, a lively railroad town somewhat larger than Kearney. We are camped about half a mile from town.

We find we are out too early as the grain will not be ready to harvest for a week or more.

Swan Nelson hired out to farmer named La Monte and Charlie Johnson hired out as a section land on the St. Jos. & Denver R. R., which has its terminus here.[1]

Hastings, July 14
This afternoon Andy Johnson and I witnessed a match game of base ball between the Kearney and Hastings clubs. The Kearneys' uniforms were red pants, white shirt, and red caps; the Hastings' [were] linen suits trimmed with blue.

The game was close and exciting and resulted in favor of the Kearneys by a score of 22 to 20. The players were all athletic, active fellows and some of them were wonderful runners.

One ball struck the Kearney right fielder in the belly and he doubled up and fell as if shot; another ball went flying way out and struck a horse in the ribs with a report like a gun. Another struck a horse attached to a buggy in which was two ladies and he started to run away but was promptly stopped by a young man with hay seed in his hair. Several hundred spectators were on the ground and there was a great deal of cheering and waving of handkerchiefs by the fair sex.

Sun. July 16
Andy Johnson and I left Hastings and started for Sutton, a small town about 30 miles east, where Andy's uncle, Jonas Johnson, lives. We walked to Inland, 10 miles, in company with Joe Clarin, a young man from Furnas county. Got a ride from Inland to Harvard, 10 miles, with some section men on a handcar. There we parted from Clarin and hunted up Andy's uncle who lives about 6 miles from Harvard in a "dugout" in a ravine. He was glad to see us, especially Andy whom he hasn't seen for many years. He will keep Andy with him.

Lincoln, Neb., July 23
Left Jonas Johnson's on the 18th and started east looking for work. Stopped overnight at Sutton and slept in an empty freight car. Resumed my journey and stopped the next night in Crete, a beautiful city on the Blue river. Yesterday I came on to Lincoln, where I passed the night in a boxcar. Yesterday as I was coming along the railroad track, I came near being bitten by a rattlesnake. I killed it and a little further on encountered a huge bull snake about 4 feet long and killed that too.

Rained pretty hard this forenoon so I could not leave the car. I was pretty hungry but I found some wheat in the car and allayed my hunger.

This afternoon the raining stopped and I went up town to a bakery and spent my last nickel for a loaf of bread. Then I walked about the town to see the sights.

Lincoln is the capital of Nebraska and is a fine city of about 8,000 inhabitants. It contains many fine buildings among which are the university, state house, high school. Near the city are the penitentiary and lunatic asylum.

Lincoln, July 25
Burr Robbins' circus and Menagerie paraded the streets. It was a brilliant pageant. Gilded chariots, cages of wild animals, elephants, camels, ponies, and a long procession of ladies and gentlemen in gorgeous attire.[2]

About 2 o'clock P.M. a female rope walker in tights gave an open air exhibition of her skill by walking up and down on a rope stretched from the ground to the top of the center pole of the circus tent. I saw the same feat years ago in Illinois when I was a small boy.

Dee Creek, Neb., July 26
Left Lincoln and came on through Waverly to Dee Creek, where I hired out to work in the harvest for Owen Marshall at $1.00 per day.

Marshall lives in a pretty white house on the bank of Dee Creek, a small tributary of Salt Creek. His family consists of his wife and three children, Martha, Tom, and Owen.

This is a pretty country being rolling, well watered, and plenty of timber along the creeks, the hillsides dotted with pretty farmhouses, groves of trees, and fields of golden grain.

Dee Creek, Aug. 3
We finished harvesting to day. I have liked it first rate. I will leave to morrow but regret parting from Martha Marshall, who has made my stay very pleasant.

Plattsmouth, Neb. Aug. 6
Left Marshall's day before yesterday. Came through Ashland, the loveliest town in Nebraska, situated on Salt Creek, a small wooded stream about 50 yards wide. I stopped over night with a kind german named Henry Mertens about 4 miles from Plattsmouth. Came here yesterday and put up last night at Hotel de Box Car.[3]

Plattsmouth is built on the bluffs on the Missouri river and as its name indicates is at the mouth of the Platte, where it empties into the Missouri.

Aug. 7
Left Plattsmouth and started back towards the setting sun. I have had enough of tramping and am going home.

Aug. 8
Stopped last night at the house of a farmer named John Filby. Had a good supper of squirrel broth, wild grapes, bread and potatoes, and was waited on by May Filby, a pretty miss of fourteen summers.

Left Filby's after breakfast this morning, walked about 25 miles, and stopped at the house of a German farmer named John Rusmuller, where I will stay all night.

Sun. Aug. 13
Arrived at Sutton yesterday on my way home. There I found a letter

from mother enclosing one from Pete Bergland. Saw a lot of Russian Mennonites at Sutton, there being a large colony of them near here.[4]

Met Andy Johnson in Sutton and went with him out to his uncles. He has finished harvesting and will go with me home.

Grasshoppers are pretty thick here but as yet have done no material damage. It is reported that they have devastated the counties of Buffalo, Kearney, and Phelps.

Aug. 16

Day before yesterday Andy Johnson and I left Sutton and last night we arrived in Kearney. Night before last we slept in a box car at Juniata. Between Sutton and Juniata we saw billions of grasshoppers. Crops were all destroyed and cornstalks eaten clear to the roots. The hoppers lay in big drifts along the railroad track and it would have been an easy matter to shovel them up like sand.

Went to Brandt's for breakfast this morning. Pete was down in the mouth on account of losing his crops. They told me every thing green in Phelps Co. had been eaten by grasshoppers. This is very discouraging, as I have brought no money to aid my folks.[5]

We left Kearney in company with Anton Peterson, Mrs. Boge, and Oscar Boge.

After crossing the Platte we stopped awhile at "Dead Man's Ranch" and so I had an opportunity of observing this place made famous by a bloody tragedy in [the] day[s] of the old Overland Stage before the U.P. was built, the facts of which are substantially as follows:

A party of big bugs from the east were coming through on the stage coach, among them being a son of one of the proprietors of the stage route, a hare brained youth of sixteen who had boasted that he would kill an Indian on this trip. This ranch was then a stage station and as the coach stopped the boy observed some friendly Indians about the ranch and before any one could devine his intention, he fired and brought one of the red men down with a ball through his brain.

The companions of the murdered brave, not being numerous enough to revenge his death, carried the body away, while the whites knowing the danger of delay hurried the murderer into the coach and galloped away at full speed.

The Indians returned with reinforcements and not finding the party they sought, retaliated by murdering the station keeper and when the next stage arrived they found his body scalped and mutilated and from that [time] on the place has been called Dead Man's Ranch.[6]

The ranch is [a] long rambling building, half log cabin and half adobe house, together with a large ruined barn all surrounded by a grove of trees.

The ranchman's daughter was quite communicative and informed us that two colts were stolen from the ranch last night.

We rode with Boges about twenty miles after which we started across the prairie on foot for home. Just as we came near the settlement a terrible storm of rain and wind overtook us, and we were forced to seek shelter in the nearest house, which was Andrew Olson's, to which we with extreme difficulty made our way, drenched to the skin.

CHAPTER 5

Back to Phelps County

Phelps Center, Aug. 17 [1876]
This morning I left Olson's and went home. As I approached home it was a sad sight to see the fields, which were waving with corn when I went away, now black as though they had been burnt, but I found all the folks in cheerful spirits and glad to see me back though I brought them no pecuniary assistance.

Aug. 24
Mrs. Brandt and Pete Brandt made us a visit and stay till to morrow.

Aug. 28
Hilda, Justus, and I went down to the Platte and picked a bushel of wild grapes on the little hay island.

Sun. Sept. 3
Justus and I went hunting. I fired into a herd of five antelope and wounded one, a doe, but she got away.

Sept. 20
I have just finished breaking 10 acres of ground, some 5 miles south west of here, for C. J. Swanberg. While there I stopped several nights with Gustaf Johnson's, the folks of Andy Johnson, who live near there. Saw a large flock of Yellow-throated blackbirds. They are very beautiful birds.

Sept. 23
Frank Hallgren, Dahlstrom, Charley Nelson, Charley Johnson, Aug. Carlson, and J. P. Swenson and father have been down on the Little Hay Island several days making hay. I went down yesterday to help them. Had an awful time last night with that pest of the Platte the

gentle mosquito. We had to build a bonfire and lie in the smoke to get rid of them. We were also annoyed by the discordant cries of crows and geese which were swarming on the river in countless numbers.

Sept. 30

Last night we had the first frost. This morning at sunrise we could see the city of Kearney, 30 miles off, quite distinctly. It appeared in the sky to the north east over the sandhills. These plains are a land of mirages and we have seen many but this beat 'em all.

On our way down to the Platte Emil, Justus, and I witnessed a novel sight—an encounter between a jackrabbit and three hawks which occurred on the prairie in full view. Every time the hawks would swoop down and think they had him they found they hadn't. The rabbit would rise up on his hind legs and fight and claw the air and jump at the hawks, which would fly off about ten yards and alight on the prairie and wait for the rabbit to move on, when the whole maneuver would be repeated. After watching the show a while, I scared the hawks away and the rabbit scampered off to his burrow.

On our way home we saw a gang of 5 wolves trot along in the road ahead of us. They, however, did not offer to molest us.

Father has plastered our house with a mixture made of sand and yellow clay.[1]

Oct. 7

Henry and Clarence Peterson, who have been hunting antelope in the sandhills, arrived at Dahlstrom's this evening and I went up to see them. They had shot 8 antelope. Clarence, the youngest of the brothers, is a famous hunter who has killed thousands of buffalo, deer, antelope, wolves, and wildcats.

Father has bought two antelope so we will have fresh antelope steak to morrow and that isn't to be sneezed at.

Sun. Oct. 8

Was at the Emigrant House with Frank Hallgren, Nick Brunzell, N. J. Peterson, Henry, and Clarence.

Oct. 10

Two days I have been helping dig a cellar on Rev. J. Danielson's claim.

We are to build a house for him. He is going to move out here from Illinois to take charge of a church which has been organized among the settlers.[2]

Oct. 13
Father and I have been helping build a sod house for Danielson these last 2 days. Most of the men in the settlement were there.

Being short of flour this morning, I yoked up my oxen and drove out to Gustaf Johnson's to borrow some. We stopped to dinner and I had a pleasant chat with Emma Johnson, Andy's sister, a preposessing young lady, whom I have not met before.

Oct. 14
Peter Bragg of Henderson Grove and N. J. Stromquist of Oneida, old friends, are with us. They are here looking at the country.

Oct. 16
Father and I attended a mass meeting at the Emigrant House. County politics and other matters of interest to the settlers were discussed and speeches made by Mr. Gronquist of Harlan Co., and Victor Rylander. Father was appointed a committee of one to take the necessary steps towards organizing a school district.

Naponee, Franklin Co., Neb. Oct. 20
Day before yesterday Johannes Anderson and I left Phelps Center to go to mill at Naponee. That day we drove down to Gronquists in Harlan Co., where we got two loads of wheat and stopped over night. While there I read an account in a paper of the death of Frank Lorelle, who was drowned in the Mississippi river at Rock Island, Ills. while bathing. Frank and I were raised together in Chicago and went to the same school and I well remember what a harum scarum scapegrace he was at school.

At the time of his death he was a student in Augustana College at Moline, Ills. and was engaged to Emma Carlson, the beautiful and accomplished daughter of Rev. Erland Carlson of Andover, Ills., formerly of Chicago, who used to be my sweetheart in schoolboy days. We left Gronquist's yesterday morning and drove down on the Republican Valley, which we struck at Melrose, a small town. One and a half miles east of Melrose we passed through a larger town, Orleans, quite a thriving place with several stores and a printing office (Republican Valley Sentinel) and kept on down the valley. The Republican river flows through the valley and is a shallow stream about 200 yards wide, bordered with a fringe of cottonwood, Elm, and Box Elder trees. It has rained at intervals ever since leaving home and the roads being very slippery we had considerable difficulty in crossing bridges across the many creeks which empty into the river.[3]

Being overtaken by night we were compelled to seek shelter in a humble cabin by the roadside which was hospitably granted.

The night was cold and stormy but we slept comfortably in a couple of buffalo robes and some quilts on the floor of the settler's cabin.

Resumed our journey this morning, passed through Alma, the county seat of Harlan, and through Republican City, a place of some importance and six miles further on we ascended a high bluff and came suddenly in sight of Naponee, which comprises a couple of houses and a grist mill run by water power and built on the west bank of Turkey Creek. The mill is so full of grist we will have to wait a day or two and here we are.[4]

Turkey Creek, Sun. Oct. 22
Our grist was ground yesterday and we stopped in the mill last night. Left this morning and drove up Turkey Creek about 20 miles and stopped in the Swede settlement at the house of Mr. Morris Sandstedt.[5]

Phelps Center, Oct. 23
We left Turkey Creek this morning and crossed the divide to Phelps Center, where we arrived safe and sound an hour before sunset. At the Emigrant House I met Swan Nelson, Frank Hallgren, Nick Brunzell, and Peter O. Hedlund, who were talking of going out on a buffalo hunt with Clarence Peterson. I guess I'll go too.

Oct. 26
Clarence Peterson, his brother John, and his nephew Pete Burgquist arrived at Dahlstrom's from a two days hunt on Plum Creek during which they killed six deer and six antelope. They said they would not go buffalo hunting yet for awhile on account of the Ute Indians being reported troublesome on the range.[6]

Father bought a deer and an antelope.

Nov. 4

Brother Emil went down to Gronquist's in Harlan County yesterday and will stay with him awhile.

Swan Nelson, Justus, and I went down to the Platte after hay. Swan's oxen became unruly, ran away with us, tipped the wagon up, spilled us out in a heap, and broke the hayrack. We were not hurt and after righting the wagon, fixing the hay rack, whipping the oxen, and picking up our pitch forks, guns, and thing[s] which were scattered along 40 rods or so, we loaded up and started for home.

Up on the divide about two miles from Williamsburg we encountered a skunk and tried to kill him, but he got the best of us. In the chase Swan lost a part of his gun, which was a breechloader and is now useless.

Nov. 6

Dahlstrom and I went up to the Emigrant House to attend a political meeting. Speeches were made by A. E. Harvey, candidate for the legislature, and Alex Hagberg of Arapahoe, Furnas Co., and by Henry V. Hoagland on the political situation. The Phelps County Ring was denounced in strong terms and resolutions were adopted to fight against and make an effort to break it.[7]

After the meeting Harvey, Frank Hallgren, Dahlstrom, Hagberg, Shafer, P. A. Brodine, Hoagland, and father went down in the southern part of the county electioneering.

This county was organized in 1873 by a ring headed by General Dilworth, and the county is already in debt some $20,000 with nothing to show for it. The ring at present comprises: C. J. Dilworth, A. S. Baldwin, and Tom Downing, County Commissioners; W. A. Dilworth, Co. Clerk; Hugh DeQuine, Surveyor, and James Sweezey, Sheriff. Gen. Dilworth's term as commissioner expires soon and we are going to run Peter A. Brodine, a young Swede, for the office. We are also running H. V. Hoagland for Superintendent of Public Instruction.[8]

Nov. 7

This is election day. The place of voting in Center Precinct was at the Emigrant House. Father, A. P. Anderson, and J. S. Salgren were Judges of Election, Frank Hallgren and Aaron W. Johnson Clerks of Election. Twenty votes were polled in this precinct and all of them went solid against the county ring. The following officers were elected for Center precinct: Assessor, John Johnson; Justices of the peace, Salgren and Dahlstrom; Road Supervisor, J. Aug. Carlson; Constables, Charley Johnson and Charley Nelson; Judges of Election, John Johnson, J. P. Landquist, and J. M. Dahlstrom; Clerks of Election, Frank Hallgren and Aaron W. Johnson.

Nov. 10
Saw a mirage this morning. The bluffs on the north side of the Platte were as plainly visible as though only a mile away and the city of Kearney, 30 miles distant, was in full view.

Justus and I were down on the Platte after wood and while on the island we suddenly heard a roaring, rushing, crackling sound and on investigating found the whole valley between us and Williamsburg in flames, which sometimes leapt upward to a height of 30 feet or more. On driving out from the island we came near being scorched by the fire. The air was full of smoke and ashes through which the fire looked like a sea of red flames.

In one place we saw a big jackrabbit surrounded by a wall of fire on every side. He jumped about from side to side trying to find some outlet to his fiery prison, which was getting smaller every moment. I jumped from the wagon thinking to have roasted rabbit as soon as the flames had passed over him. Just as the flames closed about him and were about to swallow him up he cleared [the] burning barrier with a desperate leap and came near alighting on me. He was a moment blinking his eyes at me as if to say: "How is that for high?" and then struck a bee line for the river to cool off his scorched skin.

Nov. 13
Snowing, blowing, and very bad weather.

Mr. Landquist came here muleback muffled up in overcoat and comforter. While chopping wood this morning a stick of wood flew up and hit him on the mouth and knocked him down. His under lip was cut through and through and split an inch down. He wanted us to sew it up for him which Father and I did with needle and silk thread.

Nov. 17
Frank Hallgren, Dahlstrom, Charley Nelson, Charley Johnson, and I have been down on the Platte islands after hay. While there Frank

Hallgren threw a pitchfork from the top of the load of hay, it came down prongs first, and struck Charley Johnson in the back, one prong striking him in the shoulder blade and the other in the spine, inflicting deep and painful though not dangerous wounds.

Nov. 18
Election returns show that Silas Garber was elected governor of Nebraska; Andrew Eugene Harvey, Member of the Legislature; P. A. Brodine, commissioner of Phelps Co., H. V. Hoagland, Superintendent of Public Instruction. Not so bad for the first buck at the County ring.[9]

Nov. 24
This evening sister Hilda, who been staying in Kearney sometime in the family of Jos. A. Harron, came home. She has a felon on her thumb.[10]

Sun. Dec. 3
I am reading a "History of the Great Rebellion" that I borrowed of Shafer.

I hear in a letter from Ills. that my friend, August Nelson, who had his thigh ripped open by being run over by a plow, has died from his injuries.

Dec. 4
While hauling hay from the Platte in crossing one of the channels of the river, one of my oxen, Bryan, slipped and fell on the ice, and in trying to get up, he got the wagon tongue across his back and broke it off short. Dahlstrom and Nelson helped me splice it so I could go home with the load.

Williamsburg, Dec. 14
I have been staying down here with John Shafer, off and on nearly two weeks, helping Shafer get out cottonwood poles from the islands. Shafer does the chopping and I haul them out and we take half each of the poles. I have been staying at Williamsburg with Shafer and his two boys, Bernie and Willie.

One night Old Joe Golladay, a settler on Spring Creek, stopped with us. In a fair and square "go-as-you please" talking match he has no equal. He talked nearly all night and though some of his reminiscences of frontier life, buffalo and deer hunting and adventures with Indians were interesting, yet his minuteness of detail made him tedious. He would talk himself out of breath, then recovering himself with a snort like a startled antelope, he would turn himself loose again.

Jake Moser and Elton Miller of Spring Creek stayed with us one night. They were pleasant sort of fellows. Miller is a brother of "Crazy Miller," the desperado of Spring Creek, but does not look like him.[11]

Dec. 15
The prairie fire has swept over Phelps Center. As we had "fire-breaks" and guarded them to prevent the fire leaping over, we were all right. This evening presents a fine sight as we are surrounded [by] a circle of flames. It is a grand though rather awe-inspiring scene.

Dec. 16
Mr. J. P. Swenson living west of us was a sufferer by the prairie fire yesterday. He was away from home and the fire passed over his place destroying his stable, three tons of hay, a new plow, 15 bushels of corn, and some lumber.

Dec. 21
Victor Rylander and several of the neighbors were here to dinner.

Many of the settlers make their living now by picking up buffalo bones, hauling them to Kearney, and selling them at six dollars per ton. I and my brothers have gathered a load which father is going to take to Kearney to morrow.

Dec. 24
Christmas eve, and I am reminded of the gay times we used to have in Illinois, of Christmas trees and Christmas parties. Last Christmas, I was at Mrs. Olson's in Mercer Co., Ills. and had a splendid time, and the Christmas before that we had a gay party at Mat Gibson's in Soperville.

It has snowed all day and we are having a quiet evening at home.

Dec. 26
We had a Christmas party here this evening and the following named friends were present: Dahlstrom and family; Mr. & Mrs. J. Anderson;

J. S. Salgren and family; Aaron W. Johnson; Aleck Danielson; Carl Carlson; Stenfelt; Charles Johnson; Charles Nelson; and J. P. Swenson.

Dec. 28
Attended a Christmas dinner at Johannes Anderson's. Quite a number of the neighbors were there.

1877
Sherwood, Phelps Co., Neb., Jan 2nd
Went into Kearney yesterday in company with August Carlson and his daughters, Augusta & Wilma. Came back this afternoon as far as Sherwood P. O., where I stopped with Mr. Robert M. Hindman, Co. Treasurer of Phelps Co. He is a fine old gentleman and has an interesting family.[12]

Jan. 12
We are having a regular "northerner." The snow is flying and the weather is exceedingly cold. Henry Peterson is here. He tells me that Clarence, John, and Nels Peterson, and Pete Burgquist are out on a buffalo hunt on the head of the Republican river.

Received the first number of "Vart Nya Hem," a new Swedish newspaper just started in Kearney by Rylander, Hallgren, and O. P. Pearson, and edited by Magnus Elmblad. Mr. Elmblad is the son of an eminent Swedish divine and the most brilliant journalist of the Swedish-American Press.[13]

Our School District has been organized and is to be known as School District No. 9. The School Board is Dahlstrom, Carlson, and Salgren. We are to have three months school before April 1st. A vacant sod house belonging to Charley Johnson, about half a mile from home, is to be used as school house, and a rough pine table and some seats have been made and a small stove, belonging to Shafer, has been secured and put up.

I have been engaged to teach at a salary of $22.50 per mo. and school will open as soon as the weather moderates.[14]

Jan. 15
A terrible snow storm is raging. The wind is howling and shrieking as if all Bedlam was loose. The cold is enough to freeze the hair off a cast

iron dog, and it was noon before we ventured out to feed the stock.

Jan. 16
Weather a little better than yesterday. Opened school this morning with only two pupils, brothers Justus and George.

Jan. 17
Got six more pupils, my old chum Andy Johnson and his brother, Jonas, Chas. Levin Carlson, Per Anders Salgren, and Herman and Charley Stenfelt.

The buffalo hunters arrived at Dahlstrom's on their way home. Clarence told me all about the trip. They have been gone two months and have had a hard time owing to the inclemency of the weather. They killed ten buffalo, twenty-two deer, fifteen antelope and one wildcat. Father bought a fine black-tail buck as we are very fond of venison.

Jan. 18
Have two new pupils, Charles J. Johnson, and Johnny Nelson.

Jan. 24
Got another new pupil yesterday, Alfred Nelson, brother of Johnny, and another to day, Frank Johnson, brother of Charley. He celebrated his advent by having a fight with John Nelson, knocking one of his teeth out.

Jan. 25
Old Carl Carlson chops the wood for the school, and this afternoon he came into the house to warm himself. Old Carl is a great snuffer, and knows nothing better to give his best friend than a pinch of snuff, so he hauled out his snuff box and offered me a pinch. I took a little—just to please him, and then hauled out a bottle of Marshalls catarrh snuff, which I happened to have, and asked him if he [would] like to try some of mine. He accepted with thanks, and took nearly a thimbleful. Now as it is such pungent stuff that half a dozen grains is enough to make a man sneeze violently, the effect on Old Carl was most disastrous.

He sneezed so for ten minutes he couldn't utter a word and I began to fear his head would fly off. My pupils fairly yelled with delight, and I could hardly keep from roaring myself.

Carl takes it all in good part but he won't take any more catarrh snuff.

Sun. Jan. 28
Rev. Jacob Danielson preached at the Emigrant House to a large congregation. Mr. Danielson has moved out here with his family and will make his home among us. He was our pastor many years in Henderson Grove, Ills. until the spring of 1875, when he moved to Lockport. His family is all here now with the exception of his only daughter, Clara Mathilda, who remained in Ills.

He is accompanied by Gustaf Danielson, a young man from Lockport, who is a very fine singer.

Thursday, Feb. 1
My pupils seem to take more delight in snowballing and playing ball, than in learning their lessons and I have a sorry time with them. I have no classes as no two of them have books alike.

Feb. 6
Brother Emil came home from Gronquist's on a visit. He likes to stay there very well.

Peter Brodine told me that he saw our dog Terry, which has been missing several days, lying dead on the prairie near Lee's place. He has no doubt been poisoned by strychnine, which Bill Lee had put out for to poison wolves. Terry was a beautiful dog, white with black spots, and a glass eye. I got him when a pup about 3 years ago from Jim Dusenberry.

Emil feels very badly over his untimely death as he was very fond of him.

Feb. 14
So foggy this morning that John Nelson lost his way and didn't get to school till noon. It is a hard matter to find one's way on the plains during a fog.

Emil attends school and is my best scholar.

Feb. 16
Emil has gone back to Harlan Co. Got another pupil in his place, Christina Octavia Carlson, daughter of August Carlson.

Brother Justus and Frank Johnson had a rough and tumble fight after school was dismissed so I did not consider myself bound to interfere. Victory finally perched on Justus' banner.

Feb. 20

It [seems] my pupils are making more progress in the manly art than in anything else. Yesterday brother George and Charlie Stenfelt had a pugilistic encounter which resulted in a bloody nose for Charlie. They fought like a couple of young game cocks.

To day occurred two more battles among my pupils; one between brother Justus and Herman Stenfelt resulted in a sore eye for Herman, and George and Charlie Stenfelt had another roundup. Result: nosebleed for Charlie.

Feb. 21

George had an attack of the croup last night and came near dying. Mother and I brought him around with the internal application of coffee sweetened with salt and external use of hops on his throat and skunk oil on his belly.

Sun. Feb. 25

Cold wind from the east.

A coyote, or prairie wolf, has been prowling around the premises. He chased the little pigs home from the cornfield, and if I hadn't scared him off would have got one of them.

Feb. 26

Snow — A large coyote was prowling around the house this morning and I opened the door and fired a load of birdshot at him without doing any harm. He trotted slowly away.

Feb. 28

The boys have built a fort of snow and as soon as [I] let the school out for recess, the boys who are nimblest of foot, get there first and hold the fort against all comers. The casualties of to day are [a] black eye for Frank Johnson. He was peering through a loophole in the fort when Herman Stenfelt hit him in the eye with a snowball in which he had artistically done up a pebble the size of a hen's egg. Johnny Nelson is also on the sick list; someone fired a wet snowball into his ear.

March 2

Andy Johnson has found another revolver on the prairie. Last fall he found one, a big Navy, but so rusty as to be useless. This one is also a Colt's Navy and is in pretty good condition. Arms are found frequently on the prairie. John Nelson found a shot gun one day as he was going home from school. Charlie Stenfelt found a five barreled revolver of the pepper box variety last spring, and I found a soldier's canteen last summer.

March 6

This is my birthday and I am of age. It is just one year to day since we left Illinois. I had several callers: Nick Brunzell, Swan Nelson, and John W. Holm, a young man from Jacksonville, Ills.

March 7

A party of settlers encountered a couple of wild animals in the sand hills yesterday. They claim they were bears, but I guess it must have been wild cats, or perhaps mountain lions. Father is busy nowadays assessing the tax payers of Center Precinct.

March 14

Swan Nelson and I went up to Dahlstrom's this evening after school to see August Bragg, who arrived from Illinois last night with John P. Bragg & family, his relatives.

We had a long talk and he told us lots of news of our friend[s] back east. Charlie Carlson, brother of Christine, is one of my pupils.

March 20

Taught school in the forenoon and in the afternoon I, with about 50 others, attended the funeral of Little Emily Bragg, infant daughter of John P. Bragg, who died at Dahlstrom's night before last. Rev. J. Danielson officiated. The wind was blowing hard from the north and the rain sprinkled occasionally, so the procession, instead of proceeding in the slow and solemn manner befitting the occasion, rattled along at a lively gait. The child was buried in the new graveyard which was laid out this morning by Bragg, Dahlstrom, and Father on Sec 2. Town 6, Range 19.[15]

Sister Hilda, who has been staying some time with the family of John K. Zook near Kearney, came home.

March 24
Mother had a birthday party to day, she is 45 years old. Rev. J. Danielson & family, Mr. & Mrs. J. Anderson, Mrs. Dahlstrom, and Mrs. Bragg were here.

March 27
My school closed to day and I am as happy as a big sunflower. By teaching on Saturdays I have been able to make out 3 months. I had altogether 14 pupils and there has been an average attendance of eight.

After school Swan Nelson and I went down to Williamsburg after our mail.

I got two letters, one from Hakan Johnson, and one from Pete Bergland. I also got some papers. Swan got several letters, one of them from his girl, Ida Johnson of Galesburg, Ills., enclosing her photograph and a lock of hair.

Saw John Shafer at Williamsburg, he is going out west soon.

Sun. April 29
August Bragg, J. P. Landquist, and I drove down to Knaggs' Ranch on the Platte to look at some cattle. The Knaggs are English and claim to be of royal blood, being related to Queen Victoria.[16]

On the way August shot a white tail jack-rabbit and a prairie chicken. Birds are plentiful on the plains, especially blackbirds of which there are several varieties.

May 2
Shot a prairie gull, it was a beautiful bird.

Father was paid for assessing Center Precinct in County Warrants, which owing to the bad state of the County's finances are worth only 62 1/2 per cent.

His bill was $28.

May 10
Shot a wild duck in a buffalo wallow near the house. Wild ducks are plenty.

May 11
Jack-snipes are numerous. I shot one to day. It was much larger than a common snipe.

Sun. May 13
The lagoons are full of water and ducks and snipe are plenty. Went hunting and shot a beautiful "wood-duck" on Linder's Pond, a large lagoon about 4 miles southwest of home. While setting on the bank watching [a] flock of ducks, I came near being bitten by a large rattle-snake, which crawled up behind me. In turning to watch a flight of ducks I discovered the reptile and at a distance of eight feet gave it a load of shot that settled it.

The snake was about 4 feet long and had eight rattles. The report of the gun frightened away the ducks, so I went home.

May 15
Father has bought a fine bull, half Durham, of Robt. Hindman. He is 4 years old, very gentle and broken to the yoke. $35 dollars is the price paid for him. We call him Quantrell.

May 19
We have had a shower of rain.

While breaking on the timber claim, I heard our dog "Shep" [bark] violently at something and on going to see what it was, found a large rattlesnake coiled up and rattling in defiance. I sent my brother, Justus, home after my gun and when he got back I shot the snake. It was a large one about 4 feet long and 2 inches in diameter and had a long string of rattles, but as I shot off part of them I can't say how many it had.

The air is full of grasshoppers.

May 24
Attended a breaking bee at Mr. Andrew Brunzell's. He has no team, and so a lot of us went there and broke some land for him.

May 29
Got a letter from Uncle Louis Nebbelin informing us of the death of his brother, Uncle Nels Nebbelin, at Centreville, Iowa, on the twenty-seventh day of March. He died of kidney disease.

Sun. June 3
Went out for a ramble among the prairie flowers. Saw a woman on horseback, which I at first took to be a squaw as she was riding astride,

man fashion. She rode up to me and I found it was Mrs. Joseph Johnson, who was out hunting stray cattle.

I decoyed several antelope within shooting range, but did not succeed in getting one. I, however, shot a big jack-rabbit up in the sand hills and then I went home.

Sun. June 10
Swan Nelson was out here from Kearney with a livery rig & two grey ponies and a buggy and we went out driving in the sand hills. We had lots of fun chasing antelope and did some wild driving.

June 27
Attended a revival meeting at the Emigrant House. Rev. Danielson and Rev. H. Hallner of Wahoo, Neb., conducted the exercise. Hallner is an eloquent and powerful preacher and many sinners have been converted.

June 30
Had a personal difficulty with a rattlesnake that came along and ran over my toes as I was breaking. I attacked it with my ox whip and after a fight in which I came very near being bitten, I got in a good blow on its head and laid it out. 8 rattles was my trophy.

July 4
A dull day and not at all like the fourths of Julys back in Illinois. Little Charlie Dahlstrom, however, was so full of patriotism, he tried to [illegible word] the George Washington cherry tree business on us and chopped all around one of the cottonwood trees we had planted in front of our house, and when his father asked him if he did it, he would not tell a lie, only hung his head and commenced to bawl.

I felt like making an example of him as a warning to other young Americans who want to emulate the immortal George.

July 5
Called on Stenfelt. He had a toothache, and one side of his face was swelled so big he couldn't hold his head straight. I suggested that we might hang a flat iron to the ear on the other side of his head to balance it but he didn't seem to appreciate my solicitude.

Weather red hot and still heating.

July 16
Ida is seven years old to day. Her Godmother, Mrs. J. Anderson, gave a birthday party in her honor that we all attended.[17] We are in the midst of harvest, and the song of the reaping machine is heard in the land.

July 20
The feud which has existed a long time between Crazy Miller of Spring Creek and his neighbors culminated yesterday in a bloody tragedy in which Miller was killed and Bob Dale wounded. The facts as near as I can ascertain are as follows:

About noon yesterday, while Sheriff James Sweezey, Jake Moser, Sam Moser, John Daggett, Bob and Sam Dale were engaged in harvesting wheat on the farm of Sam Moser, Miller came into the field armed with a Kentucky rifle (his famous "Long Tom") and a Spencer carbine, and swore he would kill the whole outfit. He drew a bead on Sweezey but the gun missed fire and Sweezey sank to his knees and begged for his life. Miller snapped two more caps at him and then observing that Robert Dale was running for the timber, he fired at him and grazed his leg, though at a distance of over 200 yards. Jake Moser made a break for the wagon to get his gun.

Sweezey, Sam Moser, and Daggett then jumped on Miller, who tried to use his carbine, an eight shooter. A desperate struggle ensued in which Sam Moser got his carbine away from him and shot him in the side. Jake Moser just then came up with his gun and opened fire and put another ball into him as he was walking away. He then turned around and Sweezey shot him in the breast and dropped him. His last words were: "Boys this is just what I deserve," and so he died with his boots on.

William C. Miller, sometimes called Crazy Miller on account of his eccentricities, was once Sheriff of Phelps Co. He was a crack shot and a great hunter, and claimed to be the man who killed the three Sioux Chiefs, Whistler, Fat Badger, and Hand Smeller on the Republican several years ago. Several other parties claim the same honor, however, among them being Wild Bill Cress, Newt Mullen, Pony Rogers, and others.

It is said his relations with his mistress, Old Joe Golladay's daughter, with whom he had a son, have caused most of the trouble between him and his neighbors and which led to several shooting scrapes besides this last one.

A coroner's inquest was held on his body and the jury found evidence of justifiable homicide.[18]

July 26
Pete Brandt called on me. He has just returned from his second trip to the Black Hills. He has some hair lifting stories to tell of life on the trail.

July 31
Stenfelt told me of the shooting of Turner Cannon, a Clerk in Tom Roberts' store in Kearney, who was mortally wounded by burglars at 3 o'clock this morning. It seems that Turner, who was sleeping in the store, was awakened by some noise by the burglars, and asked: "Who is there?" His answer was a shot through the stomach. He fired five shots at the burglars as they were escaping through the back window. The burglars got 18 dollars and a couple of watches.

Young Cannon was a fine young fellow about 16 years old and I had known him several months.[19]

We are through harvesting. I bound several days and nights also on the harvester.

Aug. 11
A party of land hunters from Ills. are out here and called on us this afternoon. Among them are several old friends: John Fredericks, of Altona; Alex Johnson; John Ericson; August Simpson; and Andrew Anderson of Henderson Grove.[20]

They expressed themselves highly pleased with this county in general and Phelps Center in particular.

Have been reading "Rangers and Regulators of the Tanaka" by Capt. Mayne Reid and "93" by Hugo.

Sun. Aug. 19
Was at meeting at the Emigrant House. There I met Ida Bragg, daughter of J. P. Bragg, who has just arrived from Ills. She is 15 years old, fair, fat, and red haired, but not a bad looking girl. Though so young, she is said to be of very loose morals.

Aug. 27
Hilda, Emil, Justus, and I have been down on the islands of the Platte picking grapes. We got about a bushel.

Williamsburg, Aug. 30

Went down to Sherwood yesterday to see Robt. Hindman on business. I found George Hindman at home, having got back from the
cattle range yesterday. He looked every inch a cowboy in his broad
rimmed white hat, six shooter, and cartridge belt. He told me John
Shafer is at present herding cattle at the Red Cloud Agency.[21]

Hindman's family consists at present of his wife, his sons George
and Albert, and Shafer's two little boys, Willie and Bernie.

I stopped with Hindman's over night and we had a very pleasant
evening. The old man, who is a fine musician, entertained us with
some fine airs on the flute.

Aug. 31

Stopped in Williamsburg last night at Baldwin's. Baldwin was not at
home but Mrs. Baldwin and Will Dilworth were. Had a pleasant
evening, Will giving me some reminiscences of his college life in Lincoln, Neb. and Quincy, Ills. Left there this morning and went home.

Sept. 4

Commenced to work for Rylander and Hallgren. They have about 30
"hands" at work, cutting, hauling, and scraping broomcorn and we
all board at the Emigrant House with John P. Bragg, and Ida Bragg
waits on the table.[22]

John P. Bragg is scraper "boss" and Oscar Hallgren field "boss."

Yesterday the boys had a high old time with a Texas cow that Bragg
had bought of Bill Robb of Plum Creek for beef. Bragg was to butcher
her and the broomcorn hands turned out en mass to help him. They
surrounded and attacked her with guns, pistols, and clubs and she
becoming desperate charged the crowd repeatedly. Augustus Peterson
fired six shots into her with a small revolver and Frank Hallgren fired
two loads of buck shot into her. She then charged August Bragg, who
broke for the broomcorn field shooting as he ran. She overtook him,
knocked him down, and fell over him. He was saved from serious
injury or death by Bragg's dog, Watch, which attacked her and di-
verted her attention from Aug. who got up, fired the remaining charges
out of his revolver without apparent result, and got away.

Frank Hallgren rode into the field to rout her out and she charged
his mule. She next turned her attention to J. P. Bragg, who struck her a
powerful blow between the horns with a piece of scantling, but she

came right on and he dropped his club and grabbed her by the horns to save himself from being gored. Oscar Hallgren came to the rescue with an axe and struck her blow after blow with the sharp edge of an axe, finally bringing her down with a blow in the neck.

Among the boys here are several from Ills., who came out to see the country and pay expenses by cutting broomcorn. They are Enoch Lind, Lewis Lawson, Oscar Hallgren, Alf Samuelson, Gus Charlston, August Johnson, Emil Peterson, Augustus Peterson, Wilhelm Johnson from Indiana and others.

Among others is John Nelson, alias "Indian John," who has spent some time among the Sioux at Red Cloud Agency. He is a strange fellow and the butt of all the others' jokes.[23]

Sept. 12
Still working for Rylander & Hallgren. Received a note yesterday from Will Dilworth inviting me to a dance which was to be held in the school house at Williamsburg last night, and asking me to bring my friends with me.

Accordingly Frank Hallgren, Gus Charlston, Frank Anderson, Enoch Lind, and I drove down to Williamsburg, where we found that the fiddler had failed to put in his appearance and the dance had to be postponed indefinitely. When passing Aug. Carlson's on our way down we saw through the windows, Wilma Carlson stark naked, hunting for fleas in her chemise.

Sept. 17
We told a good many white lies to the boys about the dance at Williamsburg, representing it to have been a grand affair.

Frank Boge had to leave to day to go home and take care of his brother Oscar, who is sick. I asked Frank what kind of ailment his brother had, and he said it was "forty-five fever," meaning "typhoid" I guess.

We have a good deal of fun evenings after supper, wrestling, running, jumping, boxing hats & c.

Last night I got worsted in a wrestle with Ed Swanson. "Indian John" and Frank Anderson had what they called an "Indian wrestle" in the course of which the seat of John's pantaloons split, revealing a long strip of white skin to the admiring gasp of the delighted spectators, among which was the modest (?) Ida Bragg.

At leisure times now I am reading the "Dodge Club; or, Italy in 1859," by Jas. DeMille.

Sept. 24
Frank Anderson, Ed Swanson, Alf Samuelson, Gus Charlston, and I were breaking broomcorn and encountered a rattlesnake. The other boys being afraid to go near it, I killed it, cut off the rattles and gave them to Frank, who says he will take them back to Ills. as a souvenir.

Oct. 1
Have finished cutting broomcorn. Went down to Williamsburg, killed a rattlesnake on the way by pulling off one of my boots and using it as a club. At Baldwin's I was introduced to Mr. Hugh DeQuine, our County Surveyor, a gentleman of French extraction with a bald head, short body, and very long legs.

Oct. 2
Thrashed to day. We got 114 bu. wheat; 63 Rye; barley 40.[24]

Sun. Oct. 7
My brothers and I drove out to "Lone Tree," a noted landmark about 8 miles northeast of our house. It is a large, solitary elm growing out of a small canyon or draw, and can be seen for miles. It is noted as being the only tree on the "divide" between the Platte and Republican rivers, and also as being the spot where Green Garrett was killed by the Indians some ten years ago. The story as told me by John F. Shafer, a friend and companion of Garrett, is as follows:

Green Garrett was a bullwhacker freighting between Plattsmouth and Denver in the good old days before the advent of the U.P.R.R. One evening Green Garrett and his party camped on the Platte valley near the mouth of the Lone Tree cañon. During the night one of their ponies broke his lariat and escaped. The next morning Garrett started on the trail of the pony, which led in the direction of Lone Tree and that was the last his companions saw of him alive. As he did not return, with[in] a reasonable time, his comrades commenced a search for him and found his body near the tree, scalped and mutilated by Indians and partially devoured by wolves. They picked up his remains and buried them beneath the tree.[25]

We found a lone coyote there keeping a vigil over the resting place of the dead plainsman.

Yesterday Will Dilworth was elected delegate to the State Convention at Lincoln by a county convention held at Williamsburg. Father and Frank Hallgren were delegates from Center precinct to the county convention.

Oct. 9

This afternoon, while Justus and I were plowing, we observed a badger at a distance. I sent Justus to the house after a gun while I ran after the badger and brought him to bay. When I came too near him he would make a run at me and I would stand him off with my whip. I finally drove him down into a shallow hole, where I kept him from digging by prodding him with my whip stock until Justus came with a gun, when I shot him, pulled him out of the hole, and carried him home where I proceeded to take his hide off.

Oct. 12

While coming from Kearney to day in company with "Red Oak" Johnson, we met "Indian John" and after stopping a little while to speak with him, we drove on, when Johnson told me several stories of "Indian John" I was surprised to hear. He said he knew John well and that he had a sister living near Red Oak, Iowa; that John was the incendiary who burned a portion of Red Oak, Iowa, a couple of years ago in revenge for a fancied injury, that he broke jail twice, and was regarded as a crank.

John is about 28 years old, of medium height and spare build, brown hair, blue or grey eyes, a long sandy mustache, and white teeth. He has the stealthy, gliding walk of the Indians, among which he has lived, and wears embroidered moccasins. All-together he is a strange character.

School Creek Neb., Sun. Oct. 14

Yesterday C. J. Anderson and I drove down to Gronquist's in Harlan Co. Anderson went down to preach and I went to make arrangements with Clarence Peterson to go with him on his annual buffalo hunt.

We started from home late and when night came on we were still some six or eight miles from our destination. To make it worse a heavy rain came on and drenched us to the skin. The darkness was intense. We had a miserable time getting to Gronquists, stopped there over night, and this morning went to Andrew Ruben's new log cabin on School Creek where Anderson preached to a large congregation. After services went with Clarence Peterson up School Creek to Olof Blom's where we ate dinner. Spent the afternoon and ate supper at Clarence's brother Eric Peterson, and was introduced to Clarence's two nieces Annie and Tiny and met their brother, an old friend, Pete Burgquist.[26]

Oct. 15
Staid at Blom's last night and got back home this evening.

Oct. 16
This afternoon we had a mass convention of settlers at the Emigrant House for the purpose of nominating candidates for the coming election. Father was chairman and Will Dilworth secretary of the meeting. The following nominations were made:

> County Clerk, Wm. A. Dilworth;
> Commissioner, 3rd dist., Olaf Hedlund;
> Co. Surveyor, P. O. Hedlund;
> Co. treas., John M. Dahlstrom
> Superintendent Public Inst., N. C. Christianson
> County Judge, Jonas Peterson;
> Sheriff, Rolf Johnson;
> Coroner, J. A. Burr.

The nominations for precinct officers for Center Precinct were:

> J. P.'s, John Johnson, A. P. Anderson;
> Assessor, John Johnson;
> Constables, J. P. Bragg, Solomon Linder;
> Road Supervisor, John Linder;
> Judges of Election, J. S. Salgren,
> Gustaf Johnson, and Solomon Harris;

Clerks of Election:

> Rolf Johnson and Aaron W. Johnson.

Solomon Linder was chairman and I was secretary of the precinct meeting, which was held after the county convention.

CHAPTER 6

The Buffalo Hunt

School Creek, Oct. 19 [1877]
Came down here to day and to morrow will start with the Peterson boys on a buffalo hunt to the head waters of the Republican.[1]

Oct. 20
This morning we left School Creek, heading west, bound for the headwaters of the Republican River to hunt the buffalo, the king of the plains, of whom I had heard and read so much.

We were four in our party, Clarence Peterson, his nephews Peter Peterson and Peter Burgquist, and myself.

Our "outfit" consisted of two wagons drawn by three yoke of oxen and loaded with blankets and buffalo robes for bedding and provisions, such as flour, bacon, coffee, sugar, salt, butter & c., camp oven, camp kettle, frying pan, coffee pot, tin cups & c. and our arms and ammunition. Clarence had [a]Sharps Sporting rifle calibre "44," cartridge belt, and butcher knife; Burgquist was armed with a Springfield needle gun, cal. 50, cartridge belt and knife; Pete Peterson had no arms at all; while I had a 10 shot repeating Henry rifle (which I had borrowed from Will Dilworth), a belt of cartridges and a knife, besides my old army musket shot gun.

As we crossed the divide between School Creek and Spring Creek we encountered a rattlesnake, which Burgquist killed with his bullwhip. We stopped a short while at Watson on Spring Creek, where there is a post office and store run by Fred Switzer.[2] In the store is a magnificent elk head, the tips of the antlers being over 6 feet apart. Camped this evening on the Republican valley at Clarin's in Furnas County. Clarin is the father of Jo Clarin, a young man I was acquainted with at Hastings last year.[3]

Spent the evening in pleasant conversation with Clarin, who is an old pioneer and full of interesting reminiscences.

Sunday, Oct. 21
Broke camp at Clarin's this morning and continued our journey westward up the Republican valley. About noon we passed through Arapahoe in Furnas Co., a town of some 20 log cabins and frame houses. Camped for dinner on Muddy Creek near Arapahoe. Kept on this afternoon and camped this evening at Axel Wendell's place on the valley.[4]

Dry Creek, Oct. 22
Kept on our way, passed Spring Ranch and Burton's Bend, and crossed Deer Creek, Medicine Creek, and other streams of less importance. Camped this evening on Dry Creek. We are now in Red Willow County.[5]

Oct. 23
Last night while we were engaged cooking coffee and frying "sowbelly" for supper two men drove up, unhitched their teams and came up to the campfire. They were two "cowboys" from Frenchman's Fork on their way to the ranch with provisions, and as they came up to the campfire Clarence recognized one of them as "Pony Rogers," a famous frontiersman.

He was a short man with black hair and beard and quick, restless eyes. It is claimed that he is the man who killed the Sioux chiefs on the buffalo range in 1873, but he denies it, it is said, through fear of the government.

The story as it is generally told throughout this country is as follows: "Pony Rogers" and his pard, said by some to have been Wild Bill Kress and by others to have been Newt Mullen, were hunting buffalo on a small stream since called Chief Creek emptying into the Arickaree, one of the forks of the Republican. A lot of Sioux and Pawnees were also in the country hunting and one day Old Whistler, the chief of the Sioux, accompanied by Hand Smeller and Fat Badger, two sub chiefs, came into "Pony's" camp and demanded food. Rogers stirred up his fire and set the coffee pot on to boil. The redskins seemed to think that he did not put enough coffee into the pot and [one of them] reached his hand into the grub chest to help himself when Rogers got on his ear [?] and shut the lid of the grub box down on the Indian's hand and sat down on it, pinching the red's hand so he skinned it in pulling it away.

This made the Indians mad and they commenced to cackle in their own tongue of which Rogers understood enough to convince him that they intended to bring a band of their warriors and secure the scalps of the intrepid hunters who had dared to insult them.

Rogers knew that if he allowed the chiefs to leave camp alive, his life was not worth five cents on the dollar, so he determined to kill them all and getting his pardner away from the campfire on pretext of loading some things into the wagon, he apprised him of their danger and they agreed on a plan of action, all the time attending unconcernedly to the little duties of camp life so as not to awaken the suspicions of the doomed reds. Walking about carelessly Pony Rogers got two of the Indians in line and quick as thought raised his gun and fired, killing one and wounding another with [the] same ball. His companion then shot the third one dead and Pony fired again killing the wounded chieftain and in less time than it takes to tell, the spirits of the three red chiefs were on their way to the "Happy Hunting Grounds." The hunters then shot the chiefs' ponies so they would not stray back to the Indian camp and cause a search for their missing masters. The Sioux, when they found the dead bodies of their chiefs, laid the blame of their murder on their enemies, the Pawnees, and a short time after ward revenged themselves on them by massacring a lot of them on Frenchman's Fork.

We tried to draw "Pony Rogers" out about this affair, but he was very reticent and all he said was:

"Well yes, I did have a little trouble with the Sioux that fall and lost a span of mules, damn good mules too."

This is not the only adventure he has had. He has had many hair breadth escapes and a record of his life would read like a romance.[6]

This morning we passed through Indianola, a small town of some fifteen houses, mostly log. We stopped awhile and laid in a supply of ammunition, and I wrote and mailed a postal card to the folks at home.[7] Camped for noon on Red Willow Creek, a place where "Buffalo Bill" and "Texas Jack" distinguished themselves in a battle with Indians about eight years ago. This evening pitched our camp in a bend of the river, and as here are plenty of beaver sign such as a dam, and stumps of trees gnawed off by the beavers, we set some beaver traps.

Camp at Smoky Hill Ranch, Oct. 24[8]

We caught no beaver last night. On the contrary, the beaver got away with one of our traps, the stake to which it was attached not having firm hold on the quicksand.

This morning at a place called Rock Point we met Bill Morehead and Frank Baker of Spring Creek, Harlan Co., returning from the buffalo range. They had killed twelve buffalo, and had their wagons full of meat and hides, but reported buffalo scarce.

We also met Bill Doyle, a ranchman, and Bowers, a cowboy. Doyle is a noted plainsman, and is the man who killed "Kansas Jack" the horsethief, who with his partner was surrounded and shot by the ranchman after a desperate battle last year.

One of his most notable exploits was performed in company with "Pony Rogers." The Indians attacked "Pony's" camp and ran off his mules. Rogers and Doyle concluded to retaliate, and followed the trail of the marauding reds several days and watching their opportunity, one night stampeded the herd of the reds and got safely back to the settlements with about eighty of the Indians' ponies, though they were hotly pursued by Indians. It was exploits of this nature that gave "Pony Rogers" his name.

We made our noon camp on Blackwood Creek, a well wooded stream where a detachment of soldiers were overtaken by a water spout a number of years ago while in camp and many of them drowned.[9] While the boys were frying bacon for dinner, I took my shotgun and went gunning for mud ducks—which were plenty on the creek—and shot one.

We were annoyed by a cloud of "buffalo gnats"—a small species of gnat that infest the plains. They got into our eyes, ears, and noses so we were glad to break camp as soon as our lunch was over.

A couple of miles further on we passed through Culbertson near the mouth of Frenchman's Fork (named in honor of Major Culbertson, a noted scout and frontiersman) which is the last town on the Republican Valley. It is a small place of some eight or ten houses and is the county seat of Hitchcock County. It is also the headquarters of the stockraisers on the upper Republican and tributaries. Here we crossed the Frenchman or Whiteman's Fork of the Republican and soon after we espied a badger running along the river bank, which Clarence shot.[10]

Camped this evening near a spring in the bluffs near an old deserted dugout called Smoky Hill Ranch.

Camp Creek, Oct. 25

Got an early start this morning and halted at noon on "Dry Creek" (it is a curious fact that nearly every other creek on the Republican is called Dry Creek).

This afternoon we passed a large prairie dog town, which seemed pretty lively, the whole population turning out to bark at us as we went by. I fired several shots at them with my rifle and the boys think I killed one of the little creatures, though I am in doubt about it. Soon after, I shot at a badger with better results as I brought him down with his carcass full of bird shot.

We see no more farms, only an occasional cattle ranch on some of the creeks, and "cowpunchers" are the only people we meet. They are a tough looking set, these cowboys, and are noted for their shooting proclivities and lawlessness.

The usual equipment of [a] herder or cowboy is a white, broad brimmed hat, a blue woolen shirt with wide collar and silk neck tie, leather leggins or buckskin breeches fringed at the seams, fine tight boots, an old army overcoat, a belt around his waist full of cartridges, one or two Colt's sixshooters, a bowie-knife, a Winchester rifle, a pair of big spurs, and last though most important, a small Indian pony with a big saddle. They are skillful riders too, and it is their delight to straddle a vicious, plunging, kicking, bucking bronco just out of the herd.

When sober they are perfect gentlemen and the most free hearted boys to be met, but woe to the man who dares cross them when they get full of "bug juice" and start out to "run a town."

Camped this evening on Camp Creek near a "cow ranche" and one of the "cowboys" came into camp and warned us to look out for Indians, which he said are pretty numerous of late in this vicinity and have been killing herders and committing depredations. He said a small party of Cheyennes were seen a couple of days ago on Indian Creek, a short distance west of here. "Little Pete" is frightened and wants to go home.[11]

Indian Creek, Oct. 26

This morning we passed Battle Canyon, the scene of a bloody slaughter of the Pawnees by the Sioux in 1873. It is about 12 miles above the mouth of Frenchman's Fork.[12]

It occurred shortly after the killing of Whistler, Hand Smeller, and

Fat Badger on Chief Creek, which murder (?) was laid to the Pawnees, the hereditary enemies of the Sioux, a large party of whom were at [this] time on a grand buffalo hunt.

The Pawnees were camped in this canyon when the Sioux came down on them. The Pawnee bucks all left camp to make an attack on a herd of buffalo, which the Sioux had driven up on the surrounding bluffs as decoy.

The Sioux struck the camp and had already killed some 50 or 60 of the squaws and decrepid old men in camp, before the Pawnees became aware of the trick. The Pawnees returned to camp and attacked their savage foe with desperate ferocity, but being at a great disadvantage in point of numbers, were compelled to flee leaving all their camp equipage, including a number of children, many ponies, and the robes and meat of about 500 buffalos, in the hands of the enemy. They fled down the river and sought refuge in the settlements of their friends the whites.

The Pawnees numbered some 250 bucks, children, and squaws, and were under the leadership of a white chief named Tom Williams. The Sioux engaged were Old Whistler's band, led by Snowflake, and numbered 700 or 800 Warriors.

It is claimed by many plainsmen that the Sioux were led by a white man, Col. Charles Emmett, better known on the frontier as "Dashing Charley."

About 100 Pawnees were killed in the massacre while the Sioux lost only about 20 warriors.

A detachment of troops from Fort McPherson arrived soon after the fight, buried the butchered redskins, and drove the Sioux back to their reservation. The surviving Pawnees got back to their reservation north of the Platte in a pitiable condition.[13]

Clarence Peterson with a party of Buffalo hunters passed the scene of the battle a couple of weeks after the battle. They saw a pony hobbling along the river bottom, and picked up a number of arrows. We are now camped on Indian Creek at the foot of a big cottonwood.

Camp on Frenchman's Fork, Oct. 28
Left Indian Creek yesterday morning to cross the divide between the Republican and Frenchman. The drive was uneventful save the shooting of a badger by Pete Burgquist. Camped last night in a hollow on

the open prairie, where there was neither wood nor water. We have left all timber behind and will have to burn buffalo chips from this [time] on.

This morning as I awoke I pulled away the buffalo robe which covered my face when ouch! a stream of ice cold water came trickling down off the robe into my shirt collar. We found it had snowed during the night and some of it had thawed and formed a pool in a depression of the robe with the result aforesaid. We would have had a hard time cooking breakfast if we had not brought some wood with us from Indian Creek, as the buffalo chips were too wet to burn.

We struck Frenchman's Fork opposite Rock Bluffs at a cattle ranch where we stopped awhile with the cowboys, who confirmed the reports of Indian depredations and gave us an account of how Tom Webster's outfit was attacked a few days ago while going from their place to their own ranch on the Stinking Water, when they lost some ponies and a pack mule.[14]

This afternoon we started up the Frenchman which, here, is a narrow swift stream with rocky banks.

I went gunning along the stream for ducks and succeeded in bagging one, a fine large mallard.

Oct. 29
Camped last night on the Frenchman and this morning after breakfasting on the duck I shot yesterday, we proceeded on our journey up the fork.

It snowed some last night and to day the weather has been quite cold.

While the boys were driving along the road I took my shot gun and followed the banks of the stream, which ran parallel with the road but at some distance from it. I soon espied a flock of mud-ducks in the middle of a beaver dam and got a shot at them, killing two and wounding a third, which, however, got away.

I had to strip and wade in after the ducks as they remained floating in the middle of the dam. The water was about four feet deep, very cold, and it didn't take me long to dress when I got out.

I then started to rejoin our party, which I found just parting from an outfit of four trappers from the Stinking Water who had been up in the sand hills hunting buffalo. Our party at first took them for Indians and prepared to give them a warm reception when they discovered their mistake.

Soon after, Clarence and I, who were ahead of the wagons, encountered a skunk, which I shot with my shot gun.

We are now encamped on the head of Frenchman's Fork on the banks a pond. A high rocky bluff bounds the view on one side of the camp while on the other, the plain stretches away a couple of miles to a range of sandhills.[15]

This evening I went down stream a quarter of a mile to a beaver dam and shot two more ducks. They would not float ashore so I had to wade in after them.

It became dark before I got back and I heard Clarence firing his gun and yelling so I might find my way back to camp, he being fearful that I was lost. When I got in camp I found Clarence had taken a large dose of alcohol for the ague and was drunk. He sat on the powder keg talking incoherently of buffalo, Indians, and ague until Pete Burgquist and I put him to bed.

We will camp here for several days as we expect John Peterson, Clarence's brother who is on his way from the Black Hills, to meet us here.

Oct. 30

Last night we had some rain and snow, and this morning the coyotes were howling most dismally near camp. The boys say it is a sign of a storm or cold weather.

We went down stream to the beaver dam and set some traps. We also scouted around in the hills looking for buffalo sign. Saw some tracks, evidently three days old.

I shot a duck of the blackhead variety a short distance down the fork this evening.

The boys have for several days been trying to find a nickname that would fit me and have at last decided on calling me "Sheriff Bobtail" in ridicule, I suppose, of my aspirations for the office of sheriff of Phelps County.

Oct. 31

This morning while Little Pete and I were returning to camp from a visit to the beaver traps, we heard a terrible yelling and shooting and tramping in the direction of the camp and thinking the camp was at-

tacked by Indians, we hurried to the help of our comrades. We found
the boys lying on the ground panting and exhausted. A herd of wild
Texas cattle had run through camp and stampeded three of our oxen
and the boys had to chase them several miles before they brought
them back.

On going up on the bluffs we could see thousands of cattle swarming on the flats and every once in a while a bunch of them would
come down to the water hole to drink, and we had a good deal of
trouble to keep them from stampeding our cattle.

Clarence was mad, and swore to have revenge on the "Texecans"
for his long chase, so he shouldered his "Big 44" and started up the
sand canyon after a herd. We soon heard a shot, and presently Clarence
came into camp with the hind quarters of a spring calf slung over his
shoulders.

We filled the frying pan and had a big feast. It was an agreeable
change from the "sow-belly" we had been accustomed to since leaving home.

In the afternoon another bunch of cattle stampeded through camp
and Little Pete's oxen, Swan and Duke, pulled their picket pins and
went with them. Little Pete, Burgquist, and I chased them 3 or four
miles before we caught them.

Thursday, Nov. 1
To avoid trouble with the Texas cattle, we broke camp this morning
and drove in a south westerly direction into the sand hills. We left a
notice in camp for John, written on a piece of cracker box, telling him
where to find us.

During this day's drive we crossed the dividing line between Colorado and Nebraska, where we found a large cedar post with the name
"Nebraska" carved on one side and "Colorado" on the other. The post
had been burned off by prairie fires so we took it along for firewood.

Nov. 2
We made a "dry" camp last night. This morning as Pete Burgquist
and I were building a fire, we spied a buffalo cow and calf coming
into view around a point, about half a mile away.

We woke Clarence, who got out of bed in a hurry, got his gun, and
started off after the buffaloes, which had become alarmed at sight of

the camp and were putting for the hills at a lively gate. Clarence came back in a couple of hours, not having been able to overtake his game.

Soon after, Burgquist (who had left camp to look for buffalo) returned and reported having seen a herd of buffalo crossing a ridge about 3 or 4 miles west of camp.

Leaving Little Pete in charge of camp Clarence, Burgquist, and I hunted up the buffaloes, which we found grazing on a sandy flat between the hills. There were about a hundred of them and they presented a fine appearance. Some were grazing, some were lying down, and others were pushing and jostling each other around a water hole.

We secured a position in the long grass on the brow of a hill overlooking the flat and about three hundred yards distance, and gave them a volley. The whole herd started across the flat on a lumbering awkward sort of gallop. We kept pumping the lead into them, and Clarence brought a cow down at a distance of 463 yards. As the buffaloes disappeared over a ridge on the other side of the flat, we noticed a cow that been crippled by a shot lagging behind, accompanied by two calves. Burgquist started after the herd to try and get the cow while Clarence and I went to butcher the cow Clarence had shot. She was not dead, but was very fierce and savage. As we drew near she snorted and rolled her eyes in pain and rage and tried to get at us, but she had received a shot which had crushed the hip-joint and was unable to rise.

Clarence grasped her by the horn, placed his knee on her neck, and plunged his knife in her throat.

We then skinned and cut up the cow, then went to camp where we arrived a little before sunset. Pete Burgquist got in a couple of hours afterwards and reported having killed the cow and the two calves. The cow had her foot crushed by a ball.

Nov. 3

This morning we moved our camp about a mile and a half further west on a big bottom, or flat, near a small shallow pond of water, or rather mud puddle. The water was strongly impregnated with alkali and very disagreeable to the taste, so the oxen refused to drink it, though they had been without water for two days.

Clarence, Burgquist, and Little Pete took a team and went after the hides and meat of the buffaloes we killed yesterday. About noon Little Pete came into camp with the team bringing the meat and hides. He said the wolves had partially devoured the cow Clarence had killed. He left the boys back in the hills hunting.

Suddenly we observed three old buffalo bulls at a water hole about a quarter of a mile from camp, and I got my rifle and commenced to crawl towards them to get a shot. Soon I saw Clarence and Burgquist stealing along a ridge beyond the bulls and signalling for me to lie low, and await developments.

They then opened fire on the buffaloes and as I was in line some of the bullets came whistling in unpleasant proximity.

One of the shaggy brutes staggered and fell on his haunches at the first fire, but he rallied and set off with the rest, which were all wounded, towards the hills and were soon out of sight.

Sunday, Nov. 4

Weather very cold. Clarence is sick abed with ague. The water is unfit for use and this forenoon Burgquist, Little Pete, and I dug a well in hopes of getting good water. We got down about 10 feet and then, seeing no signs of moisture, we gave it up. We had nothing to draw up the sand with except a water bucket and log chain, and I nearly broke my back pulling Little Pete out of the well hand over hand.

After dinner Burgquist, Pete, and I took a team and wagon and went off in the hills after a load of sage brush roots for fuel, the buffalo chips being too wet to burn, and the weather indicates an approaching storm. Snow is flying about, the wind is keen and cutting, and so we cower around the camp-fire, continually shifting around to keep from freezing one side and scorching the other. I begin to realize that buffalo hunting and camping out in the winter is not what it has been "cracked up" to be.

Nov. 5

This morning Burgquist and I left camp for a hunt in the hills. Clarence, being sick, remained in camp with Little Pete.

We first went to the carcass of a cow we had killed, where we had laid out strychnine for wolves. We found all the baits gone and on searching in the long grass found two dead coyotes. These we skinned and then proceeded on our way. After tramping about until noon, we sighted from the crest of a high hill, a small herd of buffalo several miles to the northwest.

We had to do so much crawling in the grass and maneuvering to get near them, that it was nearly sunset before we got within range.

Finally we got within fifty yards of them. There were about twenty in the herd lying down on the hillside, while two fine bulls were walking about, apparently on the lookout for enemies. I guess our movements in crawling through the long grass on top of the hill attracted their attention, as they came right toward us. Burgquist whispered to me to take the bull on the left while he took the one on the right. Before I could obtain a good aim through the long grass, Burgquist fired. I fired point blank at mine and the two bulls, with a snort of terror, started down hill to rejoin the herd, which was now up and fleeing. We fired several shots before they disappeared over the next ridge, then turned our attention [to] Burgquist's bull, which, having received a shot full in the breast, had run down on the flat where he was staggering about with a stream of blood running through his mouth and nostrils. Seeing us coming he got up and dusted it a lively gait. As he was running in direction of camp we concluded to let him run, as the nearer camp we got him the better. After running a couple of miles or so, he disappeared over a swell on the plain. We came up cautiously over the knoll and found the bull on the other side lying down as if taking a rest. We got up within fifty yards unobserved and Burgquist gave him a shot in the ribs. He turned his head, looked reproachfully at us, then straightened out his limbs and died.

He was a magnificent beast about 4 years old. His hair was very dark and about his head and shoulders, jet black. His short, curved horns were jet black and shining like polished ebony.

By this time the sun was setting and we didn't have time to skin the animal, so we merely removed the intestines, and as the darkness was fast approaching and hiding the outlines of the hills we started for camp, some 10 or 12 miles distant. We had one solitary star peeping from beneath the edge of a dark cloud in the west to guide us.

We had not had a morsel of food or a drop of water since leaving camp in the morning and were very hungry, thirsty, and tired.

We found a thin covering of snow in the hollows in the sandhills and managed [to] scrape up some of it with which we assuaged our thirst somewhat, but it was very gritty with sand and disagreeable to have in the mouth.

The sky overhead was dark and threatening and seemed to indicate a coming storm. We had small hopes of finding camp in this trackless wilderness and the prospect of staying out on such a night without food, shelter, or blankets was not very encouraging.

After several hours of weary tramping we ascended a range of hills, which by their height and steepness we recognized as being some three or four miles northwest of camp. On descending these hills we came to a buffalo trail which, as we knew, meandered right through our camp. Here Pete and I had a dispute as to the direction to be taken. Pete wanted to go to the left and I to the right. Finally I yielded and we went to the left about 200 yards, when we suddenly came to the end of the trail. Pete then acknowledged that I was right and we turned about and went back and after following the trail about an hour, we came in sight of the glimmering camp-fire and were soon there. Clarence told us he had fired his gun several times in hopes that we would hear it and be guided by the noise to camp—we heard no shots. Little Pete was up and had a pot of coffee boiled, a pan of buffalo hump fried, a loaf of bread baked, and some molasses and butter ready for us and we sat down and ate as if we hadn't had anything for six months.

Nov. 6

Contrary to our expectations it did not storm last night, and to day the weather has been mild and pleasant.

This morning Clarence, Burgquist, and I, with one yoke of oxen and wagon, started after the bull we killed yesterday. We brought with us a cask of water, some grub, and some buffalo robes, as we expect to remain out over night. We found the bull all right and skinned and cut him up. We also took his head, which is one of the finest we have seen. Clarence intends to take it home to Dr. Hoyt of Orleans, having promised to bring him one.[16]

We drove about nearly all day but could see no buffalo except a large herd, which we saw at a great distance shortly before night.

This evening we camped in a round basin-shaped hollow in the hills, and while we sat comfortable around a big blazing fire of sage roots, we enlivened the occasion with stories, songs, and jokes. The boys called on me for a song and I gave them the following:

> We went to hunt the buffalo
> In the Colorado sandhills;
> If you want to know the whole programme

You'll have to read the hand-bills.

We killed a lot of prairie dogs,
And skunks, and wolves, and badgers.
We stopped one night on Dry Creek
And camped with Pony Rogers.

We hunted ducks on Blackwood;
And ducks on Frenchman's Fork;
Because we had run out of meat,
And didn't like the pork.

From Culbertson to Camp Creek,
We heard of dreadful murders,
By the Indians on the range
Who were killing off the herders.

One day we went a hunting
For deer on Indian Creek;
Clarence shot one in the guts.
Just to see it kick.

On Frenchman's Fork we were attacked;
And gave our assailants battle;
'Twas "Texicans" charged through the camp,
Stampeding half our cattle.

We met the buffalo in the hills,
'Twas then our sport began;
And Burgquist killed three the first day,
Just like a little man.

Clarence shot one on the run
Five hundred yards away.
'Twas fun to see that buffalo jump,
Just like a rabbit gray.

The water being very bad
We tried to dig a well,
But we couldn't find any water there
If we'd dug way down to hell!

Burgquist and Sheriff Bobtail
Went off one day on a tramp,
And slew the king of buffaloes
A dozen miles from camp.

This was all I had composed and was received with applause by the boys. Clarence was then called on for a story and related the following experience:

He was hunting buffalo in this vicinity several years ago and got lost on the plains. He left camp one morning to try and get a shot at a couple of buffalo which he could see a couple of miles off. He succeeded in killing his game, and while skinning one of them, he noticed that a thick fog was coming on. He started to go back to camp, but soon found he was lost in the fog. He wandered about all day trying to find camp, and passed the night in a hollow in the sandhills surrounded by a pack of wolves, which stood off about 50 yards and howled. As he had no coat on and the night was cold, he had to walk about all night to keep warm. The next day was also foggy and he kept walking about aimlessly, occasionally firing off his gun and shouting in hopes that he might be heard in camp—but in vain.

That day he shot a buffalo and slaked his burning thirst by drinking the warm blood. He also ate some of the raw meat. He spent the second night the same as the first, surrounded by a gang of wolves, and though he was very cold and sleepy he dared not lie down for fear of the bloodthirsty wolves, which he kept at a respectable distance only by firing off his gun occasionally.

The next day he found the fog clearing off. He wandered about as much as his exhausted condition would admit and towards evening he happened to see something bright and glimmering like a star on top of a high hill a couple of miles away. He turned his lagging steps thither and found it was the camp of his party. He hardly recognized his own brothers and comrades, so had his terrible experience bewildered his intellect.

His party had driven a wagon to the top of the highest hill they could find in the hope that he might see it and it was the rays of the setting sun glancing on the bright wheel tire that had caught his attention and guided him to camp.

Clarence has had many thrilling adventures and hairbreadth escapes and desperate encounters with wounded buffalo bulls, but he says this was a little the toughest of them all.

Nov. 7

When we awoke this morning, we found the weather stormy. It was snowing and sleeting and as there were several bullet holes and knife cuts in the buffalo robes covering us, they leaked fearfully and we got wet, all but Clarence who had gone to bed in his buffalo overcoat.

We lay abed until about 10' o'clock A.M. dreading to get up in the storm. Then we got out, and with our knees knocking together and our teeth chattering with cold, we yoked up the oxen and took the back track for camp.

After driving several miles, we came suddenly in sight of a herd of about seventy-five buffalo huddled closely together. They were about an eighth of a mile distant, and on a flat where there was no cover. We walked toward them, stooping and keeping our guns behind us out of sight. They evidently took us for some of their own species as Clarence and Burgquist had buffalo overcoats. They kept looking at us, and occasionally shaking the snow from their shaggy heads till we got quite close. Then they seemed to suddenly "tumble to" us and with a wild snort started to run, and [we] commenced to pump the lead into them as fast as our breechloaders would work. But we were so benumbed with cold we could hardly handle our guns and all we got was one fat cow, which was wounded and took to the hills, where we captured and killed her after quite a chase.

By the time we reached camp, the storm was all over and the sun shining brightly.

Nov. 8

Cold and windy.

On getting out of bed this morning we discovered two buffalo in the sandhills about half a mile off. After a hasty breakfast Clarence, Burgquist, and I buckled on our cartridge belts, took our rifles, and started out after the buffalo, which were in full view of camp. Making a detour to get into the hills, we crawled up on them and found them to be two old bulls of monstrous proportions. One of them was standing up, while the other lay down behind him. Clarence fired at the one standing and dropped him. As the other got up to run Burgquist and I gave him a volley. He ran around a knoll and lay down, the other one then got [up], ran, and lay down near his comrade. As we came over the knoll they started to get up but we gave them another volley and that settled them.

We found several old bullets imbedded beneath their skins, which had evidently passed clean through them and the wounds afterward healed up.

Spent the remainder of the day stretching buffalo robes and coyote and badger skins on the ground to dry, which makes them lighter and more convenient to handle.

Nov. 9
Clarence, Burgquist, and Little Pete started off on a hunt taking a yoke of oxen and one wagon with them and leaving me in charge of camp. I got through the camp work, watered and picketed the stock, and went off to see the wolf baits. Found no wolves, but a skunk and two buzzards were laying around dead.

After dinner I went out hunting and about sunset I came on a herd of about 40 or 50 buffalo in the hills about two miles from camp. After much crawling through the sand and sage brush I came within twenty five yards of a fine bull, which was grazing apart from the others on a hillside while I lay on the top of the hill behind a clump of sage brush and long grass.

He had his broadside to me and taking steady aim at the place where his heart ought to be, I pulled the trigger. The huge beast gave a hoarse bellow of pain and terror and rolled over. He got up again and running to the herd about 200 yards off lay down in their midst.

Unfortunately my rifle was "out of whack" and I had some difficulty in ejecting the cartridge shell. When I finally got it in working order I commenced to fire promiscuously into the herd, which broke, panic stricken, down the flat in the direction of camp while the wounded bull started off into the hills by himself, as buffalo invariably do when wounded so badly that they can't keep up with the herd.[17]

I was fearful the fleeing herd would pass through camp and stampede our cattle, so I struck a bee line for camp. On getting there I found my worst fears realized. The cattle had pulled their lariat stakes and skipped. Being dark by this time I could not go to look them up.

Nov. 10

Fine weather. This morning I found the cattle walking around the camp dragging their picket ropes. After picketing them and getting breakfast, I went out to where I shot the buffalo yesterday and striking his trail, which was bloody, I followed it several miles till I finally lost it on a large flat covered with rank grass. I saw several places where he had been lying down, and pools of blood showing that he was badly wounded. From the top of a high hill I saw a herd of buffalo several miles to the north, but I did not care to go for them so I went back to camp, where I found the boys. They had killed two big bulls yesterday afternoon after a long chase.

Sunday, Nov. 11

This morning we struck camp and started south for Buffalo Creek, homeward bound. We have all the meat we want, and Clarence is anxious to get home on account of his ill-health.

After driving a couple miles, we met an outfit of hunters from Harlan Co., Neb., neighbors of Clarence. They were Old Sam McNeece, Bill McNeece, Lige Munro, and Frank Switzer. They had killed four buffalo and one deer and were just going into the hills to camp at the waterhole we have abandoned.[18]

We had a hard drive through the sand owing to sand, and without incident except that Clarence gave chase to a buffalo bull that ventured near our noonday camp. However, he did not get him.

Clarence, owing to his illness, is no good at running buffalo. Once he was noted for his endurance, and on one occasion he, on foot, chased a buffalo bull from Flag Creek to Watson, in Harlan County, finally killing the bull.

Just before sunset we pitched our camp on the head of Buffalo Creek and got fresh, clear, cold, water for ourselves and cattle, a luxury we all appreciated.

Buffalo Creek is about 8 miles long and runs into the Arickaree, a fork of the Republican. It used to be a famous hunting ground a few years ago, and here noted hunters such as "Antelope Jack," "Wild Bill Kress," "Wild Dick Coon," "Pony Rogers," "Buckskin Bill," "Otoe Joe," "Kiowa Bill," and other equally famous used to kill from 50 to 150 a

day each. The millions of bleaching skeletons along the creek testify
to the awful slaughter.

Nov. 12
Last night my slumbers were disturbed by the howling of wolves.
There seemed to be hundreds of them around camp, howling in every
pitch and key. This morning as daylight dawned we could distinguish
several packs near camp. We fired several shots into them, Clarence
wounding one.

We drove down to the mouth of the creek where there is a cattle
ranch. One of the cowboys told us that seventy-five Cheyenne Indians passed here about a week ago and judging from the direction they
took, they must have passed near our camp in the sand hills.
We have had fine weather for two or three days past.

Nov. 13
Camped last night half way between Buffalo Creek and Willow Creek.
This morning we got an early start and proceeded down the valley of
the Arickaree. Just after fording Willow Creek, Clarence shot a badger
in a bluff near the road.

We had a big noon camp on Rock Creek. Seven buffalo hunters under the lead of Bill Jennings, five cowboys returning from Ogallala,
and ourselves camped together.

The herders were anxious about their ranch above here, having heard
that it had been cleaned out by the Indians.

Indian Creek, Nov. 14
Camped here about 3 o'clock P.M. Here is a ranch but the two cowboys are away hunting stock on Big Timber.

While preparing dinner, a small boy about 14 years old with a broad
brimmed slouch hat came riding up. He told us his name was Billy
Myers and that he was the son of the merchant and hotel proprietor at
Culbertson, and that he came from there (50 miles) to day to see Josh
Jones and Tom Hill, the Indian Creek cowboys. As they were not at
home we invited him to stay with us till to morrow, and we'd share
our blankets and grub with him.

He accepted and producing a deck of greasy cards was soon engaged in a game of seven up with Clarence. He was as sharp as a steel

trap and full of jokes and stories. He sang several songs, among others, "Whiskey Parker's Song," a famous frontier ballad. I got Billy to
repeat it and I wrote it down. Here it is:

> Come all ye young girls,
> This song to you I write;
> We're going to the buffalo range,
> In which we take delight;
> We're going on the buffalo range,
> As we poor hunters do,
> While the soft-footed fellows
> May stay at home with you.
>
> Our fires are made of buffalo chips;
> Our beds are on the ground;
> Our tents are made of buffalo hides
> We build them tall and round;
> Our furniture is the
> Camp-kettle, the coffee-pot and pan;
> Our "chuck" is bread and buffalo meat,
> And mingled well with sand.
>
> Our game, it is the buffalo,
> The antelope, elk, and deer.
> They roam these wild prairies
> Without the least of fear,
> And when we come upon them
> Our guns have sore effect;
> We cause them to "throw up their hand,"
> And they "pass in their checks."
>
> The buffalo is a mighty beast,
> The noblest of the land;
> Sometimes he objects
> to "throwing up his hand;"
> With shaggy head thrown forward,
> And tail toward the sky;
> He seems to say, "I'm coming,"
> Now hunter mind your eye!"

Our neighbors are the Pawnees,
The Arapahoes, and Sioux;
Their mode of navigation is
Their buffalo-hide canoes;
And if they were to emigrate
I'm sure we wouldn't care,
For they have a very peculiar way
Of raising hunters' hair!

But the bloodthirsty redskins
Had better leave us alone;
Or we will give them worse pills
Than they got from Daniel Boone;
With our guns upon our shoulders,
And belts with forty rounds;
We send them up "Salt River"
To the "Happy Hunting Grounds!"

Come all ye jolly fellows
And rise with the early dawn;
Come all ye jolly fellows
And join the hunters song.
And now you've heard my story
You mustn't think it queer,
If I take a drink of whisky,
Or a glass of lager beer!

I also sang my song, the latest addition to which is as follows:

Twelve miles from camp we camped one night,
In a storm of sleet and snow;
And oh, how wet and cold it was!
And how the wind did blow!

One morning, fair, we chanced to see
Two bulls a mile away;
And after filling up with grub
We vowed those bulls to slay.

We charged upon those buffaloes,
And pumped the lead into 'em;
A dozen shots, or so, were fired,
Which was enough to do 'em.

The night we camped on Buffalo Creek
We had abundance of pure water.
I swore if I'd get home alive
I'd kiss the preacher's daughter.

Culbertson, Nov. 16

No incident occurred to break the monotony of our drive yesterday. We camped last night on Macklin Creek. Clarence is quite sick, he complains of soreness in the chest. At noon to day we camped alongside of the road, between a high bluff and the river. Burgquist and Little Pete were building a fire to cook our dinner with, when, through some carelessness, the fire got away from them and in less time than it takes to tell of it the flames were leaping skyward and roaring and crackling in the long grass in a fearful manner. The wagon[s] were in imminent danger of burning, but by tremendous exertions we succeeded in fighting it down. I scorched my hair and eyebrows, and "Little Pete" lost his hat and now wears a badger skin cap of enormous proportions, and singular cut and make.

We had considerable difficulty in crossing the Frenchman opposite Culbertson, getting stuck in the quicksand, and we had to "double up" to get out. The stream was full of floating ice and it was not very pleasant wading around with the water and quicksand running into the tops of our boots.

We camped on the main street of the town near Myers' Hotel, and spent the evening in the barroom of the hotel, among a select company consisting of Mrs. Myers, Billy, Newt, and "Chub" Myers, the buckboard driver from Arapahoe and a couple of cowpunchers in wide hats, fringed buckskin trousers, and top boots, one of whom was discoursing sweet music from a dilapidated violin, "Chub" keeping time on a tambourine.

Red Willow Creek, Nov. 17

Clarence got some medicine in Culbertson, and is a little better to day.

The only incident of to day's drive being the shooting of a grouse at 60 yards with a rifle in the hands of "Sheriff Bobtail." Camped on the Red Willow.

Spring Ranch, Nov. 18
Drove about thirty miles to day and camped at Spring Ranch, one of the most picturesque spots on the Republican Valley.

West Turkey Creek, Nov. 19
The Munro and McNeece outfit overtook us this morning at Burton's Bend and we camped together at noon on Elk Creek. They reported having had poor luck, only killed two buffalo after we left and those were wounded and crippled old bulls. Camped for supper on West Turkey Creek and had a little difficulty with a settler on account of turning our cattle loose into one of his hay-stacks. We finally "settled" the matter amicably by presenting the settler with a spoiled buffalo ham.

CHAPTER 7

Home Again, Politics and Romances

School Creek, Nov. 20 [1877]

After supper last night we yoked up and pulled out for School Creek where we arrived at 2 o'clock this morning, having driven over 38 miles since yesterday morning.

The folks were glad to see us safely back. Pete Burgquist's mother and pretty sister, Annie, got up and rustled some grub for us and we had to recount the incidents of the trip before going to bed and Annie gave me some news from Phelps that Emma Johnson and Solomon Harris are married and that my old friend and playmate, Thilda Danielson, has arrived from Illinois.

Burgquist has another sister, older, but she is not at home.

John Peterson, Clarence's brother, whom we expected to meet on the head of Frenchman's Fork, is here. He arrived a couple of days ago from the Black Hills by way of the Platte.

This afternoon was spent by the Peterson boys, a hunter named John Crockford alias "Barefoot John," and I in shooting at a target and in trying to break to harness a Mexican mule that John brought from the Black Hills.

Phelps Center, Nov. 22

Home again!

Yesterday morning after we had divided the spoils of the chase, I started for home in company with Charley Nelson of Phelps. I stopped at his house last night. Nelson told me some interesting stories of his wolf hunting in Sweden and I had to tell him all the adventures of my trip to the buffalo range.

I got home all safe and sound this afternoon, none the worse but a good deal healthier for my five weeks of "roughing it" on the plains.

They were glad to see me at home especially mother, who has been full of vague fears for my safety. She says she was sure that I would be killed by the Indians or buffaloes.

I have finished my song of life on the buffalo range and the last verses are as follows:

> I scorched my hair in a prairie fire;
> And Little Pete lost his hat;
> It lay smoking in the ashes,
> And stunk like a dead polecat.

> And now our trip is over
> Again we are at home,
> We'll often think of our hunting trip,
> Where reds and buffaloes roam.

> In remembrance of our buffalo hunt,
> These lines I here now trace;
> And "Sheriff Bobtail" bids adieu
> To his comrades of the chase.

Nov. 23
Went to the Post Office and got my mail. While I have been gone a P. O. called Phelps has been established at C. J. Anderson's, 3 miles south of our house.[1]

Nov. 24
Father and Dahlstrom went to Williamsburg to investigate the affairs of Robert Hindman, the County Treasurer, who moved to Dallas, Texas, some time ago leaving, it is alleged, his office in a muddled state. They found that the deficiency was imaginary and gotten up by the Dilworth faction to scare the Swedes, as Father, Dahlstrom, Frank Hallgren, and August Carlson were Hindman's bondsmen.

Sunday, Nov. 25
Attended meeting at the Emigrant House in the forenoon. Took dinner with Ida, August, and Johnny Bragg and called on Brunzells this afternoon.

Nov. 26
Cold wind from the north.

It transpires that at the election held on the 7th day of Nov. I was elected County Clerk and Clerk of the District Court in the place of Sheriff, Frank Hallgren being substituted as I had anticipated. Will

Dilworth was dropped altogether on account of some sharp practice on his part in trying to put up a job on the anti-ring party.

Owing to a mistake the Judges of Election of Center Precinct sealed up the ballots and poll book of said precinct in one envelope and presented it to the Board of Canvassers at Williamsburg. These, being members of the ring, saw here a pretext for throwing out the vote of Center Precinct and refused to count the votes, claiming they had no right to open the envelope containing the ballots.

So not taking the vote of Center Precinct into consideration they claim to have won the office of Clerk and Treasurer by five or six majority and presented Certificates of Election to William A. Dilworth and Christopher Jensen instead of Dahlstrom and I who, counting the 24 votes of Center precinct, were elected by a large majority.[2]

Frank Hallgren, Olaf Hedlund, P. O. Hedlund, and Jonas Peterson we elected by a majority outside of our precinct.

Sun. December 2
George Steward called this morning. He lives on Spring Creek now and is married to a daughter of Old Sam Moser.

August Bragg called also, and we amused ourselves with target shooting. At Aug.'s suggestion I, in fun, fired a couple of shots at Dahlstrom's dog, which was trotting along the end of the field over 600 yards away. At the second shot the dog gave a yelp and struck out for Dahlstroms like greased lightning. Aug. and I went over to see how badly he was hurt and found the ball had grazed his nose and torn a patch of skin off as big as a silver dollar.

If I had done as good shooting as that while on the hunt, we would have got more buffalo, I think.

Dec. 3
Charley Nelson, Emil, Justus, and I have been down to the head of Spring Creek after two loads of poles and crotches for the stable we are building.

We came near being lost in a snow storm on the way home this evening.

Dec. 6
The Hon. A. E. Harvey of Arapahoe, [Furnas] Co., is here. We are going to contest the election of last fall and bring a case of Quo Warranto

before the Supreme Court and have engaged Harvey to attend to it. He says we are bound to win, and thinks he can put the case through for thirty dollars and his expenses to Lincoln, which will probably be $30 more. Harvey, Dahlstrom, Frank Hallgren, P. A. Brodine, father, and I discussed the situation this evening. We concluded to call a mass meeting of settlers at the Emigrant House to morrow evening and lay the matter before them.

The County Ring has expelled Brodine from his office of Commissioner, claiming he had removed from the county, which is untrue as he was absent only a short time from the county to earn his living.

The County Ring sees that its days are about over, and it is trying to do all the harm it can before breaking up entirely.

Dec. 7

Attended mass meeting at the Emigrant House. The Anti-Ring party was strongly represented. Mr. Harvey made a short speech on the exigencies of the occasion which was well received. A subscription was started to defray the expenses of contesting the Election and $19 in cash were collected on the spot.

Dec. 10

Leander Hallgren and John W. Irvin of the Grand Central Hotel, Kearney, took dinner with us. Irvin is out buying broomcorn. He bought ours at $40 per ton.[3]

Dec. 26

Borrowed August Carlson's pony, Billy, this morning and started horseback for Arapahoe to consult our lawyer, Mr. Harvey. As it was snowing a little I was afraid to take the short cut across Devil's Gap for fear of getting lost so I rode by way of Rock Falls and Watson, and arrived at Harvey's place, a large, gloomy-looking frame house situated on a bluff a mile or so from Arapahoe at dusk having rode about fifty miles.[4] After stabling my horse at a Dutchman's farm on Elk Creek near by, I had supper with Harvey and was introduced to his wife, Mrs. Clara H., a young, refined lady, and to his little son Edward.

Spent the evening very pleasantly.

Dec. 28
Staid night before last at Harvey's and in the morning found the prairie covered with about 6 inches of snow. Mr. Harvey wanted me to stop a day or two and join him in a rabbit hunt. I declined, with thanks, and after breakfast went over to the Dutchman's to get my pony. The Dutchman was not at home, but his wife, a fat goodhumored woman, and his daughter, a well developed and goodlooking damsel of fifteen were. I tendered the old lady half a dollar for keeping my horse, but she said it was too much and directed her daughter to get an old sugar bowl from a top shelf in the cupboard and find some change to give me. She climbed up on the back of a chair and reached for the bowl when down came the girl, chair, and sugar bowl. She came near falling on to me and as her skirts flew over her head, I involuntarily had a vision of the female form divine such as I had not seen since the times I used to catch the girls in swimming back in Illinois. It was several moments before she recovered her equilibrium, when she went into the adjoining room and I saw her no more.

I then struck for home via West Turkey Creek and Devil's Gap. As I was making a short cut cross the plain from Devil's Gap to the head of Spring Creek it commenced to snow, and as I had no road to follow, I soon found I was lost. I rode about hither and thither until three o'clock this morning when I got to John Sandstrom's, having been over twenty hours in the saddle. I was so exhausted with cold, hunger, and hard riding I could hardly get off the pony.

I stopped at Sandstrom's the remainder of the night and came home this morning after breakfast.

At Sandstrom's I found a cowboy from Frenchman's Fork named Henry Burger. He informed [me] that Pony Rogers killed an Indian last fall on the buffalo range.

Sun. Dec. 30.
Mother and I went over to Johannes Anderson's. There I found sister Hilda, Aaron W. Johnson, and Miss Clara Mathilda Danielson, the daughter of Rev. Jacob Danielson and [an] old playmate of mine lately arrived from Ills. We used to have lots of fun together back in Ills. and I was glad to see her. Had a pleasant visit.

Dec. 31
Aaron Johnson has commenced to drill a well for us and henceforth we will not have to haul water.[5]

Tuesday, Jan. 1st, 1878
Cold and windy weather.

Andy Johnson, "Thilda" Danielson, Aleck Danielson, and Annie Johnson called on me this evening. By the way there is [a] good joke on Annie in which Mr. Harvey of Arapahoe is also involved.

Jan. 2
Lawyer Harvey advised me when I saw him to get my Official bond for $3,000 as County Clerk signed and present the same to the commissioners for approval at their first annual meeting, so I have been skirmishing around for signers. My bondsmen are Aaron W. Johnson, Solomon Linder, Fridolf W. Stenfelt, Andrew Olson, and Charley Nelson.

Jan. 8
Last night we had a prayer meeting at our house and after it was over I escorted Thilda Danielson to her home. We had a pleasant walk and a long talk over the good old times when we were "children in the wood." Got back home at 2 o'clock this morning.

Olaf Hedlund, County Commissioner Elect, P. O. Hedlund, Surveyor Elect, P. A. Brodine, and I took a flying trip down to Williamsburg and filed our Official Bonds with the County Clerk.

Attended prayer meeting this evening at Dahlstroms and escorted Miss Danielson home from there.

Thilda and I used to be pretty intimate back in Illinois where she used to claim me as her lover. Even now after several years separation the old affection seems still burning and she shows in various ways that she is not indifferent to me.

Kearney, Jan. 10
Father, Justus, and I left home yesterday morning with two loads of broomcorn, bound for Kearney. Night overtook us on the Platte valley and we stopped over night with Manlius Lucas and Charley Alexander in a little shanty on the valley. Got into town this afternoon and put up at Brandts. There we found Pete Brandt and Eric Ericson, brother of Sam Ericson and a distant relative of ours.[6]

Kearney, Jan. 11

Went to the P. O. this morning where I got a letter from A. E. Harvey together with some affidavits in our Action of Quo Warranto, which he instructed us to swear to before Col. Sam L. Savidge, a Notary Public, and then forward them to the Hon. Guy A. Brown, Clerk of the Supreme Court at Lincoln.[7]

I hunted up Dahlstrom and Brodine who were in town and we fixed the papers up in good shape and mailed them.

Saw a monster wildcat, which was killed by a party [of] hunters a couple of days ago on Dismal River.

I have concluded to stop in Kearney a while to get some points from Simon C. Ayer, Clerk of Buffalo County, so that I will be qualified to take charge of my office if the Supreme Court should decide in my favor.[8]

I am boarding at Brandt's. My old friend Indian John is there also.

Lost 40 cents this evening playing "Pigeon hole" with Pete Brandt, Nels Nelson, and a big Irishman.

Kearney, Sun. Jan. 13

"Little Redbird" (Ida Bragg), who is employed at the Grand Central Hotel, called on me at Brandt's this afternoon. "One-Armed Johnson" and John P. Nelson, two store clerks, called also.

This evening Pete Brandt and I "took in the town" and in the course of our rambles called at Alice McDonald's to see the girls.

Jan. 17

I spend several hours every day at the Office of the County Clerk of Buffalo Co. to get posted on a County Clerk's duties. Mr. Ayer, the Clerk, is a fine gentlemen and Sam Nevins, his Deputy, is one of the boys and I get along first rate with them.

I received a letter from Thilda D. commencing: "My Darling Rolf" and signed Madcap Tillie, in which she informs me she will be in town to morrow.

Kearney, Jan. 18

Thilda came in this afternoon with her brother, Aleck. They put up at Brandt's. This evening Thilda, Ida Bragg, Carrie Johnson (Pete's girl), Pete, Aleck, "Indian John" and I had a gay old time at Brandt's after which we took a promenade around town.

Kearney, Sun. Jan. 20
Played cards and checkers with Thilda Danielson most of the day. This evening, Thilda, "Little Redbird," "Little Carrie," Miss Mathilda Broman, Miss Gussie Carlson, Mr. John P. Nelson, Mr. One-Armed Johnson, Pete Brandt, "Indian John," and I had a good time together.

Kearney, Jan. 23
Thilda D. is now staying with the family of B. H. Bicknell. I see her every evening. Weather rather cold to day. Has been warmer and pleasant most of the time for the last two weeks.

Met Miss Tinie Nelson, Sister of Swan G. Nelson, this afternoon. Took her to Brandt's, where she remained a couple of hours I then escorted her to her residence.

Phelps Center, Jan. 24
Rode from Kearney home with Lewie Swanson. Took supper at the Emigrant House with Lewie and his sister Ellen. This evening Aaron Johnson, Johnny Bragg, and Norwegian Johnson called on me. "Norwegian" has been a sailor and gave us an interesting account of his trip to Egypt.

Jan. 29
We have the mail once each week. This is mail day and I got a letter from Miss Elma Johnson, Soperville, Ills., and one from Thilda Danielson.

Jan. 30
Fine weather again.

P. O. Hedlund and P. A. Brodine arrived at Dahlstrom's from Beaver City, Furnas Co., this evening. They told me they saw A. E. Harvey, our lawyer, who said he had sent the Summons in our action of Quo Warranto in a registered package addressed to me at Kearney, Neb. I will have to go to Kearney to morrow and get it as the summons have to be served on defendants before Feb. 4.

Jan. 31
Rode into Kearney with Frank Hallgren in his buggy, got to town about 2 o'clock, went to the P. O., got my mail, and in less than an hour was on

my way back to Phelps Center riding Frank Hallgren's mare pony, Fanny.

Got home after dark all right but very tired, having rode bare back.

Found Dahlstrom, Brodine, and Aaron Johnson, at our house, awaiting me. Brodine, Johnson, and I set to work and copied the summons as the originals have to be returned to Lincoln.

The day has been gray and dull, hoar frost falling all the time.

Friday, February 1st

This morning about 3 o'clock Dahlstrom and Brodine started in a buggy for Rock Falls, where they got Sheriff Sweezey. From there they went to the southeast part of the county and served the summons on Christopher Jensen. They came back to Dahlstrom's this evening.

To morrow Sweezey, Stenfelt, and I will go to serve the Summons on Will Dilworth and Harry Mudge.

Kearney, Feb. 2

Sheriff Sweezey, Stenfelt, and I drove down to the residence of Gen. Dilworth on Plum Creek in the northeast [sic] corner of the county. The ranch is a low rambling structure of wood and sod. We found Will Dilworth at home and served the summons on him in the case of Rolf Johnson Vs W. A. Dilworth. The summons in the case of P. A. Brodine vs H. W. Mudge were next served on Harry Mudge, a brother-in-law of Gen. Dilworth, who is employed as a herder at Dilworth's Ranch. We then drove to Kearney, stopping for dinner at Baldwin's in Williamsburg, and returned the original summons to Lincoln. Sheriff Sweezey put up at the Grand Central while Stenfelt and [I] went to Brandt's.

Sheriff James Sweezey is a small, spare, man with treacherous grey eyes, dark hair and beard. He talks in short jerky sentences. He is, however, courteous and gentlemanly in deportment. He gave me a detailed account of the killing of Ex-Sheriff Miller on Spring Creek last summer, which was substantially the same as I first heard the story. He said this was not the only shooting affray in which he had been engaged since the war.

Sunday, Feb. 3

This afternoon Tinie Nelson called and Pete, "Indian John," Tinie, and I played a four-handed game of cassino. I afterward took Tinie up town, left her, and called on Ida Bragg at the Grand Central. Thilda is living 3 miles out in the country so I can't see her.

Stenfelt and I drove back to Phelps Center this evening, taking Sweezey with us as far as Williamsburg.

John Shafer has got back from the cattle range, and is staying on Spring Creek. Bill Lee accuses him of having seduced his wife, and has sworn to kill him on sight. Shafer goes armed all the time and if the two meet there will be war.

Feb. 5
There is a touch of spring in the air, I might almost say, of summer, so clear is the sky, so beautiful is the sunshine. Got a postal card from Swan Nelson and a letter from Thilda D. in which she accuses me of faithlessness. Says her heart is broken and mixes reproaches, love, and other nonsense up in an awful mess.

She is sore because I called on Ida Bragg last Sunday while in Kearney, and did not go to see her. From what I can understand John P. Nelson, who is trying to pay attentions to Miss Thilda, has "given me away."

Feb. 14
Brother Emil received a letter from his second cousin, Charles Atle Nelson of Soperville, Ills., in which he relates some of his experiences while traveling in Europe last summer with his father and mother. They crossed the ocean in the same steamer with Gen. U. S. Grant and his family. He says they became quite intimate with the Grants, Nelson often playing cards with the General, and Atle beat Jesse Grant playing checkers.[9]

Kearney, Feb. 16
Went with Frank Hallgren to town. Met Leander Hallgren at the Grand Central Hotel just back from Minnesota. He presented me with his photograph. Found a letter [from] Thilda at the P. O. in which she begged forgiveness for writing the other letter. She wants to make up.

Kearney, Sun. Feb. 17
Beautiful weather. This afternoon I went out in the country to Bicknell's and visited Thilda D. She was over-joyed to see me, said she thought

I had gone back on her. Spent a pleasant afternoon and evening. Got back to Brandt's 9 P.M.

Kearney, Feb. 18
This evening Pete Brandt and I called on Ida Bragg and "Little Carrie" at the Grand Central. Ida did not seem as pleased to see me as usual and in a short time excused herself, and went up town with Rachel French, another hotel girl. Pete and I soon took our departure, and I determined to revenge myself for Ida's unaccountable conduct.

Kearney, Neb., Feb. 19
Spent most of the day in the Clerk's Office. In a conversation with Sam Nevins, he gave me an account of the various encounters between cowboys and citizens of Kearney, of most of which he had been an eyewitness. He told how "Texas Spence" was shot off his horse and killed in front of the Harrold House, how "Peeler" was shot down in front of "Mother Alice's" bagnio; how Ed Smith was killed on the street by City Marshall Dick Stimpson; of the murder of Milton Collins by Jord Smith, and the pursuit, capture and trial of the murderers. Sam says times used to be considered dull here if they didn't "have a man for breakfast" every day.[10]

I have found out that Ida Bragg is trying to play sweet on John P. Nelson, while that festive individual fights shy on account of her red hair. In revenge for the scurvy trick she played on me last night I wrote a letter in a disguised hand to Ida purporting to be from John P., in which he ask[s] her to meet him at Roberts' store this evening at nine o'clock as he had an important communication to make. This I mailed and this evening Pete Brandt, "Indian John," whom I had let into the secret, and I were on hand anticipating some fun. We waited near Roberts' store till long after nine o'clock and then as the gentle Ida had not appeared, we concluded the plot had miscarried and went home considerably disappointed.

Kearney, Feb. 20
Thilda Danielson walked in to town three miles this afternoon to see me. She will stop over night with us.

Pete Brandt called on "Little Carrie" this evening to try and find out through her why Ida did not make her appearance last night. Carrie told him that last night, a little before nine o'clock, Ida came down from her room arrayed in her most stylish togs and upon Carrie's question as to where she was going, she answered that she had an appointment for 9 o'clock and upon Carrie's further questioning she confided to her how she had received a letter from Mr. Nelson asking an interview and how happy she was.

Carrie "smelled a mice" and told Ida not to make a fool of herself, that "if John was so anxious to see her he could do so any day without making such an appointment, as he was boarding at the same hotel," and much more to the same purpose and finally persuaded Ida to stay at home.

Kearney, Feb. 21
Fine weather.

Pete hitched up his ponies and we took Thilda D. out to Bicknell's.

Met Sam Ericson. He had just got in from North Platte where he has been herding cattle. Sam is one of the boys.

Kearney, Feb. 22
Father arrived in town this evening with a load of wheat. He told me that A. S. Baldwin's house in Williamsburg has been burned, the fire supposed to have been incendiary.

Kearney, Feb. 23
This evening I dressed myself in some of Mrs. Brandt's clothes and then, disguised as a female, with a veil over my face, I made the rounds of the town with Pete Brandt, Oscar Boge, and "Indian John." We attracted a good deal of attention, and had lots of fun.

Kearney, Feb. 24
This evening Pete and "Little Carrie," "Indian John," and I attended a religious meeting at Akey Themanson's to hear Mr. J. P. Johnson of Galesburg, Ills. preach. We had a high old time as Indian John by his devilment kept nearly the whole audience on the broad grin.

Kearney, Feb. 25
Pete and I called on "Scandy," a prisoner in the Buffalo County Jail. We also saw and conversed with Haralson of Kearney County, called

the "bridge lumber thief," and with Harry Underwood of Texas, a notorious frontier outlaw and member of the Sam Bass gang of train robbers. He was arrested and brought here charged with complicity in the Big Springs train robbery when a band of six prairie pirates, under Sam Bass, robbed a passenger train on the Union Pacific at Big Springs, Neb. of $60,000 in gold.

Underwood is a tall, dark complexioned, well-made man, and looks like a hard customer.[11]

Kearney, Feb. 26
Tinie Nelson called to day and we had some pleasant games of "cassino." After this "Indian John" beat me in a game of checkers. This evening Sam Ericson, Pete Brandt, and I played poker until about 10 o'clock when Sam left.

Kearney, Feb. 27
This morning early Sam Ericson came to Brandt's and informed us of a fire in town last night. Three buildings were burned and the fire was evidently the work of an incendiary. It was first discovered about one o'clock A.M. in A. L. Webb's Agricultural Implement Warehouse, where hay and other combustibles had been heaped against the wall and set afire. The flames soon spread to Marsh and Roe's Hardware Store and Frantz Drug Store and all three buildings were burned to the ground with most of the stock they contained.[12]

After breakfast Pete and I went over the scene of the conflagration, where we found a large crowd of citizens and heard mutterings both loud and deep of revenge on the incendiary, should he be caught. We heard that "Indian John" is suspected of the crime, it being known that he had a grudge against Webb. This seems very likely in view of his known character and of the fact that he left Brandt's last night about 8:30 o'clock and had not returned. He was seen this morning at Horn's house in the sand hills south of the river. A party consisting of Eugene Hall, Constable Marsh, and H. H. Achey have gone out to bring him in.[13]

Poor John! I am afraid it will go hard with him if he is caught.

Thilda Danielson is in town and is stopping at Brandt's.

Kearney, Febr. 28
Last night about 11 o'clock, we were awakened from our slumbers by

shooting and yelling up town. Instantly it flashed across my brain that "Indian John" had been captured, brought to town, and was being lynched. I proposed to Pete that we go up town, but he replied that the fun would be all over before we got there. We had just composed ourselves to sleep when we were again disturbed, this time by a man tapping at the window and calling Pete's name. It proved to be H. H. Achey, a neighbor of Pete's who said:

"We caught the son of a bitch! He confessed the crime and we tried to hang him but the officers got him away from us."

This morning we went down town and learned all about the capture and attempted lynching from participants.

He was captured in eastern Phelps County, twenty-seven miles from Kearney. He was first sighted on the prairie, and when he saw his pursuers he started to run and they had quite a chase before they overtook him. He was armed with a bowie knife and billy and at first seemed disposed to turn on his pursuers, but on being covered with the shotguns and revolvers of the party, he dropped his weapons and threw up his hands. He was then handcuffed and brought to town. They drove past the jail up town, firing their pistols to draw a crowd and in a few moments over a hundred men had gathered, crying: "Lynch him! lynch him!" John was pulled from the buggy, a rope was thrown around his neck, and he was dragged to the railroad track, where it was proposed to string him up to a telegraph pole. At this stage of the proceedings, Constable John Hoge appeared on the scene with Pete Frithiof, a cowboy, and a number of influential citizens who rescued John and lodged him safely in jail. Sheriff David Anderson, who also came to the rescue, was overpowered and held fast by the mob. "Indian John" exhibited the most wonderful nerve throughout the affair. He did not plead for his life, seeming to think it useless to ask for mercy at the hands of the howling mob.[14]

There is a plot on foot to make another attempt to lynch him if he is taken up town for his preliminary trial, but it is generally understood that he has waived examination and will not at present venture out of jail, where he is comparatively safe.

This afternoon Pete and I went down to the jail to see him. We found him in the cell with Underwood, the road agent, and Haralson, the bridge lumber thief. He seemed in pretty good spirits and not much cowed by his dangerous position. I asked him if he didn't think he was in a pretty tight place last night with the rope around his neck. He smiled, twisted the ends of his long mustache and replied: "Yes, but I have been in some tight pinches before, and got out all right." He denied the crime and expressed sympathy for the sufferers by the fire.

This evening Thilda and I went to the Union Pacific Depot where we met Frank Hallgren and John Shafer. Shafer was going west to Sidney.

Phelps Center, March 1.
A wet, rainy, drizzling day. Got back from Kearney in company with Mr. Stenfelt. We, together with Dahlstroms and P. A. Brodine, made a visit to Rev. J. Danielson's.

March 6
Celebrated the 22nd anniversary of my birth by harrowing in the fields all day. Got letters yesterday from cousin Josie, and Hakan Johnson. Father has commenced his duties as assessor of Center precinct.

March 8
Some time ago father traded off two oxen, Jerry and Bryan, for a pair of horses. To day he sold the horses to Rev. Jacob Danielson.

Wed. March 13
Beautiful weather.

Miss Ida Bragg, Mrs. Bragg, and Mr. Nels Rylander visited us to day. Ida expressed contrition for the trick she played on me some time ago in Kearney and laid the blame on Rachel French and "Little Carrie," who, she says, put her up to it.

Nels Rylander is just out from Kearney. He told us that Thilda Danielson is so sick she is not expected to live.

March 15
Father came home yesterday from Deer Creek having bought a pair of horses.

Called on Ida Bragg this evening and found Miss Selma Peterson with her.

Kearney, March 16
Ida Bragg, Johnnie Bragg, Sister Hilda, and I took a buggy ride to

Kearney and on our arrival we went to Harry Hatch's Art Gallery, and had our pictures taken. Then we called on Thilda at Aitkins Hotel. Thilda was a little pale and thin from her recent illness.

After taking Ida to the Grand Central, I went to Brandt's while Hilda and Johnnie Bragg started back for Phelps. At Brandt's I found Anton Peterson and family, old friends of mine late of Henderson Grove Illinois. His oldest daughter, Rosa, is now sweet sixteen, tall and slender with fair hair and the bluest of eyes. I took her out for a promenade and we had a long and interesting talk about the old friends back east.

Underwood and Haralson broke jail last Wednesday night, stole two of the best horses in town, and skipped for Texas. They have not been recaptured and the chances are all in their favor.

Harry Underwood left a very sarcastic letter in his cell for Sheriff Anderson, who was absent at Sidney, saying he was sorry he could not wait for him to get back, and regretting that they had to cut the jail up so to get out. Saws in shoes and bucket of butter.

Kearney, March 17

Spent the forenoon in company with Pete Frithiof. Pete is a tall, well-made fellow about 30 years old. He's a Swede but was raised in this country. At the age of 14 years he joined the army and fought through the war under Gen. Canby. At the close of the war he went to Texas and was engaged in oyster fishing on the Gulf several years, making considerable money. He then went to Cambridge, Ills., married, and went into business. About four years ago he came west and has passed the time since then roving over the plains of Nebraska, Kansas, Indian Territory, and Texas as a hunter and cowboy. He is well educated and his stories of life on the plains are very entertaining.[15]

This afternoon John P. Nelson, Thilda Danielson, and I were at Brandt's and John proposed to play me a game of cassino to see who should escort Thilda home. I assented, we played a game, John won and went off with the girls. I consoled myself with Rosa Peterson.

Kearney, March 18

Practiced target shooting in "Shorty's" Saloon, where Gardner Keneval, a young friend of mine, runs a shooting gallery.

Spent the afternoon at Brandt's in the society of Rosa Peterson.

Phelps Center, March 22
Got back from Kearney several days ago. Went over to Danielson's in the after noon, where I was introduced by Aaron Johnson to his fiancee, Miss Augusta Gronlund, and her sister Thilda, two young ladies, who with their parents arrived yesterday from Lockport, Ills.

March 23
Mother, Hilda, and I went over to Danielsons to supper, Aaron Johnson and the Gronlunds were there too.

Sunday, March 24
Mother, Hilda, and I went visiting Mr. Gust Danielson at his homestead about 4 miles southeast. We stayed to dinner, took supper at Andrew Olson's and came home.

I have had my eyes opened to the fact that Gus. Danielson aspires to becoming a member of our family. He has been paying his attentions to sister Hilda some time, but I had no idea it was anything serious until now.

March 29
The ground is covered with snow. Father took mother and Hilda sleigh riding out to Solomon Linder's. I helped Dahlstrom write up his Annual Report as District School Treasurer.

April 1st
"All Fool's Day" and the only fools I saw was a flock of prairie chickens I encountered on Rylander's timber claim, which were too foolish to get out of the way until I shot one of them, a fine cock. I fired from the wagon, and the report of the gun frightened the horses, which started to run away and nearly upset the wagon.

April 2
Shot a prairie chicken at a distance of ninety-six yards.

Got two letters, one from Thilda Danielson, and one from Tinie Nelson who lives at Gibbon east of Kearney and signed Maud Bostford, which, I suppose is one of her aliases, another one being Ella V. Rice. She is scarcely sixteen, but is a pretty hard case all the same.

April 4
Wrote and mailed three letters, to Elma Johnson, Josie Hawkinson, and Tinie Nelson. Augusta Gronlund called on us this afternoon.

Sunday, April 7
Nick Brunzell called on me and we were engaged in a game of cards when the folks came back from meeting, bringing with them Thilda Danielson (who came out from Kearney yesterday). She seemed very cross and snappy about something, and as I did not know that I had merited her displeasure I went with Nick out in the granary and played poker until Her Royal Highness was gone.

April 8
This morning Hilda received a note from Thilda D. inviting her to come and visit her in the afternoon and to coax me to go along. I wouldn't go so Hilda went alone, and on returning brought Thilda with her. She, however, did not seem any better disposed than she was yesterday.

April 9
Owing to the inclemency of the weather Thilda remained with us last night. She passed a very restless night and several times I awoke to hear her sobbing. Conjecturing that I, though innocently, was the cause of her grief I pitied the poor girl.

This morning, [she] swallowed her pride and begged my pardon for her behavior of the last two days, and then proceeded to explain the reason. She said she came from Kearney last Saturday, happy in the prospect of meeting me, but when she got home her folks took her to task and upbraided her for her intimacy with me, telling her that I was only fooling with her, that I did not care for her, and I had several other sweethearts with whom I corresponded regularly, and much more to the same effect, bringing her into such a state of excitement, she wept all of Saturday night and on Sunday went with my folks from meeting with the intention of securing an explanation from me. But her pride got the better of her resolution, and in her resentment she treated me harshly.

Of course we kissed and made up, which is the usual ending of lover's quarrels.

Sunday, April 14
Weather foggy and misty.
Received a note from Thilda inviting me to call this afternoon as she would be alone. Called and found her all alone, her folks having gone visiting. Spent the afternoon very pleasantly and staid until about ten o'clock this evening, and we played "love in the dark" as we lighted no lamp not wishing to be watched from without through the windows. When I heard her folks drive into the yard I tried to slip from the house unobserved, as I knew there would be hell to pay if they found us together with no lamps lit.

I did not succeed as I met the old man just outside the door. I passed on without speaking.

April 15
My girl went to Kearney. She had a stormy interview with her father last night after I was gone. He was very severe, called her a prostitute, and accused her of being my mistress. Says she won't go back on me, no matter what the old folks say.

April 16
Received two letters, one from Elma Johnson and one from Tinie Nelson. Tinie writes that there is to be an Odd Fellow's ball at Shelby soon and she wants me to come and take her to the ball. She finishes her letter with the couplet:
   "My pen is bad my ink is <u>pail</u>;
   My love to you shall never <u>fale</u>"
which seems to indicate that she is "mashed" or something.

April 19
Called at Swanson's to see John P. Nelson, who is very sick with rheumatism.

Kearney, Apr. 24
Went with August Bragg to town. Went to the Office of Col. John H. Roe and filed my application for Pre-Emption Entry on the N.E. 1/4 of Section 24, Town 6, Range 19 W. This land is in the same section in which my father lives.[16]

Phelps Center, Apr. 25

Last night I hunted up my girl. As I approached the house where she lives the door was open and I heard Tillie singing, "I'm waiting to night to meet my darling," and just then, as if in answer to her song I appeared on the threshold. She was considerably surprised, but very glad to see me.

Staid at Brandt's last night. This morning August Bragg and I had an interview with "Indian John" through the bars of his jail window. He seemed cheerful and contented and said he could have made his escape with Henderson [Underwood] and Haralson had he been so disposed.

Left town after dinner and started for home. When we got to Williamsburg it was dark. Here I shot a big jack-rabbit.

May 4

Yesterday morning I started for Bloomington, Franklin County, in company with August Jacobson, J. P. Erikson and Red Oak Johnson to transact some business at the U.S. Land Office. We passed Walker's Ranch about noon and arrived at our destination about 4 P.M. As the Land Office was closed we drove a short distance out of town and camped on a small creek. This morning we went into town, which is a small town on the bluffs north of the Republican. After settling our affairs August Jacobson and I started off into Kearney Co. to get a cow that Aug. had bought of John Lynn, a settler. We stopped for the night at Nels Olin's about 2 miles west of Fredericksburg.[17]

May 6

Drove on yesterday morning and found John Lynn living on the Dry Fork of the Blue some 6 miles east of Fredericksburg P. O. Lynn was a Swede and was married to a German girl. After dinner, we took a ride with John Lynn and his brother Charley to the North Blue, got the cow, and started for home. Drove about 18 miles and stopped last night at John Rothsten's, where I met some old friends, among them Fred Holmquist. Got back home this afternoon.

May 10

This forenoon I with about 30 others attended the funeral of Little Otilia Johnson, infant daughter of Chas W. Johnson.

Sunday, May 12

I attended meeting and was present at the confirmation in the Lutheran faith of Selma Peterson, Olga Swanson, Gussie Carlson, Annie Johnson, Charley Peterson, and Johnnie Bragg, by the Rev. J. Danielson. I am now reading, for the second time, "Rob Roy" by Sir Walter Scott.

May 17 [13?]

Got letters from Swan Nelson and Thilda D. Thilda writes that "Indian John" had his trial last week and was sentenced to twenty years in the penitentiary for arson. Tillie was summoned as a witness in the case. John took his sentence very cooly, acknowledged his guilt, and confessed a long catalogue of crimes.

May 15

Rained nearly all day.

My prospective brother-in-law, Gus. Danielson, is here. The wedding is set for Saturday, [Friday] May 24.

There is rumor that John F. Shafer, Ex-Sheriff of Phelps County, has been shot and killed at Sidney in a quarrel about a woman.

I have commenced to read another of the Waverly Novels: "Old Mortality" by Sir Walter Scott.

May 30 [20]

Borrowed one of C. J. Anderson's ponies and rode down to Judge Fritz G. Wilke's in the south eastern part of the county. Got a marriage license for Swen Gustaf Danielson and Hilda Johnson. Judge Wilke is a very tall, slim man and his wife is a short, fat, goodlooking woman. They were very nice people and invited me to dinner, which I of course accepted. We had Turkey for dinner and I did full justice to it.

On my way home I stopped at Old Jonas Peterson ['s] and got him to go on my bond as County Clerk. (My other bond was not approved because I had no free-holders as bondsmen.)

Friday, May 24

The wedding is over. It passed off without a hitch. Gus. was dressed in black and Hilda in grey with a sprig or two of myrtle in her hair. The ceremony was performed by Rev. Jacob Danielson, at our house, in the presence of: Mrs. Danielson, Thilda Danielson, Gussie Carlson,

Mr. and Mrs. A. P. Anderson, Mr. and Mrs. Henry G. Thorell, C. J. Anderson, Mrs. Dahlstrom, Mr. and Mrs. J. Anderson, Mr. and Mrs. Andrew Olson, Mr. and Mrs. C. M. Christianson, Carl Carlson, Nels Peterson, and our folks.

Thilda D. was radiant in white dress with blue silk sash trimmings, ruffles and flowers, and told me confidentially she wished I would stand up with her and be "spliced" so we could have a double wedding, "it would be so nice." But I "couldn't see it." I am not quite prepared to leave the state of single blessedness for that of double misery.

This evening after supper I accompanied Thilda D. and Gussie Carlson to their respective homes.

May 25
Warm weather. Shot a big turtle in the sand hills.

Sunday, May 26
Warmer!

Mr. and Mrs. Gus. Danielson received a number of their friends and Nels Lundquist and family, Solomon Linder and family, J. M. Dahlstrom and family, Squire Salgren and family, Stenfelt, J. C. Bragg, and others called to present their congratulations to the newly wedded couple. I spent the afternoon in a spring seat on the shady side of the house with my girl.

May 27
Hot!

Gus and Hilda commenced housekeeping. Called on Thilda this evening.

May 28
Hotter!

Stayed last night at Thilda's house, much to the disgust of her folks. Got a letter from Selma Johnson.

May 29
Red-hot, and still heating!

Thilda D. stayed with us last night and this morning she left for

Kearney riding with the mail carrier. She was reluctant to leave me.

> "When thou art by, I know not why
> I love thee, but I love thee not so deeply;
> When thou art gone, and I'm alone,
> I marvel that I held thee then so cheaply."

June 1st

This morning I found that a swift, or prairie fox, had "jumped my claim" and dug a den in the north west corner, so I armed myself with a Sharp's rifle and belt of cartridges and proceeded to eject the trespassers. I shot at the old one and missed and then shot four cubs as they came one by one out of the lair.

June 3

Went down to Williamsburg to see William Lee. Found him lying sick at Old Jim Steward's. He signed my bond as County clerk. On the way home I fired at a jackass-rabbit as he was setting on his haunches and shot off both his forelegs. I went up towards him and he started off, kangaroo fashion. I had no more cartridges so I tried to run him down, but he jumped so fast on his hindlegs, I couldn't catch him.

June 4

C. J. Anderson has appointed me Assistant post-master of Phelps P. O. and to day, as Anderson was absent, I discharged my duties by receiving and distributing the mail. I got a letter from Tillie and a postal card from Swan Nelson. At the Emigrant House I met Ida Bragg, just out from Kearney, and escorted her home for which I was amply rewarded before we parted.

June 8

A protracted meeting commenced the day before yesterday at the residence of C. J. Anderson, and is now in full blast. A number of friends from Harlan County are in attendance, among the[m] Clarence Peterson, who is stopping with me.

Spent the afternoon with Ida Bragg.

I am now reading "The Pirate" by Sir Walter Scott.

Annie Peterson of School Creek called and took dinner with us.

Sun. June 9

Attended meeting. Rev. C. J. Magnuson preached. Went with August Bragg and Ferdinand Johnson to Bragg's to dinner. This afternoon Clarence and I stopped with "Little Redbird" while the rest of the folks went to meeting. We had a pleasant time, might have had more fun if either Clarence or I had been alone with the girl.

June 10

The big meeting broke up last night and most of the visitors went home. Clarence, however, concluded to stay a little longer and go antelope hunting with me. He had his "big 44" with him and this morning we struck out in the sand hills and tramped about till noon. We laid down to rest awhile and then went down on the level prairie. We saw numbers of antelope and got in a few shots, and crippled two or three, but did not get them. On our way back, we came on a doe and two kids in a small draw, about two miles east of the house. We both fired at the doe at a distance of some 300 yards. The doe commenced to limp and the two kids ran over a ridge and got away. We went about 100 yards nearer the doe and both fired again and she dropped. As we came up to where she was struggling we found three shots had taken effect. One foreleg and one hindleg were broken, and her intestines protruded from a hole in her belly. Clarence gave her a kick in the head to "settle her," but instead of settling, she got up and hopped about one hundred yards on two legs while the other two swung back and forth and her bowels dragged on the ground. We soon dispatched her. She had horns like a buck. We removed her intestines and I carried her home on my shoulders, getting my shirt and hat bloody all over.

June 11

I had promised to give Clarence a ride as far as the head of Flag Creek on his way home. So this morning we hitched up and started, taking Justus along. About 12 miles south on the head of Turkey Creek we saw an antelope run down into a "break." We left Justus in charge of the team and went down the canyon. We soon found the antelope, a doe, and Clarence shot her through the neck, killing her almost instantly. We put the carcass into the wagon and soon after reached Flag Creek, where Clarence left us and we drove back home.

I am reading "True Stories of Wild Bill" by Leander P. Richardson.

June 13
Met William Johnson, alias "Spotted Bill," alias Spot Johnson, at the Emigrant House. He is an old plainsman.

June 15
Shot a big rattlesnake on Salgren's "firebreak." The heavy ball from my breechloader traversed him lengthways about a foot and ripped him open. He had eight rattles.

Sunday, June 16
Spent the forenoon at Brunzell's playing cards with Nick Brunzell and Pete Peerson. This afternoon played "croquet" at the Emigrant House with Ida Bragg, Nick Brunzell, Olof Hoag, Johnny Bragg. Had a nice time.

June 21
Went antelope hunting and shot a big rattlesnake, which came near biting me as I was rolling down the side of a canyon to get out [of] sight of a gang of antelope I was stalking. The antelope were frightened at my shot and skipped away. I went home and spent the remainder of the day with Ida Bragg, who with her mother was visiting at our house.

June 24
Attended a mass meeting at the P. O. where county affairs were discussed. Dahlstrom, Salgren, A. W. Johnson, John Lindbloom, and father were appointed a committee to circulate a petition for the Co. Coms. to call an election for the relocation of the county seat.[18]

Got a letter from Thilda. When she is away, I get, on an average, two letters a week from her.

June 27
Yesterday Pete Brodine and I took a trip down to Rock Falls to get our petition for relocation of county seat signed by the Spring Creekers. We also visited "Crazy Miller's Dugout," which is perched like a swallows nest on the side of high bluff with a grinning human skull stuck on a pole keeping guard over the chasm below. We also visited Miller's grave

and the scene of his tragic death, a short distance from his dugout.

We saw Sheriff Sweezey, who told us that Dahlstrom and I lost our case in the Supreme Court and would have the costs to pay, some 20 dollars.

As were returning I shot a large jack-rabbit with my rifle.

Night overtaking us we stopped at the residence of Charles Nelson at Industry, where we obtained food and lodging. Tinie and her sister Ellen were at home and we had a pleasant evening.

Got back home to day, and to morrow Brodine and I will go to Arapahoe to find out the issue of our case in the Supreme Court from our lawyers, A. E. Harvey and W. S. Morlan.

Arapahoe, June 28

Brodine and I drove down to Arapahoe by way [of] Devil's Gap. We had a pleasant ride, the prairie was bedecked with flowers of many colors, and even the cactus was in bloom.

On our arrival at Arapahoe we found Lawyer Morlan and learned from him that the Supreme Court decided in favor of defendants in cases of Dahlstrom vs. Jensen and Johnson vs. Dilworth on the ground that Dahlstrom and I could not give sufficient bonds. The case of Brodine vs. Mudge was decided in favor of Brodine.

June 29

Stopped last night at Alexander Hagberg's a couple of miles east of Arapahoe. Hagberg is an old pioneer well fixed and has a fine farm. Got back home in good time.

July 2

Staid at Charley Nelson's last night.

Attended to the Post Office. Passed a couple of hours in company with Annie Johnson, who is keeping house for the P.M. temporarily, then went down to Charley Nelson['s] with Nick and Billy Brunzell. On the way down we saw a skunk in a ravine which I shot with my breech loader. Found the Nelson girls at home.

July 3

We stayed at Charley Nelson's last night. Went back home this afternoon and found Thilda D. there. She came from Kearney yesterday.

Thilda and I went to my Sister Hilda's to stay till to morrow. I and Nick Brunzell are going to Wood River day after to morrow.

July 4
Thilda Danielson, Tinie Nelson, Nick Brunzell, and I passed most of the day together, part of it in playing croquet at the Emigrant House. The girls are very blue because Nick and I are going away.

CHAPTER 8

The Harvest Circuit

July 5 [1878]
Nick Brunzell and I went to Kearney. As the day was hot, we cooled off by taking a swim in the Platte.

This evening we encountered a couple of drunken streetwalkers. One of them was a white woman and the other was the notorious "Nigger Liz," one of the characters of Kearney. She is very black, very short, and weighs in the neighborhood of three hundred pounds. She raised such a racket we were glad to get away.

Shelton, July 7
Stayed in Kearney until this morning. After breakfast at the Delmonico Restaurant we struck out on foot for Wood River. Passed through Gibbon about noon and struck here this evening.[1] On inquiring for Swan Nelson, we find that he lives about half way between here and Wood River. He is well known in this place and is noted as a rough and tumble fighter, wrestler, and athlete. As a fellow waxing enthusiastic over the subject told us, "You bet I know Nelson—He's the greatest feller for fighting, scuffling around, running, jumping, and betting I ever see! He's a good hearted boy though and won't go back on a friend. Why only a couple of weeks ago he had sort of a duel with a feller down at Wood River, and broke the other man's arm, and now the boys call him the 'Champion of Wood River.'"

Wood River, July 8
Stopped at Shelton last night and this morning we set out to hunt up Nelson, whom we found at Pat Nevill's, a fine place on the banks of Wood River. Swan was glad to see us and told us we could get work in the vicinity as soon as harvest commenced in about a week. Swan took us around among the neighbors and made us acquainted.

Wood River, July 9

Swan, Nick, and I went to Shelton last night and drank a bucket of lemonade. We got back to Nevill's about 11 P.M. and stopped overnight. To day we have been at Wood River Station on the railroad, a small place, containing two hotels, two stores, two blacksmith shops, and one saloon.

Swan got me into a foot race with Johnny Britt, a noted runner. We ran 50 yards and came out even as the referees decided. Nelson then ran 100 yards against Britt and got beat. Went swimming in Wood River, which has a fine sandy bottom.

Grand Island, July 12

For the last few days, we have been bumming around Wood River having a good time among the Irish settlers. Then we concluded to take a trip to Hastings before harvesting commenced, so last night Nick and I travelled to Grand Island partly on foot and part of the way by rail.

Hastings, July 13

Left Grand Island yesterday after breakfast and went south across the country to Hastings, getting to ride most of the way with farmers. Passed the day loafing around town with a couple of the boys, Aug. Thompson and Roby, who runs a shooting gallery.

Hastings, Sunday, July 14

Very hot weather.

In the outskirts of the town is a settlement of Russian Mennonites, called the "Russian Camp." They are a peculiar people and we had lots of fun watching them. Tom Smith, one of the boys, had a bottle of very strong vinegar which he would hand them to take a drink, they thinking it was whiskey. After taking a swallow they would make a wry face, say it was "goot wix" and walk off shaking their heads. We also encountered "Dublin Jack," a notorious bummer and dead beat, of whom it is said that he was once a professor in a college.

He was drunk but on a passing invitation from Tom Smith took a drink of the vinegar and remarked that it tasted more like vinegar than whiskey.

This evening Nick and I encountered three ragged tramps near the "Russian Camp." They tried to make very friendly with us but we soon "tumbled to their racket" their intention being, evidently, to rob us as we had a gold and a silver watch and some money. On discovering that we were both armed with revolvers they evidently considered us "bad medicine" and allowed us to depart in peace.

Wood River, July 15
After breakfast this morning we left Hastings and started back across the country on foot for Wood River. Got our dinner at the "Sand Krog," a picturesque German inn on Grand Island, a large island in the Platte River. We went in swimming in the river, after which we kept on and soon fell in with "Old Peck of Wood River" and his daughter, Mollie, and got to ride the rest of the way. Mollie was a lively, vivacious young lady and made the time pass pleasantly.[2]

Wood River, July 17
Yesterday Nick and I bound wheat for Bill Hollister near the station. Bound wheat this forenoon also.[3]

This afternoon we engaged to work for William Harnan, an old Irishman living a couple of miles from town. On arriving at his place I was surprised and pleased to meet my old Kearney chum, Gardner Keneval, alias "Kearney Kid." He seemed equally pleased to see me.

Since we last met he has been on a hunting expedition up the Dismal and helped to find and bury the bodies of Luther Holbrook, Herman Allen, and the Sutton boys who were killed by the Hargrove boys. Gard had a span of mules stolen from him during the trip by Tip Smith and "Persimmon Bill."[4]

Gardner is a relative of the Harnans and has been making his home with them for some time.

July 18
Bound wheat for Bill Hollister. This evening had a high old time at Dick Smith's singing, joking, and telling stories. Bob Kennedy, one of the boys, was the life of the party and sang a very comic song called "The Dutch Volunteer."

July 19

Bound wheat at Harnan's.

Harnan has several daughters. Three of them, Belle, Fanny, and Mary Ann, are at home. Fanny is about 15, Bell is older and is a school marm, Mary Ann is an old maid of vinegar aspect, and peppery temper. Had a good time this evening. Fanny and Belle sang "Gathering Up the Shells on the Shore." Nick and I sang "Whiskey Parker," and then Bell and Fanny and Gard Kenevel sang a ballad entitled "Chris Rafferty's Doom," supposed to have been written by Chris Rafferty, who was hung several years ago for the murder of Policeman O'Mara in Chicago. It is as follows:

> Come all ye tender christians;
> I hope ye will draw near;
> And likewise pay attention,
> To these few lines I've here;
> For the murder of O'Mara
> I am condemned to die;
> On the twenty-second of February;
> Upon the gallows high!
>
> My name, it is Chris Rafferty-
> A name I never deny-
> I left my aged parents
> In sorrow for to cry;
> And little did I think,
> In all my youthful bloom,
> That I would go to Chicago;
> And there I'd meet my doom.
>
> Policeman O'Mara
> Came into the saloon;
> Says he to me: "Chris Rafferty
> I want you mighty soon!"
> 'Twas then I pulled my pistol;
> And shot him through the heart;
> Which caused a loving wife
> And husband for to part.

On the day of my trial,
'Twould please your heart to see,
My friends and associates
All standing up by me;
I bade them all a warning
To take by my sad fate;
And leave off their night-walking,
Before it was too late.

On the day of my execution,
It pierced my heart to see,
My sister came from Bridgeport;
To take farewell of me.
She fell into my arms;
And so bitterly did cry.
Says she: "My dearest brother
This afternoon you die!"

And now my trials are over;
And from this world I part.
For the murder of O'Mara
I'm sorry to the heart.
Come, all ye young and older men,
And warning by me take!
And leave off your night walking;
Before it is too late.

Sunday, July 21

Nick and I went to Maher's where Nelson is staying. Took dinner there and made the acquaintance of Honora Maher, a lively damsel of sweet sixteen. She was born and raised here, and never was 30 miles from home in her life and though she lives within a mile or so of the railroad, she has never traveled by rail. She is clever, well educated, and has taught school.

We played ball with the boys in the afternoon.

July 24

We quit working for Old Daddy Harnan last night and this morning commenced working for John A. Connor, binding grain on a Harvester. Mrs. Conner is a darkling woman with black curly hair and black eyes. It is reported that Connor is very jealous of her. The Connors have a pretty girl named Rosa Jessop working for them. She is a daisy. Black hair cut short, fine dark eyes, pearly teeth, and beautiful complexion. In the afternoon Nick and I went over to Maher's farm ostensibly to see Nelson, but really to see Honora, the maid of Wood River. We got a ride from Wood River out to the farm with Mrs. Maher and Honora, who had been in town shopping. Nora handled the reins with the skill of a John. Nick is rapidly surrendering to her charms.

July 26

We got Mrs. Connor to drive the harvester team to the intense disgust of Connor, who turned green with jealousy.

Fred Risland or "Rosa's Dutchman" as Connor calls him, called to see Rosa. He is a young blacksmith of Wood River. He is a fine young fellow. He was one of the seconds in the Nelson-Voland fight and gave us a full account of it substantially as follows:

Nelson and Voland, who is a big athlete weighing over two hundred pounds, got into a difficulty at a dance, but their friends prevented a fight. Soon after this John Voland sent Nelson a formal challenge. Nelson promptly accepted. Time and place were named, and Fred Risland and Ed McDermott chosen seconds. At the appointed time Nelson and Voland met at Wood River Station in the presence of a large crowd of friends and backers at 1 o'clock P.M. The men toed the scratch and shook hands and the fighting commenced. In the first round Voland was so badly used up he was unable to continue the fight and his second threw up the sponge. His arm was broken, and shoulder dislocated and he had to go to Grand Island 20 miles to have his damages repaired. Since then Nelson's popularity has greatly increased and he is styled the "Champion of Wood River."

Fred has spent some time in the western mountains and tells some pretty tough yarns of frontier life.

July 31

Connor calls me "Rosa's Dutchman" now as he says it is an open question whom she likes best, Fred or I. Nick and I went to Wood River this morning. As we approached the station the Emigrant Train from the east stopped at the depot. We observed a commotion among the passengers, who were crowding to the windows and platform to stare at us while the word "Indians" passed from mouth to mouth.

They were evidently deceived by our peculiar appearance, as we wore red flannel shirts, broadbrimmed white hats with buckskin fringes, and pistols in our belts. We boarded the train and gave the passengers "chinmusic," telling an inquisitive young lady that we were "Indians," that our names were "Big Wall of Pine" and "Shack Nasty Bill" and that we belonged to the "Squawpuncher" tribe. She retired discomfited amid roars of laughter.

Went to Harnan's this evening to see Gardner Kenevel and the girls.

Phelps Center, August 2

Finished our job yesterday noon and spent the afternoon very pleasantly with Mrs. Connor and Rosa. In the evening we bade them farewell and they seemed sorry at our separation. I know I was, and I fancied I detected tears in Rosa's eyes as she reached me her hand and said "goodbye." She made me promise to write to her.

We stole a ride on a freight train from Wood River to Kearney. Staid over night at the Junction House Livery Stable and rode out to Phelps Center to day with the Swanson boys, Lewis and John Erick.[5]

Rolf Johnson, photographed in Denver, 1880. Courtesy of Mrs. R. Bruce Chamberlin.

The John Johnson home, ca. 1880. Courtesy of Grace C. Johnson.

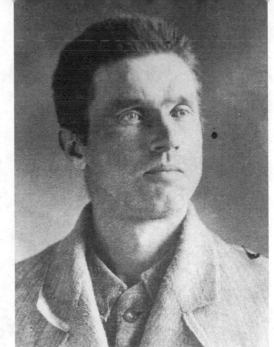

John "Indian John" Nelson, photographed at the Nebraska State Penitentiary. Nebraska State Historical Society, RG2418.

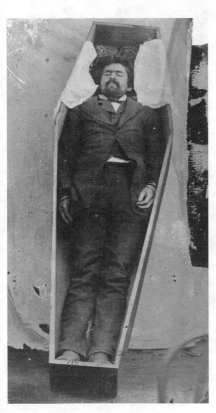

The body of Stephen D. Richards after his execution, 1879. Nebraska State Historical Society, PC1799-1.

Judge William Gaslin, Jr. Nebraska State Historical Society, P853.

The grave of Peter Anderson, Bethany Cemetery, Axtell, Nebraska.
Courtesy of James E. Potter.

Jordon Smith, photographed at the Nebraska State Penitentiary. Nebraska State Historical Society, RG2418.

Phelps Center, ca. 1880. Nebraska State Historical Society, RG2389.PH:7-1.

Rolf Johnson later in life. Courtesy of Grace C. Johnson.

Rolf Johnson's Nebraska

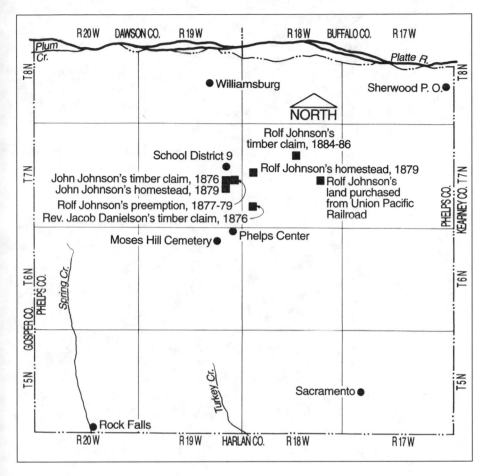

Phelps County, 1879

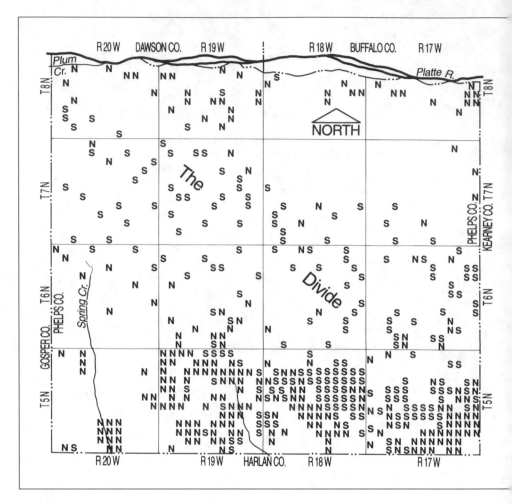

Swedish and non-Swedish settlement in Phelps County to 1879

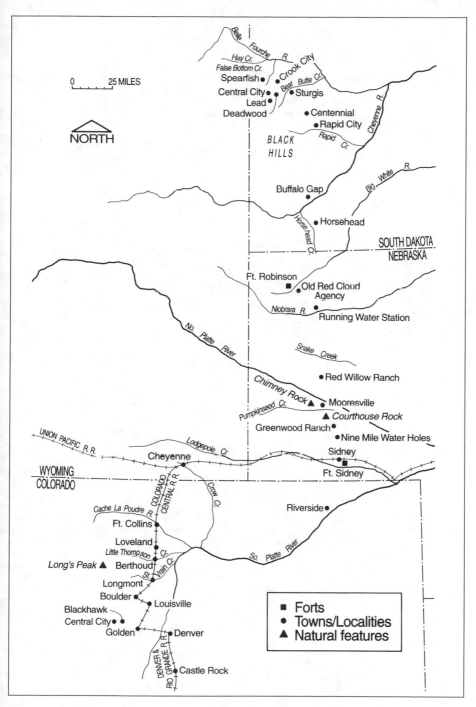

Rolf Johnson's travels, June 1879 to May 1880

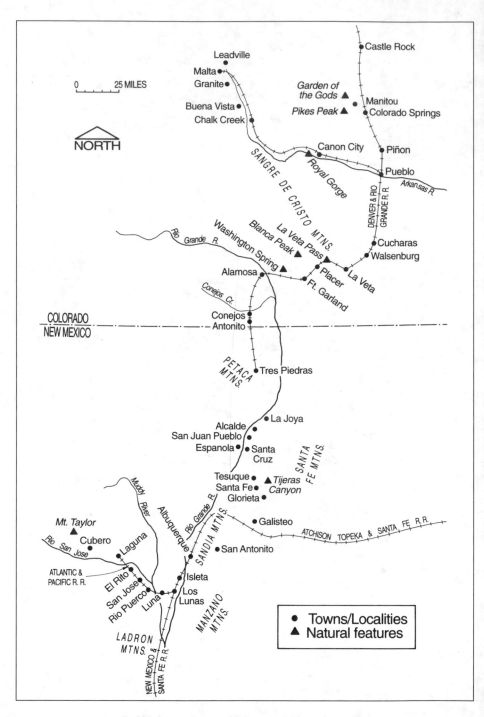

Rolf Johnson's travels, June to November 1880

CHAPTER 9

More Politics and Romances at Home

Aug. 7 [1878]

I have been helping father stack his grain these last few days.
Nick Brunzell brought me my mail. I had a letter from Clarence Peterson, one from Cousin Josie, and from Elma Johnson and two from Thilda Danielson.

Aug. 10

Thilda Danielson rode over on horse back to our place this morning to see me. She was so sick she could hardly keep her place in the saddle. She told me J. P. Nelson had told her I was to start for the Black Hills immediately so she came out from Kearney yesterday to see if it was so. I told her John had been fooling her. She stopped only an hour or so, then she rode home. August Bragg and I went buggy riding this afternoon. We took Tinie Nelson riding as far as Danielson's where we left her. We then took a drive up into the sand hills where Aug. shot a jacksnipe on the fly with his carbine, and I shot a bullsnake with my revolver.

Sunday, Aug. 11

Spent the day at Danielson's with Thilda Danielson and Tinie Nelson. Had a good time and lots of watermelons.

Aug. 12

Tillie and Tinie came to see me to day. They told me Danielson raised hell last night when he came home and found out I had been with the girls.

Aug. 16

Went down to my sister Hilda's day before yesterday, where I had an appointment to meet Thilda. Found her there and staid with her until this morning when I went home to help father make hay. This year we make hay at home on the timber claim where the grass is long and heavy. This is an improvement on last year when we made hay in a lagoon about seven miles from home.

Sunday, Aug. 18
Nick Brunzell and I went over to Danielson's to see Thilda. She was very cross and acted in an unaccountable manner and would give no explanation of her conduct, so we left.

Aug. 22
Last night I attended prayer meeting at Dahlstrom's. After meeting Thilda D. who was there, [she] asked me to take her home, which I, of course, did. On the way she asked my pardon for her strange behavior last Sunday and told me that it was owing to the machination of her folks, who were all the time trying to set her against me, saying that I was working her rein and never meant to marry her. They brought up so much evidence to sustain their assertions that she was convinced against her will that such was the case and resolved to leave me alone and promised them not to see me anymore. They have been very kind and attentive to her since then but she has not slept for two nights and has hardly eaten anything since last Sunday. She saw this kind of thing was killing her and she resolved to go back on her resolution and seek a reconciliation with me. Said she would rather go to hell with me then go to Heaven without.

I am cutting broomcorn at J. P. Bragg's these days. Nick Brunzell, Aug. Jacobson, Ferdinand Johnson, and Aug. Bragg work there too.

Aug. 23
Thilda went back to Kearney this morning. She tried to appear happy and gay, but it was a miserable failure as the tears sparkled in her eyes as she said "good bye."

Aug. 26
Ida Bragg got back from Kearney and called on me with a message from Thilda D. After supper I took her home.

Aug. 31
Went in to Kearney yesterday and last night I got played for a sucker

by a lottery swindle and lost five dollars, for which all I have to show is a five cent collar button. I ought to have known better and it was worth five dollars to find out what a derned fool I was. Before leaving town to day I bought a new suit of clothes.

Sunday, Sept. 1
Put on my new clothes and stand up collar and went out to make a "mash." Had a fine moonlight stroll this evening with Ida Bragg and Tinie Nelson. The girls said: "It is never late till the moon goes down." So it happened. The folks had been in bed several hours when I brought the girls back home.

Sept. 2
Father, brother Justus, and I went down to the Platte and picked about 1 1/2 bushels of wild grapes on the island.

Sept. 4
Ida Bragg and I with others cut broomcorn at Holm's. Good time. John Hendricks and I called on Tinie Nelson this evening.

Sept. 7
Sheriff Sweezey and Dave Nash of Spring Creek called and presented me with a bill for $8.60 costs in our case of Quo Warranto. I refused to pay.

Sunday, Sept 8.
Passed the Sunday at Brunzell's very quietly playing domino with Nick and a young nursery stock agt. named George Vinsel.

Sept. 14
Alex Hagberg and Vincent of Arapahoe are camped near our place with a herd of ponies.

Sunday, Sept. 15
Fred Rosso and I took a buggy ride down to Watson, Harlan Co. Fred is full of fun and a good boy to travel with. He has been a cowboy in Texas and has seen some tough times.

Just about dusk, while on our way home, we ran across Pete Johnson and Tinie Nelson out walking near Nelson's place. We took Tinie into the buggy between us and brought her up to Dahlstrom's where Fred is stopping. On the way we met her parents, but I put my big slouch hat on her head and in the dusk her folks did not recognize her, though her folks stopped and talked with us a little while. It was fortunate as her father has forbidden her to go with me and Nick Brunzell and he would have raised hell I guess. Good time.

Sept. 16
Fred Rosso, Tinie Nelson, Ida Bragg, and I went out walking this evening. Somehow Ida and I became separated from the others and lost them altogether, which was very strange, as the moon was shining very brightly and we could see a long distance.

Fred has proved himself as good at making a "mash" on the susceptible female heart as he is a lassoing a wild pony.

I am wearing Ida's gold ring for luck.

Sept. 18
Ida and Tinie called on me this evening and when I took them home it was so pitch dark I could hardly see to kiss them good night.

John Young killed a wildcat in John Hendricks' broomcorn field.

Sunday, Sept. 22
John Hendricks, Ida Bragg, Tinie Nelson, and I spent a very pleasant evening out on the prairie singing and talking.

I now wear Tinie's ring on the same finger with Ida's.

Sept. 24
Attended a caucus at the P. O. for the purpose of nominating candidates for the coming election. The following nominations were made:

For County Clerk, Leander Hallgren;
    "   "   Judge, Dwight Whitcomb;
    "   "   Sheriff, William J. David;
    "   "   Treasurer, Thomas Squires;
   " Commissioner 1st Dist. Olaf Hedlund;
   " Commissioner 2   " T. M. Hopwood;
   " Supt. Pub. Inst. Mrs. Ella Rowland.

After the county officers were nominated we had a precinct convention and nominated the following officers for Center Precinct:

For Justice of the Peace, C. J. Anderson;
    "   "   "   "   , Peter Peerson;
  " Constable   , Gustaf Johnson;
  "   "   , John S. Salgren;
  " Assessor   , John Johnson;
For Judge of Election;   John Johnson;
  "   "   "   J. M. Dahlstrom
  "   "   "   Albert Sundblad;
  " Clerk of Election   Frank Hallgren;
  "   "   "   Aaron W. Johnson.

For Delegates to Republican County
Convention at Williamsburg Sept. 28.
  Frank Hallgren and Rolf Johnson

Called on Ida this evening; her folks were all away.

Sept. 26
Tinie Nelson, alias "Shoo Fly," and I are cutting broomcorn together at Dahlstrom's.

Sept. 28
Frank Hallgren, Victor Johnson of Lake Precinct, and I drove down to Williamsburg to attend a Convention for the purpose of electing delegates to the senatorial Judicial and Representative convention. It was a packed convention and we could not do anything against the ring, though we voted against all the nominees but Jim David. Frank Hallgren, Hugh DeQuine, and Elton P. Miller were appointed a Committee on Credentials and reported as follows:

    Center Precinct: F. Hallgren, Rolf Johnson;
    Rock Falls   "   James Sweezey, Elton Nitter;
    Lake   "   Hugh DeQuine, Christ Jensen;
    Williamsburg "   A. S. Baldwin, Daniel Lute.

The other precincts were not represented
Sweezey was chairman and Baldwin was Secretary. The nominees were:

    Delegate to State Convention: James Sweezey;
     " Senatorial   "   Hugh DeQuine;

" Judicial   "   W. J. David;
" Representative "   Jim Sweezey & Dan Lute.
On our way home I shot two rattlesnakes with my revolver.

Sunday, September 29
Nick Brunzell and John Hendricks called on me. Nick told me he met Belle Harnan of Wood River at the Post Office to day. She has been engaged to teach the center school.

Some time ago the school board asked me to teach the coming term at $30 per month, but I declined and recommended Belle Harnan.

Sept. 30
Cut broomcorn for August Bragg. Quite a number of others were cutting and Charley Nelson and Ferdinand Johnson on one side and August Bragg and I on the other had a breaking match in which Aug. and I came out ahead though our opponents were big powerful men.

October 2
Am cutting broomcorn for J. P. Bragg. Last night after supper one of his cutters, Swen Magnuson, a big good natured hearty fellow, was taken suddenly ill with cramps in his stomach and vomiting and in less than half an hour he was all drawn up in a heap and could hardly speak. Julius Carlson, alias Frank Boge, and I sat up with him all night. He suffered great agony and the only thing that seemed to relieve him was when we rubbed his muscles with Turpentine and he asked for water every few minutes. He kept getting worse all day and died at 10 o'clock this evening. His sister, Mrs. Skoog, had been sent for and was present at his death. He leaves a wife and several children in Indiana.

Tinie Nelson was present, but the presence of the destroying angel did not seem to awe her as she tried to keep up a flirtation with August Bragg and me.

I read a piece in the "Police News" about Veen Dusenberry, who has been captured in Utica, N.Y. on a charge of burglary and arson committed in 1854. I knew him well. Solvinus Dusenberry lived close by us in Henderson Grove, Ills. a long while; he was a half brother of Jim, Ed, and Cal Dusenberry. He was quite a clever fellow and one of the best speakers in our Debating Club. He swindled Henry Burgland of Galesburg out of $22.00 and absconded, since which I haven't heard from him until now.

Oct. 5
Attended the funeral of Swen Magnuson. About 40 persons were present. Rev. J. Danielson preached the funeral sermon and performed burial services.

Sunday, Oct. 6
Met Belle Harnan at church and had a short conversation with her. She complained of being very lonesome out here among so many strangers.

John Hendricks, Ida Bragg, Tinie Nelson, and I were out walking this evening.

School Creek. Oct. 10
Deputy U.S. Marshall Frank Baker stopped with us last night. He was returning from an unsuccessful chase after Persimmon Bill and Dutch Henry, the noted horse thieves. To day I rode down to Baker's Place on Spring Creek. On the way Baker, who was armed with a fine Sharps rifle, proved his fine marksmanship by shooting a crane at long range. The wind blew fearfully and covered us with dust. Stopped at Baker's cabin for dinner and was introduced to Mrs. Baker, a very nice little woman. After dinner I went over to Clarence Peterson's on School Creek. The boys were glad to see me.

School Creek, October 12
A revival meeting is in full blast down here and a good many Phelps County people are in attendance. Clarence's mother is sick and his cousin, "Little Carrie" Johnson, is keeping house for the boys.

This evening Clarence, Sam Wright, and I rode over to Watson to attend the Lyceum. It was held in a small log school house and was well attended, the fair sex being also pretty well represented. Songs were sung by Smith Waller, Billy Beam and Charles Zenoue. Then the subject for debate: "Resolved, that labor is more honorable than speculation," was discussed. Frank Baker and a little Irishman named Conley were on the negative and got the best of the argument, but the Wooden-headed judges decided in favor of the affirmative.

Miss Ella Thrasher read the "Watson Investigator," the literary production of the Society, which contained some good hits of local interest.

Adjourned.

Oct. 16

Had a nice time these last few days on School Creek. Went home to day in company with Rev. Joe Allen. Weather was cool and windy. Found the prairie fire had passed over Phelps County during our absence and occasioned a great deal of damage to grain and hay stacks, stables and such. Brunzell's stable, hay, and straw stacks, and Nick's pony were burned. August Bragg and Ferdinand Johnson lost most everything except their teams and wagon. A Swedish lady, Mrs. Foreman, was burned to death in Lake precinct, but the story of the great Indian scare of last Monday beats anything.[1]

It seems that Mrs. Nels Nelson, a late arrival who was living at Eric Olson's, had her mind so excited by the stories of the recent Indian massacres on Sappa and Beaver Creeks that she lived in constant dread of an Indian raid.[2]

Last Monday the air was murky with smoke from the big prairie fire and objects assumed distorted proportions to the eye at a short distance. She happened to see a large herd of antelope run by near the house, and in her disturbed state of mind took them for a band of Indians on horseback. She ran to the nearest house and reported what she had seen. The alarm spread through the settlement like wildfire and the settlers fled for their lives, many leaving everything and taking only their families.

Mother says the first she knew of it Oliver Peterson came running from Dahlstrom's, his hair on end and eyeballs protruding. He burst open the door and breathlessly gasped, "Indians!"

When he had recovered his breath sufficiently to speak he related that the Indians were as thick as grasshoppers between Carlson's and our place.

Mother was incredulous and concluded to send Justus to investigate before she would flee, so Justus mounted Mack and rode over to Carlson's where he found Carlson, Salgren, L. M. Anderson, and Charles A. Nelson were preparing to go over a scout in the direction of Olson's. Justus accompanied them, and after going half way, they saw a woman come running toward them. She had on a white dress and black cloak and on account [of] the smoky condition of the air they couldn't see very plain and concluded it was an Indian on a white pony. The woman saw the scouts and took them for a band of Indians and ran into a broomcorn field to hide. The scouts thought the Indian was trying to surround them and started back for Carlson's as fast as their horses could run. Justus rode home, Mother and the rest of the family had fled and he found them at the Emigrant House where a good many settlers with their families had taken refuge and Lee Hallgren was in command. Scouting parties were sent in different directions, Aug. Bragg, John Hendricks, Pete Peerson, Frank Hallgren, John A. Ward, Sol Linder, John P. Nelson, Olof Hoag, and others, but reported "no signs of Indians."

A good many of the settlers were in Harlan Co. attending the revival, among them, father and Emil. They returned just as the fugitives were dispersing to their respective homesteads.

Many amusing incidents and anecdotes are told of the great panic. Stenfelt with his family and several other fugitives, among whom was Ida Bragg, drove as fast as the mules could run down to the break of Spring Creek where they passed the night, suffering a good deal from cold, as in their hurry they had forgotten to take any bed clothes with them.

The scare extended all over the county, and even into adjoining counties. Even the city of Kearney was in a fever of excitement, fugitives arriving constantly with terrible tales of Indian ravages, one man reporting that he had seen 300 Cheyenne setting fire to the prairie.

Oct. 18

Alf Larson and Daniel Monson called on me. Alf has spent some time on the frontier and was with General Custer on his Yellowstone Expedition.[3]

We all went together to meeting at the Emigrant House where I had a good time with Ida B. and Tinie N. in the kitchen.

Oct. 19

Went with Victor Friberg and Pete Holm to attend a Mass Meeting at the Emigrant House for the purpose of considering the relocation of the county seat and deciding upon a site for the same. Thos. Squires of Cottonwood was Chairman and I was Secretary.

A proposition by L. Hallgren was considered: "That in consideration of the county seat being located on the N.W. 1/4 of the N.E. 1/4 of 1-6-19, he would bind himself to remove the present county buildings to the proposed site, erect a pump and windmill, deed 10 acres of land to the county, plant thereon on and cultivate a sufficient number of shade and ornamental trees, and if the commissioners did not see fit to remove the present building he would agree to haul lumber from Kearney for a new courthouse."

Sunday, Oct. 20

This afternoon the prairie fire, driven with the speed of a race horse by a hard wind, came down from the north and came near sweeping everything before it. The flames leaped skywards, roared like a hurricane, the long dry grass crackled like musketry, and the smoke obscured the heavens, and the air was hot as the blast of a furnace. Father, John Young, Dan Monson, J. P. Bragg, Aug. Bragg, Ferd Johnson, Victor Friberg, Pete Holm, Oliver Peterson, Dahlstrom, J. A. Halin and I saved Halin's place by means of back fires. It was in imminent danger a while and we had to work like fun. Aug. Bragg, Vic Friberg, and Pete Holm rode down to Aug. Jacobson's to try and save his place as he was not at home, but they could not stem the resistless sea of flames and very narrowly escaped a fiery death, their horses being singed and Aug. losing his coat.

When I got tired of fighting fire I went out on the prairie with Ida Bragg and Tinie Nelson, where we lay down and watched the rest of the folks fighting the flames. All at once we observed August Carlson's place in flames and Aug. Bragg, Ferd Johnson, and I mounted our horses and rode over there. On arriving we found all Carlson's hay, grain stacks, stables, broomcorn & c. in flames. Carlson, Charlie Carlson, John Hendricks, and John A. Anderson were there exhausted by fighting the fire, saving the house and live stock. Carlson's loss is 15–20 tons of broomcorn, 13 stacks of wheat, 40 tons of hay, stable and broomcorn shed, lots of lumber and poles, and a number of chickens.

This is a hard blow to Carlson as he is heavily in debt, which he was expecting to pay this fall.

Oct. 21

John Young, Dan Monson, Oliver Peterson, and I were up at Carlson's last night keeping guard over the burning stack so the fire would not spread. Had a wrestle with Oliver, and got away with him.

Oct. 22

The Election for the relocation of the County seat was held to day. The place of voting for Center Precinct was at the Emigrant House. I was appointed Clerk of Election in place of Frank Hallgren. The other clerk[s] was A. W. Johnson, Father, Dahlstrom, and Peter Peerson. 46 votes were polled in this precinct. The different sites voted for were 1-6-19, 16-6-18, and 26-6-19.

I cast my maiden vote.

At noon Miss Hedwig Hallgren spread the table and asked the board of Election to dine, which the board did not refuse.

Nels Lundquist had not made his appearance at the polls this evening and as we needed his vote, I rode up to his place and brought him in time to cast his vote before the polls were closed.

Oct. 24
Rode down to Deputy County Clerk Dan Lute's with the returns of Election. From [there] I went to Bill Lee's and got my dinner, then went home.

Oct. 25
Nick Brunzell and I went to Norwegian Johnson's and he told us some yarn[s] of the sea.

I am reading "Black Dwarf" by Sir Walter Scott.

Oct. 26
P. A. Brodine and I went to Williamsburg and attended a meeting of the board of canvassers of the recent Election. A. S. Baldwin, Will Dilworth, and Dan Lute were present. As the returns from all the precincts were not in the board adjourned till next Tuesday. From the returns already in we found that so far 1-6-19 had a big majority.
The board of Co. Coms. were in session and among other things allowed my claim of $3.30 for Election services and the Co. Clerk drew a warrant for the same which I sold to Will for 65 cts. on the dollar.
I made a bet with Will Dilworth of a dollar on the result of the Election, I holding that Phelps Center would get the county seat, while he claimed Williamsburg would come out ahead.

I am reading "The Monastery" by Sir Walter Scott.

Oct. 31
Threshed our grain yesterday and to day. Got 250 bushels of wheat,

140 of barley, 114 of oats, 85 of rye, and three of peas.[4] Lewis and John Erick Swanson ran the machine, John Hendricks drove the horse power, A. Aspelin measured grain, Dan Monson and Dahlstrom stacked straw, Oliver Peterson cut bands, Sol Linder, father, and August Carlson pitched bundles, Gus Danielson and I carried the grain into the granary.

November 1

Brother Justus went out to Dan Monson's place in Harlan Co. with a load of straw. On his way home, as he was coming through a draw, the hayrack slid ahead onto the horses, which became frightened and ran away. Justus fell off the hayrack between the horses and the wagon, the horses kicked him, the wheels passed over his legs, and a bolt struck him on his head cutting a gash about 3 inches long. Justus, nothing daunted, started after the horses which ran about a mile and a half and were caught at Phelps P. O. Justus got them, drove home, and put up the team before mentioning anything about the ugly gash in his head.

The Co. Coms. have changed the commissioners' districts so that both our nominees, Hopwood and Hedlund, are in the same district so this afternoon a number [of] homesteaders met in Convention at the P. O. and nominated Mr. Ingel Rodstrom for commissioner of Dist. No. 1. We also concluded to run Old Jimmy Steward for States' Attorney against Gen. C. J. Dilworth. The General is sure to be elected but we will vote for Old Jimmy, who can't even write his own name, just to spite Dilworth and show how he stands in the estimation of his own county, because he has been blowing in his campaign speeches that "at home, where I am known, there is where I expect to get the votes."

Wm. Lee was chairman and Lee Hallgren secretary of the caucus.

Mr. O. P. Pearson of Kearney was present and spoke in behalf of Mr. J. D. Seaman, who is running for the State senate.[5]

Sunday, Nov. 3

Rode over to Charley W. Johnson['s] to see Julius Carlson and his sister Thilda, who were there visiting.

Nov. 5

Election day.

The General Election has taken place and we have elected state, district, county, and precinct officers.

A. W. Johnson and I were clerks; Dahlstrom, Salgren, and father were judges for this precinct. We voted the straight Republican ticket with the exception of Gen. Dilworth, whose name we scratched and substituted the name of James Steward.

Forty-four votes were polled in Center precinct.

County Officers:

> Clerk - Leander Hallgren;
> Treasurer - Thos. Squires;
> Supt. Pub. Inst. Mrs. Ella Rowland;
> Judge - Ole D. Whitcomb;
> Sheriff - W. J. David;
> Com. 1st Dist. Ingel Rodstrom;
> "   2nd "   T. M. Hopwood.
> J.P.'s Peter Peerson and C. J. Anderson;
> Assessor, John Johnson;
> Constables, J. S. Salgren, and Gustaf Johnson;
> Judge of Election - Johnson;
> "   J. M. Dahlstrom;
> "   Albert Sundblad
> Clerk "   "   A. W. Johnson;
> "   "   "   Rolf Johnson

Nov. 7

Co. Judge Wilke and Mr. Kinnear of Lake stopped with us last night. Ida B. came to see me this afternoon.

Nov. 9

Rained all day

Broke one of Joe Allen's ponies to ride and had a lively time.

In the afternoon I went to Williamsburg with the returns of the Election.

It is reported that John Shafer was not killed [as] rumor had it some time ago. He is "cowpunching" near Sidney.

Nov. 13

This morning we were scraping broomcorn and Frank Hallgren, who was feeding the scraper, accidentally caught his hand in the gearing, broke a finger, and crushed his hand badly.

John Hendricks and I called on Ida B. this evening.

Nov. 16

Last night John Hendricks, Johnny Bragg, August Bragg, and I went over to *Chivari* John Olson and Carolina Aspelin, who were married several days ago. We were armed with shotguns and revolvers and the first intimation they had of the racket was when we fired a volley under the windows followed by an unearthly yell. We then retired to reload, then returned to the attack and after keeping up the noise for a time without bringing the bridal pair out, we went home.

I guess they were too frightened to come out, thinking it an Indian attack.

Nov. 21

Was husking corn this afternoon in the field when Thilda Danielson unexpectedly appeared on the scene, having come from Kearney yesterday.

Sun. Nov. 24

Quite cold. Passed the day with Thilda at sister Hilda's.

Election returns show that our ticket was elected by a large majority.

Nov. 28

Last night as Mr. Danielson, Alex Danielson, Old Carl Carlson, Mrs. Johannes Anderson, brothers Emil and Justus, Thilda Danielson, and I were returning from prayer meeting at Christianson's, the night was very dark as we neared Danielson's place. Danielson, who was driving ahead, ran against the wire fence around his pasture. His ponies became frightened and started to run away breaking the buggy tongue and doubletree; it was only by the combined efforts of Aleck and Mr. Danielson that the ponies were finally stopped. Mrs. Anderson got scared and leaped from the buggy spraining her knee so badly she couldn't get up.

I was driving along at a brisk trot, but as I was paying more attention to Thilda, who was riding with me, than to my horses, I didn't know anything of what was going on ahead of me until one of my horses, Rock, ran against the wire fence and fell. As soon as he got up I came near driving over Mrs. Anderson, who lay on the grass groaning in agony. I stopped the horses in time and went to help Mr. Danielson unhitch his frightened ponies. We then lifted Mrs. Anderson into my wagon and took her home.

This afternoon Mother and I went over to see how Mrs. Anderson was getting along. Her knee was very much swelled and she couldn't walk. I left mother there and went over to Danielson's and took supper with Thilda.

Nov. 29
Went with Rev. Danielson to Dilworth's Ranch on business. On our way down Danielson had a shotgun lying in the bottom of the wagon and the jolting firing it off. The whole charge tore through the end gate of the wagon.

On arriving at the Ranch we found no one at home except Charley Peterson, the cowboy, and his sister Selma, the housemaid, so we couldn't transact our business and after lunch drove back home.

Danielson is quite friendly now. He sees I won't try to curry favor with him and as it is a ground hog case, he has to grin and bear it.[6]

Sun. Dec. 1st
Saw a mirage this morning. Could see the city of Kearney quite plain, apparently in the sky.

Dec. 2
Yesterday August Bragg and I drove down to Julius Carlson's in Lake precinct and spent the afternoon and evening with Julius, his pretty sister Thilda, and Rosa Peterson. Had a good time and plenty of fun. We got back about 3 o'clock this morning.

Cedar Bluffs, Dec. 5
At 4 o'clock yesterday morning Aleck Danielson and I, with two teams, started for the Cedar Bluffs to get cedar for fenceposts. Camped for breakfast on the Platte after which we drove up the valley of the Platte passing Dilworth's Ranch, Robb's Ranch, and camped for the night at Nickoll's Ranch, where the extensive stables and corrals gave evidence of the proximity of the Cedar bluffs, as the broken hilly country south of the ranch is called. A deer hung up to one corner of the cabin showed the presence of game in the vicinity.[7]

This morning, acting on instructions from the cowboys at the ranch, we drove 3 or 4 miles up Big Tree Canyon where we found the cedar growing in deep precipitous "pockets" branching off from the main canyon. It grows upon the steep sides and takes a good deal of climbing to get at.

We are camped this evening in a narrow canyon with perpendicular walls. We are pretty tired as we have done hard work chopping and loading our wagons.

Dec. 7
Got back from Cedar Bluffs about noon to day. Camped last night on Plum Creek. Weather rough and cold.

Sunday, Dec. 8
Spent the afternoon with Thilda.

Dec. 9
The county seat election will take place tomorrow and Dahlstrom and father have been down in Lake, Prairie, and Divide precinct[s] electioneering.

Dec. 10
Served as Clerk of Election of Center Precinct. Aaron Johnson was also clerk and father, Dahlstrom, and Salgren were Judges. 49 votes were polled in this precinct, all for 1-6-19.

Dec. 11
Rode to Williamsburg with the Poll book and ballots of Center precinct.

Bloomington, Neb., Dec. 12
This morning Jacob Danielson, John Anderson, Carl Carlson, Fridolf Stenfelt, L. M. Anderson, A. P. Anderson, Andrew Olson, J. P. Bragg, J. S. Salgren, Nels Rylander, Frank Hallgren, Father, and I started for Bloomington on land business. The weather was raw and windy and we had to walk part of the time to keep our feet warm.

Upon our arrival at Walker's Ranch in Kearney Co., we were told that five persons had been murdered recently in the neighborhood by a man named Richards.[8]

It seems that last summer S. D. Richards was in jail at Kearney for stealing a watch. At the same time Mrs. Mary Haralson, the wife of the bridge lumber thief, was in jail on suspicion of having aided in the escape of her husband and Harry Underwood, the train robber, from jail. The two became acquainted and upon their release from jail it appears that Richards continued his intimacy with her and went to live with her on her homestead in Kearney Co.

About a month or six weeks ago the woman and her three children disappeared and Richards told the neighbors they had gone to Texas to join her husband.

He stayed about the place, jumped her claim, sold and disposed of her property claiming to have bought her out.

Last Monday he murdered a Swede named Peter Anderson some half dozen miles from the Haralson place and escaped. He was last seen in Bloomington, with the sheriff two hours behind him.

As soon as the murder of the Swede was discovered the people in the neighborhood of the Haralson place began to suspect that he had also made away with the Haralson family, and instituted a search, which resulted in the discovery of the mangled bodies of Mrs. Haralson and her three children buried under a strawstack about 100 yards from the house.

We were told that the victims of this atrocious murder were then lying at the Haralson place about half a mile from Walker's Ranch and that an inquest had been held on them this morning. So Stenfelt, A. P. Anderson, L. M. Anderson, J. P. Bragg, father, and I went over there to see the bodies.

We found them lying on some straw and presenting a horrible sight. The woman was covered with blood from head to foot, one eye was knocked out, and her face beaten out of all shape. She had on a dark green underskirt and a pair of stockings. The three children, ranging between the ages of two and eight, had their heads crushed and [the] smallest also had a leg broke. Their limbs were fearfully shrunken and hands and feet devoid of flesh.

It spite of the cold weather the stench of the bodies were intolerable, and we soon left the awful scene.

They are supposed to have been murdered with a flat iron, which was found covered with hair and blood in the house.

They were to be buried this afternoon.[9]

The feeling against the brutal butcher is intense and the chances are that he will be strung up with out Judge or Jury if he is captured.[10]

We arrived in Bloomington all right and transacted our business at the Land Office, Father and the others getting the benefit of the "grasshopper" law, which gave them a year's extension on their pre-emptions.

Bloomington, Dec. 13
The hotels were so full and crowded last night we could not obtain shelter so our lawyer, J. Woodson Peery, kindly placed his office at our disposal and we slept on the floor. During the night a regular Nebraska blizzard came on and snow has been flying around so to day we could not start for home, and we have been baching it at Peery's office.

Phelps Center, Neb., Dec. 14
Staid in Peery's office last night, and started from Bloomington after breakfast, weather very cold. Stopped at Julius Carlson's in Lake precinct and Thilda Carlson got up a good dinner for us.
Got back home this evening.

Sunday, Dec. 15
Nick Brunzell, John Hendricks, Thilda D., and I have had a good deal of fun sleigh riding.

Dec. 16
Very cold weather.
John Hendricks staid with me last night and to day and we passed the time popping corn.

P. A. Brodine told me this evening that he was one of the board of canvassers of the ballots at the recent election, and that 16-6-18 received about 90 votes for location of county seat while 1-6-19 received 110, but as no place received 3/5 of all the votes, the county seat will remain at Williamsburg until next fall when the question will again come up for final settlement.

I am reading "Irish Legends" by Samuel Lover.

Dec. 19
Cold weather.
Went to the P. O. and got my mail. In looking it over I ran across an

account of the death of my old friend, Gardner Keneval, in the "Kearney Nonpareil."

It seemed that Joel Gardner Kenevel, who had been for some time employed as brakesman on the B & M. R. R., was climbing from one car to another when he slipped and fell between the cars. His right arm and left hand were cut off, and he was bruised about the head. This happened at Hastings in the morning and he died before night leaving parents, sisters, a brother, and many friends to mourn his untimely fate.

Called on Thilda this afternoon.

Dec. 20
John Hendricks and Three cowboys from Nickoll's Ranch named August Johnson, Charley Swanson, and Pete Ericson stayed with us last night.

Dec. 24
Christmas eve.

Got a letter from Swan Nelson at Wood River in which he tells me that my favorite at that place, Rosa Jessop, is married to Fred Risland.[11]

Spent the evening with Thilda Danielson, Annie Allen, and Anna Maria at the Danielson homestead.

The old folks have gone down to School Creek to spend the holidays and the girls had fixed up a Christmas tree (a small straight cedar, which I brought from the bluffs) with candles, gilt paper, and rosettes presenting a pretty and attractive sight. We had an elegant supper and a pleasant evening.

Dec. 25
I slept at Danielson's last night and this morning we got up at 5 o'clock and Thilda, Annie Allen, and I went over to the Emigrant House to attend "Jul-otte," a time honored custom of the Swedes.[12]
There was quite a press of people and the house was prettily lighted with a large number of candles.

The services were over about 9 o'clock A.M. and I went with Nick Brunzell home and staid to breakfast and dinner.

Took supper with Tillie this evening at Johannes Anderson's.

The weather is pretty cold.

Dec. 26
Father, Emil, and I took a sleigh ride to church. We brought Thilda D.,
Julius, Oscar, and Thilda Carlson with us home to dinner and had [a]
pleasant afternoon. After supper Julius and Oscar went away and I
accompanied the two Thilda's over to Danielson's, where we spent
the evening in a wild Christmas frolic.

Dec. 27
The girls would not let me leave them, so I staid there last night and
slept upstairs.

   Thilda Carlson's brother called for her about 10 A.M. and she went
away. I spent the remainder of the day with Thilda D. and went home
this evening.

Sun. Dec. 28 [29]
Thilda Danielson, Aaron Johnson's brother Charley, and I spent the
day at my sister's.

Dec. 30
Thilda Danielson, John Danielson, and Annie Allen spent the afternoon at our house.

   I hear that a fracas occurred last Saturday at a school meeting near
Williamsburg between William Lee and John Holmes in which Lee hit
Holmes on the head with a cedar pole and knocked him down.

   George Steward, charged with burning Will Hagen's [building?],
had his trial at Plum Creek last week, was found guilty and sentenced
to one year in the penitentiary.

   I find through the papers that Richards was captured.

Jan. 1st, 1879
We had a sort of New Year's gathering to day and the following named
persons were present:

> Dahlstrom and family; P. A. Brodine;
> Mr. & Mrs. Salgren; Mr. & Mrs. Bragg;
> sister Hilda and Gus; Thilda,
> John, and Alex Danielson.

We had a pleasant time.

Jan. 3

Just got back from Kearney this evening. I went in with father and came back [with] August Bragg and Will Anderson.

The weather was so bad I froze my nose.

S. D. Richards, the murderer of the Haralson family, is now in the Kearney jail. He was captured at his old home Mt. Pleasant, Ohio, and brought back to Kearney. He is bold and defiant and boasts of nine murders.

Jan. 4

Weather very cold. I have been reading "The Silent Hunter; or, The Scowl Hall Mystery," by Percy B. St John.

This evening, the weather having moderated somewhat, we went over to Jacob Danielson's and took supper. Got a letter from Clarence Peterson, who has just [returned] from a buffalo hunt on the headwaters of the Republican. The boys had a hard trip and one of them, Barefoot John, froze his feet. They killed 6 buffalo.

Jan. 6

Attended a big supper at J. P. Bragg's in company with Thilda Danielson. Present: Aug. Bragg, Mr. Skoog, Charley Skoog, Nels Rylander, Wilma Carlson, and many others.

Jan. 7

Got a very interesting letter from my Illinois correspondent, Elma Johnson.

Jan. 9

We had lots of visitors to day. Rev. J. Danielson and family; Mr. and Mrs. Johannes Anderson; Old Carl Carlson; Mr. and Mrs. Solomon Linder; Anna Maria; Gus and Hilda; Joe Allen and his girls, Annie & Leanda; Nels Rylander and Charley Johnson; and others.

Jan. 10

Attended a big supper at J. Danielson's, many guests were present; among others Nels Rylander, Charles and Louisa Skoog.

Sunday, Jan. 12

Last night I went to see Thilda. Got back at two o'clock this morning.

Jan. 17

Was present at a sort of party at Jacob Danielson's. Among others present were the Lindbloms; C. J. Anderson and family; Mrs. John Peerson, Lewis Swanson, Ellen Swanson, Andrew Falk and Christine Swanson, a young lady from Beaver City, to whom I was introduced.

Had a good time.

I learn from the papers that S. D. Richards had his trial at Minden, Kearney Co., last Tuesday. He was indicted for the murder of Peter Anderson, tried, found guilty, and sentenced to be hung at Minden on the 26 of April.

He exhibited the same remarkable *sang froid* which has characterized him since his capture, and laughed and joked with all around him.

Sunday, Jan. 19

A very fine day.

We had a good deal of company: the Lindbloms; The Thorells; Gus and Hilda; John Hendricks, Thilda Danielson, and others.

Nice time.

Jan. 22

Got letters from Clarence Peterson, Swan Nelson, and Cousin Josie.

Thilda D. called on me.

Jan. 24

Thilda sent word for me to come over and see her, as she had something she wanted to tell me. I went and found she wanted me to go with her and her father to School Creek to morrow. I made all kinds of excuses, but she gained her point.

Jan. 25

About 11 o'clock this morning Jacob Danielson, Thilda, and I started for School Creek. We had gone but a mile or so when one of the ponies kicked and got his leg over the buggy-tongue and the ponies started to run away. They were very hard to hold but by our united efforts we brought them to a stop and I got off and unhitched the tugs.

They commenced to rear and struggle and as I had hold of their bridles they made it pretty lively for me. I got the best of them however, and after hitching up we resumed our journey without further incident.

The pony which kicked over the tongue had all the skin rubbed off his leg.

Got to School Creek about 3 P.M. and were warmly welcomed by our friends.

Sunday, Jan. 26
Attended church this morning and Sunday school afternoon. I was urged to take Miss Maggie Cooper's class in Sunday school but declined. Peter Burgquist taught one class and Mr. Keeney one. One of the prominent members of the school was Cab. Adams, a noted hard case and horsethief, who is now supposed to have reformed. He is small and slightly built; black hair, mustache and goatee, brown eyes, and a dare devil look which gives him away.

He is a partner of the notorious Lank Sherrick and Fred Ferguson and a brother of Clarence Adams, who was recently shot and captured at North Platte.

Cab was himself shot some two months ago while attempting to steal a horse on West Turkey Creek. He is now a professor of religion claiming to have been converted at the late revival. I was introduced to him by Clarence Peterson and found him full of fun.

After supper I went with Clarence to meeting at Old Man Wright's held in a long rambling building, half dug-out, half log cabin. There I was introduced to Clarence's girl, "Chubby" Wright, to Miss Ella Wright, and to the McNeece girls, Lena and Jane.

Jan. 27
Thilda and I staid at Burgquist's last night. Passed the day pleasantly. John, Clarence, and I were shooting at a target and John and Clarence did some tall shooting.

Attended school afternoon. Thilda D., Annie and Tinie Peterson, Clarence, Jane McNeece, [and] Sam Wright were there. We had a good time, especially at recess, where we played "Drop the Handkerchief" "Blackman" and other games in which kissing the girls was part of the programme. Miss Cooper, the teacher, joined in the game with the rest of us.

After supper we attended prayer meeting at the school house, and at its conclusion I accompanied Annie Peterson home, much to the disgust of Sam Wright, who expected to be her escort.

Jan. 28
Thilda and I stayed at Burgquist's last night and we had some fun this morning.

About 10 A.M. we took leave of our kind friends and started for home. The weather was as pleasant as we could wish. We arrived at Danielsons about 3 P.M. and while waiting for dinner to get ready I sat down in a pan of hot rolls Mrs. Danielson had sat down in a chair to cool covered with a cloth, which I in my innocence took to be a cushion.

I squashed the rolls flat as a pancake to the consternation of Mrs. Danielson and the great delight of Thilda and the other members of the family. After dinner Thilda went with me home to stay a day or two.

Father got back from a trip to Kearney, where he met Bill Brumbaugh, who confirmed the report that Little Bernie Shafer, son of Ex-sheriff John Shafer, was murdered north of Sidney by the Cheyenne last fall.[13] Bernie was a bright boy and it is too bad he should meet such a horrible fate, but such are the vicissitudes of frontier life.

Jan. 31
John Hendricks is staying with us. Thilda went back home yesterday. It snowed all last night and until noon to day. The snow is 8 inches deep on a level and has formed big drifts around the house and stables.

February 1, 1879
John Hendricks, father, and I drove over to Ericson's where we found the Danielsons. We staid to supper.

Sunday, Feb. 2
Staid at Danielson's last night and all day. We organized an im promtu Sunday school of which I was the superintendent.

Feb. 7
John Hendricks and I took a team and gun and went out rabbit hunting. Shot a big jack-rabbit about half a mile from home.

Feb. 8
Thilda D. stayed with us last night and this morning John Hendricks took us sleigh riding down to Gus and Hilda's, where we'll stay a day or two.

Febr. 10

Hendricks and I went jack-rabbit hunting. John drove the team and scared up the game and I manipulated the gun. We started up three rabbits one after the other and had some fine chases, but couldn't get them. On our way home we started one about a mile from our house and I shot it. About five minutes afterwards I shot another one, and soon after this we had an exciting chase after another near L. M. Anderson's place, which I got after shooting at it three times.

Joseph Allen and his daughters Anna and Leanda are staying with us this week.

Took Thilda sleighriding this evening

Feb. 11

John and I went hunting. We had a long drive and were finally rewarded by bagging a magnificent whitetail on Solomon Linder's timberclaim.

Joseph Allen is keeping a private school in L. M. Anderson's house 1/2 miles away. He boards with us. When he and the children get home they look like a lot of street gamins they are so dirty from the dust of the sod walls, dirt roof, and dirt floor.

Febr. 13

Weather colder, so we didn't go hunting, but I made up for it by shooting a bush-rabbit in a grove of cottonwoods near the house.

Febr. 14

Father and I drove out to Landquist's, where we stopped for dinner. On the way back I shot a big jack-rabbit.

In the afternoon John and I went hunting and I shot a rabbit which dodged into its hole. The hole was so deep we could neither see nor reach him, so I resorted to a trick we used under similar circumstances in Illinois, where we used to tree rabbits into hollow logs and stumps. I took my ramrod, pushed it into the hole till it touched the rabbit, then twist[ed] it around till I had a good hold on the rabbit's skin and then pulled it out. The rabbit was quite dead.

When we got home we found Nick Brunzell, Jim Stanley, and Thilda at our house. Nick and Jim brought her in a sleigh.

Feb. 18

Went home with Thilda yesterday and staid all night. She left this morning for Kearney. Did a lot of writing for Danielson.

The boys at the Emigrant House had rare sport last week in running down and capturing an antelope.

August Bragg and August Jacobson encountered a wild-cat a day or two ago, about a mile from here. As they had no arms they dared not attack the cat, which was very large and fierce.

Feb. 21

John Hendricks and I went rabbit hunting. After driving a mile and a half a big jack jumped up and I popped it over. We then drove out to Charley Johnson['s], and took dinner. On our way back we had a long chase after a rabbit and finally succeeded in shooting it.

Feb. 22

Hendricks and I drove out to Harris['s] and took dinner with Mrs. Harris, after which we drove down to Brunzell's and spent the afternoon.

Feb. 26

Rode to the P. O. with Geo. Bedillion, the buckboard driver, and got letters from Thilda D., Elma Johnson, and Cousin Josie.

Feb. 27

Miss Annie Nelson is now a visitor in our family. She came from Ills. last month. She is a tall, slim girl about 18, a sister of Tinie Nelson.

Feb. 28

Alfred Christianson brought me a dog with the request that I would shoot it as he was too tenderhearted to do it himself. I put two or three ball[s] from my pistol through the dog's head and killed it. Annie seemed to take delight in watching the poor beast's death struggle. She must be hard hearted; she says she would like [to] witness the execution of S. D. Richards, condemned murderer of Kearney Co., but thinks that hanging is too good for him and that he ought to be burned at the stake.

Hendricks and I took her over to Danielson's this afternoon.

March 5
John Hendricks and I rode over to John Olson['s] where I was introduced to Olson's handsome wife.

March 6
I am twenty-three years old to day. August Bragg, Julius Carlson, Chas. W. Johnson, and Chas. A. Nelson took dinner with us. This also Aug.'s Birthday and he is twenty-one.
Gus and Hilda also spent the day with us in honor of the occasion.

Sunday, March 9
The new meeting house on Moses Hill was opened for services to day. It is a frame structure, 30 x 36, with three windows on each side and a door in the south end. It is built on Moses Hill, the highest point in the whole county, and can be seen for a distance of 20 miles.
Father, Justus, John Hendricks, and I attended the opening ceremonies.

March 11
We are sowing wheat nowadays.
Got letters from Thilda Danielson and Cousin Josie. Thilda sends me her portrait and Josie tells me of the marriage of cousin Celia Johnson to Mr. John Norlund at Peoria, Ills.

Sunday, Mch. 24 [23]
Rode down to Dilworth's Ranch at Plum Creek to see about buying a pony. Took dinner there with Miss Benedick, Charley Peterson, McCall, Co. Clk. of Dawson Co., Jim Robb, and Noble, a cowboy, and Charley Nelson of Williamsburg. There were no ponies for sale at the ranch so I had to go home without.

March 25
Shot a big jack-rabbit about 40 rods from the house this afternoon.
Dan Monson and Alf Larson called.
Am reading "Life in Danbury" By J. M. Bailey.
Got letters from Thilda D. and Elma J.

March 29
Father has finished assessing and taking the census of this precinct. In

looking over his blanks I find there are over 290 inhabitants in the precinct [compared] to about 200 last year, when the precinct was larger.

April 1

All fools day passed without incident except I shot a large jack-rabbit. I have received the first number of the Phelps County Pioneer. Vol 1. No 1. published at Sacramento by Bert O. Wilson. It is a small paper about twice the size of a sheet of writing paper and is full of bright locals and interesting state and county items. It begs its readers as a favor, "not to judge of the Pioneer's quality nor the editor's ability as a journalist by the present number as it was issued under very discouraging circumstances."[14]

It is the first attempt at a newspaper venture in this county and I hope it will succeed.

April 4

Shot a bush-rabbit in the wood pile.

I am reading "Seven and Nine Years Among the Comanches and Apaches" by Edwin Eastman.

April 7

School District no. 9 had its annual meeting to day at Aug Carlson's. Father was elected Treasurer, Salgren Director, and Dahlstrom Moderator. Other business relating to the school was transacted.

April 8

Went to the P. O. and played "Nosby."

Got a letter from Thilda.

We are to have the mail twice a week after this, commencing on Monday.

Kearney, Apr. 21

Went to Kearney in company with Gus Danielson. Met John Hendricks in town and this evening after supper John and I called on Thilda D. at the residence of Frank Gibbs. We found her entertaining a couple of lady friends, Thilda Brown and Ida Sall. We passed a very pleasant evening.[15]

Phelps Center, Apr. 22

Thilda hunted me up this morning and monopolized my attention for an hour or more.

Left Kearney about 10 A.M. in company with Aug. Carlson and got home without incident except getting caught in a hail and rain storm.

I have sold my pre-emption claim to Aaron Blomquist for $50, half in cash and the other half Oct 1st.

CHAPTER 10

The Execution of
Stephen D. Richards

Saturday Apr. 26th [1879]
About 4 o'clock A.M. Nick and Gus Brunzell and I started for Minden, Kearney County, distant some 25 miles east.[1] We had borrowed father's team and Dahlstrom's buggy. We had a splendid drive, and we enjoyed it as well as if we were going to a picnic instead of going to attend the execution of S. D. Richards, which was our purpose.

We arrived at Minden shortly before 10 o'clock, and found it to be a small town of a dozen of houses surrounding a square in the center of which was erected an enclosure of boards about 14 feet high inside of which was the scaffold, the top of which showed above the enclosure with the fatal rope dangling from the cross beam. Outside the enclosure, posts were set in the ground and a new inch rope stretched around them to keep the crowd away from the enclosure. A large crowd was already on hand, and before long it had increased to some 1,500, many being ladies. I met a number of friends and acquaintances in the crowd, among them Victor Johnson, Oscar Skoog, P. O. Hedlund of Phelps county; John B. Peterson, Spot Johnson, and Fred Rosso of Kearney and Pete Frithiof, whom I supposed to be in Texas.[2]

He told me he went to Texas last spring and while crossing Red River with a herd of cattle, he became sick from exposure and came near dying of fever. Upon recovering he went to Indian Territory, where he has been serving as government scout for Col. Dodge between Camp Supply and Fort Reno until a short time ago.[3]

Richards arrived at Minden last night from Lincoln, where he had been confined since his conviction. He was under guard in a one-story frame courthouse, but we got a glimpse of him through a window.

Shortly after our arrival he was brought out and driven slowly around the square in a spring wagon. As he passed the enclosure in which the scaffold was erected, he gave it a searching look but made no remarks. He was then taken back to the courthouse.

Richards was a handsome man. He was about 23 years of age, over six feet tall, well proportioned and muscular, and weighed 180 pounds. His eyes were steel gray, about blue, very keen and penetrating, and also restless and suspicious. His forehead was rather broad but low, and his dark brown hair, which was wavy and inclined to curl, fell over it like a mane. A large sensual mouth, shaded by a dark mustache, good teeth, high cheek bones, and protruding chin—in all a face not very handsome, but striking and one not easily forgotten. He was dressed in a light brown coat and dark pants, white shirt, collar and necktie, and black hat—altogether his appearance was very prepossessing.

The Statutes of Nebraska require executions be private and as Kearney county has no jail, the scaffold had been enclosed according to law but this was an eyesore to the crowd, who all wanted to witness the execution, and toward noon it was understood in the crowd that the enclosure would have to come down. The Sheriff, Matt Kieran, anticipating this, had placed a large posse of guards around the enclosure inside of the rope to keep the crowd back.[4]

As the hour of execution drew near, the crowd became demonstrative and commenced to cut the rope to pieces. The guards were unable to prevent this and while tying it together in one place it would be cut in another. We then pulled the posts out of the ground and dragged them out on the prairie. Then about 25 or 30 of us would get hold of one end of the rope and the guards of the other and there came the "tug of war." We, however, proved too much for them, would drag them out on the prairie and get the rope away from them.

The Sheriff and guards did all in their power without resorting to violence. We finally made a break for the enclosure, led by Pete Frithiof and Fred Rosso, and soon the boards commenced to fly and in less than five minutes three sides of the enclosure were razed to the ground. The Sheriff, seeing that there was a determination on the part of the crowd to witness the execution and that he was powerless to prevent it, mounted the scaffold and made a speech to the crowd, saying that "he was sorry to see such a spirit of lawlessness and disorderly conduct, but he couldn't help it and as they now could all see he hoped they would leave the north wall of the enclosure standing." It was accordingly allowed to stand.

At 14 minutes to one o'clock Richards was brought out of the courthouse with his shackles and handcuffs off, seated in a carriage drawn to the gallows by the people. He alighted firmly on the ground and walked up the scaffold stairs unassisted. He was neatly dressed in a brown coat, black pants, black hat, white shirt, standing collar and black necktie, and polished boots. His appearance was very prepossessing. Sheriff Kieran, Rev. Sandford Gee of Lincoln, and County Clerk Kent also mounted the scaffold.[5]

Richards took his position on the fatal drop as cool and unconcerned as if he was not the principal actor in the terrible drama. He ran his fingers through his dark wavy hair several times and looked at the crowd with a pleased expression.

The sheriff then read the death warrant and asked Richards if he had anything to say. He then spoke substantially as follows:

"Ladies and gentlemen. I stand here a victim of the law. You have your opinion, I have mine. I was condemned to die on a charge of murder in the first degree, but I am not guilty of the crime as charged. I have made my peace with God and have no desire to roam this world any longer. I hope to meet you all in Heaven. I bid my friends all farewell. I look upon these beautiful prairies for the last time and I only regret that I have a father, brother, and five sisters to mourn my fate. Would to God they had been so far away they had never heard of this. I am going to meet my mother and other dear friends in a better land where parting never comes. I am not afraid to die though this is a hard place to stand. Young men take warning by me! If I had listened to the prayers of my dear mother I would never have to die such a death as this far from friends with none to mourn my loss."

He stood erect while speaking while occasionally his eyes looked over the crowd at the green prairies, while the fresh spring wind waved his hair and swung the hangman's noose against his face and neck. Rev. Gee then read from the Bible, Isaiah 1:16-19, St. John. 3:14-15-16, offered up a fervent prayer for the soul of the condemned man, and asked the audience to join in singing "There is a fountain filled with blood," stating that it was at Richards' own request. We all joined in, and Richards sang bass in a rich, melodious voice.

The Officers then prepared for the last act in the drama pinioning his hands, knees, and feet. While this was doing he spoke again:

"Young men, take warning by me. I am here, far from home, native land and friends, but I put my trust in God and he gives me strength to stand here. I prayed to him while in my cell for grace and strength and he has given it to me. Some may laugh, some may chuckle and turn their heads and make cruel remarks on the personal appearance of the poor man who is standing here to day, but I have a free soul and God will save it. Many of you who are standing around are travelling in the downward road to ruin and will be lost, but I hope none of you will ever stand where I stand to day. I am to Suffer for the crimes they say I have committed. This is in accordance with the laws of the state. I am the first one executed in Nebraska for 12 years and I hope to God I may be the last. I have no hard feelings against the Sheriff, he is doing his duty and may God bless him. I shall not be surprised to meet some of you on that beautiful shore where sorrow never comes. If I have any enemies here I forgive them and hope to God they will forgive me. Young men let this be a warning to you to keep from evil;

> 'Let not sin enter at the door
> Lest you can drive it out no more'

Ladies and gentlemen kind friends I am sorry that we must part, but I hope to meet you in Heaven. I bid you all a last farewell."

During the latter part of this speech the sheriff stood with the noose in his hand working it to make it limber, but Richards never flinched, though once or twice a slight tremor was perceptible in his voice. He seemed desirous of impressing the crowd with his courage under such trying circumstances and it required a nerve of iron which he unquestionably possessed to maintain the perfect composure which characterized him throughout this trying ordeal.

When he had finished speaking he said to the Rev. Mr. Gee, "Mr Gee, write to my folks." He then turned to the sheriff saying, "Sheriff I am ready." The sheriff then placed the rope around his neck, tightened the noose and placed a black cap or bag over Richards' head. As he did so Richards took his last look at the sky and the beautiful prairies and murmured: "Sheriff meet me in Heaven." These were his last words. It was now 15 minutes past one o'clock and the Sheriff stepped back, touched the lever with his foot, and Richards dropped through the trap door about 5 feet or more with a dull thud. Twice he swung up, lifting his body and legs with the muscles of the neck. He then hung motionless for about 10 minutes when his breast and shoulders heaved as if trying to breathe. He then hung motionless about 5 minutes longer, when he was pronounced dead. His body was then taken down and laid in a plain pine coffin painted black, the black cap was removed, and the crowd filed past to view the remains of what a short time before was a perfect specimen of physical manhood. His face was not distorted though very pale, and around his neck was the mark of the rope, green-blue and ghastly.[6]

Having now seen what we came for, the last of S. D. Richards, we started for home where we arrived without further incident than that I shot a jack rabbit with my revolver and that Gus Brunzell became ill and was taken with a violent vomiting and racking pains in his stomach.

During the execution I noticed Harry Hatch, the Kearney photographer, taking views from the top of a sod house about 200 yards away.

Richards' Confession:

While in the Nebraska Penitentiary awaiting execution Richards made the following confession:[7]

"I was born March 18, 1856, at Wheeling, W. Va. My parents are American born and were always considered good, reliable people, though my father made no profession of religion. My mother was a Methodist, and quite strict in the faith. When I was six years old, my parents removed to Monroe County, Ohio, and afterwards to Noble County, the same state, where they lived till I was eleven years old, when they went to Warren, in Jefferson County, and soon after to Mt. Pleasant, in the same county where my mother died Sept. 16, 1871, when I was 15 years old. Mt. Pleasant is largely inhabited by Quakers, and when I lived there was a very orderly town. My parents were not strict, but my mother used her influence over me as a Christian woman, and I regularly attended Sunday School and some of the different churches of Mt. Pleasant. During the time I lived there I went to school and learned something of arithmetic and grammar, and was not considered a very bad boy by my teachers. I was a little wild at times, and sometimes attended dances and other evening entertainments, but did nothing positively wrong while there.

"A short time before I came West, I sought and won the affections of a virtuous young lady by the name of Anna Millhorne. We were engaged to be married, and would have been in a year or two if I had not been arrested, for in all my wanderings and wickedness, I kept up a correspondence with her; I may say that I loved her; at any rate I loved her as much as I can love any one.

"From the time my mother died until leaving Ohio, I was most of the time at home, but was working around among farmers and others.

"At this time I opened correspondence with a number of bad men in the West, among whom were notorious desperadoes. I also began to pass counterfeit money, which I got of a New York man through one of my acquaintances, and through them and in various ways picked up the correspondence I have above referred to. In February 1876 I came West to seek my fortune. I had no definite object in view, or any definite destination, but wanted to see the country and live easy and avoid work. My first stop was at Burlington, Iowa, to visit Bill Lee, one of my correspondents, who kept a house of ill fame opposite Burlington. This man has since been hung for killing Jessie McCarty, an inmate of his house, and a bad crowd both of them. From Burlington I went to Morning Sun, Louisa County, Iowa, where I worked for Myers Jarvis on a farm, and then I went to Mt. Pleasant, same state, and engaged [in] the capacity of an attendant in the Insane Asylum. While there I had my first experience in handling 'stiffs,' and it didn't strike me as being very disagreeable either. I remained here until the fall of 1876, when I began tramping the state in regular style. I went to Kansas City, then up to Hastings, and thence to Kearney Junction.

"Two weeks after my arrival at Kearney I was coming in on horseback from the south and fell in with a stranger, also on horseback; we went on in company; at dark we lost the road, and finally camped between Dobytown and the wagon bridge. Here we built a fire and played cards for money and I won nearly all the stranger had. He claimed that it was not honorably done, and we got into a quarrel, but went to bed finally, and next morning started for Kearney. We had not gone far when the stranger, stopping his horse, said: 'We may as well settle this matter between us here and now.'

'In what way?' I asked.

'Either give me back my money or fight,' he replied.

"I refused to refund, and he got kind of savage, and so I shot him. The ball struck him above the left eye, and killed him almost instantly. After killing him I dragged him down to the river and pitched him in. He was a man near six feet high, weighed about 150 pounds, dark hair and eyes, and wore a good suit of dark clothes, and was about 35 years of age. I took his horse and went to Kearney and traded it for another, and went from there south to Phelps county; was gone two or three days and when returning, while near the old 'Walker's Ranch,' I overtook a stranger on foot. He asked me if I knew what had become of the man I was in company with on a certain day, referring to the man I had last killed, and said he had seen me with him and that he had disappeared.

"On inquiry I found that the two were friends and land-hunters. I denied any knowledge of the man or ever having seen him. He called him John; I did not learn the last name. The stranger asked me so many questions that I got nervous and it seemed to me it would be safest to kill him to stop his mouth; and for that purpose I asked him to ride an extra horse I was leading which he did; and the first opportunity I got, when he wasn't looking, I shot him, the ball passing through the back of the head, killing him dead. He was a younger man than the other and dressed about the same. I never heard of either of them afterwards.

"This occurred about 15 miles northwest of 'Walker's Ranch' and there I stayed all night and slept in the barn.

"I sold the extra horse in the morning and started for Kearney. On the way I stopped at Jasper Haralson's, and while there Mrs. Haralson, being a very free talker, asked me if I had been fighting. I asked her why she asked me that question; and she replied that there was blood on my shirt bosom and collar. I did not know it and was startled but remarked, in a joking way, that it must be the blood of some of the men I had murdered. The subject was then dropped.

"I do not remember how long I stopped in this vicinity, but it was only for a day or two, when I went to Kearney and then started for Cheyenne via the U.P. Railroad, stopping at Plum Creek, North Platte, Ogallala, and Sidney, and occupying in all ten days in the trip. I had no particular business at Cheyenne or along the road, but I was uneasy and restless, and all I cared for was adventure, and that too of the most exciting kind. I do not remember all what I did in Cheyenne, but I passed the time principally with the 'boys,' and think I had my share of the fun. However, my sojourn in that place was not long when I fell in company with two young men who were on their way to Kansas City. I joined them, not caring much where I went. I had been calling myself William Hudson up to this time, and went by this name till I reached Kansas City, when I 'shook' my friends and once more took the name of Richards. At Kansas City I took my first glass of liquor. [I] Thought I should be arrested for murder, or for passing counterfeit money, of which I had a good supply. My first streak of conscience struck me at Kansas City, and I determined to reform. So I went about twenty miles outside of the city and went to work as a farm hand. Here I took sick with a fever and lay six weeks and was well cared for. I bore a good name while here, and left the last of October and went north into Iowa, and stopped three weeks at Mt. Pleasant, Morning Sun, and other points; the last one was Maquota. I then went to Cedar Rapids and while there, bought a span of horses and a buggy of a stranger, paying for the same mostly in counterfeit money. On trying to pass it, the young man of whom I had made the purchase discovered the nature of the cash, and about three days after the same was made, hunted me up and wanted good money or the property returned. I refused to do either, and he threatened to have me arrested. Then I made some concessions and began to talk business. All this happened in a strip of timber about three miles from Cedar Rapids. It was just about dusk and raining. The young fellow had followed me out there, and the end of it all was that I shot him. He was a young man, about 19 years of age, rather tall and slim, and with light hair and eyes. I felt a little squeamish, but got over it in a moment, and at once set to work burying the dead. I did this by throwing brush over him, and then I left taking the team with me. I did not know the young man, but I think he was a stranger in the neighborhood.

"I left there as soon as possible, and never heard of the affair afterwards. Soon after I sold the team for good money and started West again. About the last of January 1877 [1878] I reached Lincoln, Nebraska, where I stopped about ten days. Then I went West via the B. & M. R. R., making short stops until I reached Kearney Junction, where some persons were waiting for my coming. My object in stopping at Kearney was to visit Jasper Haralson, husband of the woman I since murdered, and Underwood, alias Nixon, a notorious desperado who was then awaiting trial for alleged complicity in the Big Springs Train Robbery, and who has since been leader in the robbery of the Santa Fe Train. Haralson was awaiting trial for stealing lumber off the Platte River bridge at Kearney.

"Both these men cut their way out of the jail by means of instruments furnished them by outside friends (I among the number), and made good their escape. The excitement over this was great in Kearney and I kept away for a few days, spending the time in riding about the country, but after awhile, everything seeming quiet. I returned to town and shortly afterwards went to Hastings, about 40 miles east of Kearney, to see a lady friend and from there I crossed over to Grand Island, a small town 30 miles north on the U.P.R.R.

"About March 19, 1877 [1878], I left Grand Island in company with a young man by the name of Gemge, to ride to Kearney on horseback. Night overtook us when we were between Lowell and Kearney, and we camped for the night near the south end of the B.&M.R.R. bridge across the Platte river. About 3 o'clock in the morning I awoke, and as the moon had risen and was shining brightly, I thought we had best continue our journey, so I awoke my companion and told him that I had concluded to start on. He was furious at being aroused, and swore at me for doing so. I told him it was almost morning, and he replied that it was a d—d lie; it was not after midnight. I told him I had looked at my watch and it was after three o'clock. He replied that my watch was as big a liar as I was. I told him it was well for him he did not mean what he said, and he replied that he meant just what he said and had the tools to back it up. I told him I had said I would shoot the first man that called me a liar, and he said: 'You do lie, and I have got right here (laying his hand on his pistol) what will back me up.' After a little more quarreling, in which he made repeated threats, I suddenly drew my revolver and shot him as he was sitting on the ground with his hand on his sixshooter. He fell back, shot just back of the ear with a 32-calibre 'blue jacket' ball. I then gathered the traps [personal effects] together and taking both horses started on going up the river toward Kearney.

"After daylight I left the horse with a settler and told him that my partner and I were looking for land and to keep the horse until called for, and for what I know the man keeps the horse yet, for I am sure my 'partner' never called for him.

"On the bridge south of Kearney I met some friends and with them I went to town and registered at the Commercial Hotel as F. A. Hague, and in answer to numerous inquiries I said I had just arrived from Colorado. In Kearney I met several old acquaintances, among others George Johnson, better known as 'Dutch Henry,' and a partner of his by the name of Hurst, also a Mr. Burns, who was around town with me nearly all day. March 21 Burns and I were arrested by the officers of the town and placed in jail. We did not know why we were arrested that night, but were told the next morning that we were suspected of the murder of Peter Geway [?]. I was acquitted, however, on examination but Burns was held on the testimony of a sporting lady he had previously met. Burns was held until court set and was then discharged, no evidence of guilt having been found against him. This was my first arrest, and before I was told what it was for I supposed it was for the murder of the young man, Gemge. I was very uneasy, and felt greatly relieved when told it was for the murder of Peter Geway, for of this crime I was entirely innocent.

"I now come to that which has given me notoriety, and for which I am to suffer death, April 26th—the murder of Mrs. Haralson and her three children and the killing of Peter Anderson, the Swede. It is not necessary for me to detail the events that occurred from the time I last left Iowa until the above murders were committed; I will simply describe the killing.

"After I was liberated from the jail at Kearney, 1878, where I was confined on a false charge of larceny, early in June 1878, and having met with Mrs. Haralson, she being confined in jail for supposed complicity in the escape of Mr. Haralson and Underwood, alias Nixon, [I] called on her at her home, remaining over night. The Haralson family were originally from Illinois, and were considered a bad 'crowd.' Haralson was a no-account fellow, and his wife was little better, though she was a shrewd woman, a great talker, and very inquisitive. She was of medium height, rather slender of build, sandy brown hair, grey eyes, rather large, and withal not a bad-looking woman. The oldest child, Daisy, was about ten years of age, rather delicate build, sharp, spry, and pretty. The next was Mabel, a pretty little girl of four years and my favorite. Then came Jasper, or 'Jesse,' the little boy, two years old. I thought a good deal of the children, and they in turn hung around me constantly and seemed to be very fond of me.

"At this meeting in June I came to an understanding with Mrs. Haralson that she would give me a deed of property—quarter section of land—at the expiration of six months, when she would 'prove up.'[8] Price $600 for farm, crops, etc. After making this bargain I began to work around and traveled about the state a good deal, part of the time in Kearney, Hastings, Bloomington, in all of which places I formed many acquaintances. July 2d I was in Hastings and made my head-quarters there until October 17th. In the meanwhile I was at Grand Island some while, and other places, and on one occasion met Mrs. Haralson, who was at Grand Island canvassing for subscribers for a book, and gave her some money. [I] agreed to go to her place September 15th, but it was October 18th before I reached there. At this time Mrs. Haralson made transfer of property to me, and I settled down for awhile at her house.

"I have been asked a good many times why I killed the Haralson family, and I have kept people in ignorance until now. They are simply these: First, she talked too much; second, she was too inquisitive; third, she would have 'given me away' had I let her live. I had told the woman a good deal about myself and she had gone through my trunk and looked over my letters. More than once she had told me I was guilty of murder; and so, knowing what she did, I thought it the safest plan to put her out of the way.

"I had come to this conclusion some while, and set the time Sunday morning, November 3d.

"The house is a sod one, contain[s] two rooms—the first with two beds and a crib, and the other a kitchen, where the cooking was done. In one corner of the room was the bed occupied by Mrs. Haralson and the two little girls. At the foot of the bed was the crib, wherein slept the baby boy, 'Jesse.' In the opposite corner of the room was my bed, and on the night of the murder this was occupied by a man of the name of Brown, a friend of Mrs. H. and myself. It was about 10 o'clock when I went to bed; Brown had gone a few minutes before. At this time the children were asleep, and shortly after retiring myself, Mrs. Haralson went to bed. We had no word of dispute in the evening and nothing unusual happened. I slept some during the night, but not sound; once I awakened Brown, and he growled considerably, and for a moment I had a notion to kill him along with the rest. This was Sunday morning and about dawn I got up. I had slept with my clothes on, and therefore did not need to dress. The first thing I did was to awaken Brown, who got up at once and went to feed the team and do other things about the stable. It was scarcely light at this time, and I went out and when about twenty rods northeast of the house near a straw stack on the plowed ground, I dug a hole with a spade and then returned to the house. This occupied about thirty minutes, and was not very hard work. When on the road to the house I stopped two or three times and looked around me and listened. I was ready for any sort of murder then and would have killed my best friend had he been in my way.

"Previous to going out I had placed an axe near the door of the house and immediately on returning, I took this and cautiously slipped in the house and approached the bed in which lay Mrs. Haralson asleep. She did not hear me; she was breathing regularly and the children were also sleeping soundly. I looked over the situation pretty well before I made the first move. Once more I listened—I could hear nothing but the steady breathing of the sleepers, and it seemed to me then that my heart stood still. At this moment—I do not know what tempted me—I passed across the room and pulled aside the curtain just a trifle. A ray of sunlight came in and slanted across the face of Mrs. Haralson, right over the partially covered face of Daisy. At this she moved a little, and murmured something like 'Mamma, mamma!' and then went on sleeping. If she had said anything more I might have lost my courage; but the time had come—now or never and, without waiting any longer I approached the bed of the mother and, getting good aim at her head, raised the axe and struck her once very hard on the left side of the head. The blow must have killed her almost instantly for she never spoke and scarcely stirred. To make sure of my work, I hit her a second time near the temple, and then I turned to Daisy, who was still sleeping with one little hand over her head and a few curls and part of her face visible. She laid between her mother and Mabel, with her head toward the foot of the bed; Mabel laid next to the wall. I struck her twice with the flat of the axe on the left side of the head near the temple. She too stirred but little and made no noise. Next I killed Mabel—struck her on the forehead with the flat side of the axe, one blow, and killed her dead.

"Then I killed 'Jesse,' who laid sleeping in the crib at the foot of the bed. I struck him three blows and killed him dead. I then stood still a moment, looking at the bed and as Daisy moaned and murmured, and writhed around some, I struck her two or three times more and then she laid quite still! All this time Brown was at the stable and did not return to the house for some time.

"The question now was how to get the bodies out of sight. I had not much time to lose. First I took the mother to the grave I had dug and threw her in. Then I came back and carried both girls at the same time and chucked them in the same hole with the mother; then I took the baby, 'Jesse,' and threw him in with the rest, covered them all over with a blanket, and scattered straw and dirt over them.

"The mother was dressed, but the two girls were in nightclothes and the baby had on a wrapper. After all this was done, which did not occupy thirty minutes, I returned to the house, washed my hands which were slightly bloody, and then went to the stable where Brown was fooling around, and after doing a few chores, he and I started for Hastings, and were two miles away by sun-up. At Juniata Brown left me. At Hastings three days, I made a few calls, but returned Tuesday evening home, or at Haralson's, and the next day bought a load of corn and went on as if nothing had occurred. When asked about Mrs. Haralson, I said she and her children had gone off with Brown, and probably would not return soon, if they did at all.

"I killed Peter Anderson, December 9, 1878. He was a Swede, though he spoke good English. He lived all alone in a little house seven miles southwest of Minden. He was a bachelor. I had agreed with him to change work in building sod buildings, and on or about the 1st of December, I went there and commenced to help him in his labor. His place was about 5 miles from the Haralson property. I worked there December 9, when, between the hours of twelve and two o'clock Monday in the daytime, as he had been sick a day or two, he accused me of poisoning him. I denied it and he called me a liar.

"We were in the house at the time and he was preparing dinner. When he called me a liar, I told him if he repeated it I would hit, though I had no idea of killing him at the time. He was not at all frightened at my words, but called me a liar again at once; then I knocked him down, and hit him two or three times and then let him up. I thought he would not care to repeat the trouble, and asked him if he would not give up. He replied, 'No; I'll fight you all day,' and at once started to pick up an axe; but I was too quick for him, and seizing a hammer that lay near by I struck him a blow over the left eye. He fell, and I struck him twice more on the forehead, breaking his skull. He threw up his hand, uttered a cry, and fell to the floor dead! I was not mad or excited at the time, but was altogether very cool. I simply was bound to protect myself and I did it. I pushed the body [to] one side, and sat down and ate my dinner. After doing this I took the body, carried it down cellar, and covered it up with clay and coal. Then I came up stairs and looking out of the window, saw some men coming in a wagon. I thought at first they would not stop but they did, and after rattling at the door awhile, called out, 'Pete, Pete!' but Pete didn't answer.

"Then they went away but soon returned with more men, and I thought something was going to happen then sure. I was out then hitching up the team when they arrived and one of the men asked me where Pete was, and I told him he had gone to see a man he had bought some wheat of some time before. I was about to go away then, but they stopped me and said they wanted to see Pete before I went away, and I said, 'I will wait till he comes; or you can go and see him.' They asked for the key of the house, which I gave them, and they went in, and while they were in the house, I fed the horses hay, and taking the gray horse, rode home.

"I was quite sure these men would find the body, and then I knew the game was up.

"As I rode home, I thought it all over, and concluded it was getting too hot for me there and that I had better skip. So I went home, changed my clothes, arranged with my neighbor's boy to have my trunk taken to Kearney and shipped to Omaha and by Friday night I was on my way out of the country. I determined to travel under the name of Galagher, and so registered wherever I stopped. Went to Bloomington, and from there to Red Cloud by conveyance and then took the train for Hastings. Here I stayed several days, and then took the B. & M. to Omaha, and from there east via the C. B. & Q.

"I need not detail the incidents of my trip to Ohio. I went there expecting to stay, as I knew it would be dangerous for me to return to Nebraska. In due time I reached my old home at Mt. Pleasant, Ohio, and found part of my friends there. I was not there long when one day, while in company with two young ladies, on our way to attend a party, I was arrested and soon after taken to Steubenville, and from there brought to Nebraska.

"What I have written may not be a full history of my life, but all the important events are given, and as nearly correct as possible. I have killed in all nine persons. I am 23 years of age, and am to be executed on the 26th of April, 1879. I cannot say that I regret what I have done—I can't say why—but I don't. I am a member of no church and no society. I never played a game of cards until I came west, or drank a drop of liquor. It has been thought by some that I am insane, but this is all a myth. I am perfectly sound in mind and body and never felt better in my life than I do at present.

"There is one thing more of which I wish to speak. I have taken particular pains not to bring my lady friends—of whom I had a good many—into any of my scrapes. Near Hastings there lived one whom I called 'Dolly.' I thought a good deal of her, but I think it was she who directed the officers of the place to find me. She must have done this through fear, for otherwise I think she would not. I passed a good deal of time at her house, and was always well entertained.

"And now I have little more to tell. My trial was a short affair, and like a small horse, quickly curried. I was taken from the Kearney Jail to Minden early Wednesday morning, January 15th, and the trial commenced before Judge Gaslin and a jury of twelve citizens at 9 o'clock of the same morning, and by four o'clock in the afternoon, I was convicted of the killing of Peter Anderson and sentenced to be hanged on the 26th day of April, 1879.[9]

"I pled not guilty to the charge of murdering Anderson, for I killed him in self defense, and I think was perfectly justifiable in doing it. It was simply a matter of death for one of us, and so I killed him to save myself. After the trial I was brought direct to Lincoln and lodged in prison for safe keeping, and here am now with a full consciousness that I am to swing in a short time. I should like to explain to you what a man's feelings are who is about to be hanged. It seems strange that I should sleep and eat well, that I should be anything but gloomy and despondent; but that is something, the explanation of which I do not know myself. Since my coming here, I have done considerable reading—have read history and travels, with a few biographies, all of which I have enjoyed. The Warden and Mr. Nobes, the Deputy, have been very kind to me, and I have not wanted for anything to make me comfortable, if there can be such a thing as 'comfort' to a man who is about to be hanged.

And here I may as well close the chapter.

Respectfully,
Stephen D. Richards.
Nebraska State Prison, Jan 23, 1879."

[Rolf's narrative resumes.]

Sunday, Apr. 27

I have been very stiff and sore to day from a blow across the knees received yesterday, while helping tear down the enclosure at the hanging.

Apr. 28

Joe Allen, Pete Brodine, and Gus. Pelander took dinner with us. Went to the post office and got a letter from Elma Johnson in which she tells me some interesting news about the Stenfelt girls, Ida and Vendla; they are inmates of a Chicago house of ill-fame under the names of Ida Cooksey and Ella Stone.

I have heard of a cruel practical joke that was played on John N. Peterson last Sunday while he [was] up at the Emigrant House visiting his girl, Miss Ebba Peterson.

It appears that John, who is working for Dahlstrom, rode up there on a steed which by a casual observer might easily be mistaken for a hat rack or a rail fence. When he got there he took his girl out for a ramble among the prairie flowers. Young Axel Hallgren and Andy Samuelson took advantage of their absence to deck Peterson's horse in the most fantastic style imaginable. They dressed him up in a pair of old over-alls and gunny sacks; tied an armful of hair to his tail; stuck a piece of dried antelope skin up like a plume between his ears; stuck a large, wooden maul under the saddle; and put a pair of old no. 14 brogans in the stirrups. The poor animal looked like a fourth of July rag company, and when Peterson returned from his promenade he was at first astonished, then disgusted, and then angry, while the boys hid behind the straw stack and laughed like hyenas. Peterson will go afoot next time.

May 3d

Served as Clerk of Election of Center precinct at the Emigrant House. The election was for voting "For or Against Bonds," the bonds being to fund the old county debt.[10] Forty-eight votes were cast in Center precinct, all "against bonds." The rest of the board of election were Aaron W. Johnson, clerk; Dahlstrom, Albert Sundblad, and John Johnson, judge.

May 5th

Aaron Blomquist and I drove to Bloomington to homestead land. We passed through Sacramento, a new town just started in the south eastern part of Phelps County, composed of three or four sod houses and one frame building and contains a store, a blacksmith shop, and newspaper office.

Got to Bloomington about 3 o'clock P.M. and found the town much improved since the advent of the Republican Valley Railroad, which is bringing the town right up.[11]

I homesteaded the S.E. 1/4 of Section 18, Town 7, Range 18 West and Blomquist homesteaded my old pre-emption claim.[12]

May 6

Got back from Bloomington.

May 9th

Went out to view my new homestead, which I found in possession of a herd of Antelope, which I put to flight with my rifle.

Ida Bragg and her mother visited us this afternoon.

Wrote 3 letters, one to Thilda, 1 to Elma Johnson, and a communication to the Phelps County Pioneer signed "Johnny Hayseed."

The results of the last election have been announced: For Bonds 9; Against Bonds 200.

May 13

Have just got back from a trip to the mills at Orleans with a load of grist. Started yesterday morning, stopped in the mill over night, and got back this afternoon in company with Jim Lukecart of Industry.[13] The last copy of the Police Gazette contains an illustrated account of the hanging of S. D. Richards. Both the account and illustrations are remarkable for its variance with facts.

May 14

Miss Annie Nelson and her father took dinner with us.

May 16

I was surprised this morning to receive a call from Thilda Danielson and a young lady from Kearney, who was introduced to me as Augusta

Winholz. They staid with us all day and this evening we went out walking, taking Ida Bragg with us.

May 18
I am reading "Wanderings in Caanan" by John Ashworth.
Called on Thilda D. and Augusta Winholz this evening.

May 19
On returning from a drive with John P. Nelson, I found a note from Thilda awaiting me in which she stated that she was sick and wanted to see me immediately. As I braced up and went to see her, found her with her folks and friends visiting at J. P. Ericson's. I was invited to stop to supper which I did. Thilda was not very sick. While there a heavy storm of rain and hail came up and the water poured down as I have never seen before. In a short time the canyon below Ericson's was a rushing torrent and almost impassable with a team.

May 20
At the earnest solicitation of Thilda I stayed at Danielson's last night. Lee Hallgren was there also. Thilda was very sick and was afraid she would die, but as good luck would have it she didn't.

May 21
This morning Gus and Hilda came home on a visit and I took one of Gus' mules and rode down to Bragg's to see Ida. Stayed there awhile and was well entertained by Ida showing me her photographs and some love letters, among others one from Aug. Jacobson in which he offered her his heart and hand, but which as she informed me, she respectfully declined.

This afternoon Ida Bragg paid me a return visit accompanied by Thilda Danielson.

May 22
Thilda stayed with us last night.

May 26
Got a letter from Bert Wilson of the "Pioneer" in which he requests me to take subscription for his paper and also to continue to write up

items from Phelps Center. I also got a postal card from S. C. Nelson in which he states that he is [at] Granite Cañon, Wyo. Ter.

May 27
Dahlstrom, Stromquist, Pete Holm, J. P. Bragg, and I have been down to Crazy Miller's claim on Spring Creek after 4 loads of poles for Stromquist's house.

Had to work hard and had a tough time getting out of the canyons.

May 28
Called on Thilda this evening.

May 30
Bill Robb, a Gosper county ranchman, came here and wanted me to sign a bail bond for Old Bill Lee to get him out of jail. I did.

May 31
Thilda, who has been staying with us a couple of days, went home this evening.

Sunday, June 1st
John Hendricks and I called on Ida Bragg, whom we found at home all alone. We had not been there long when Gus Anderson, Will Anderson, Gus Pelander, and John N. Peterson hove in sight. We were there first, however, and the boys soon took their leave. We then took Ida with us and went over to Danielson's and spent the evening.

June 2
Last night Pete Holm, the Danielson boys, and myself stayed up all night at Johannes Anderson's armed with shotguns to kill some coyotes that have been prowling around and killing 8 of Anderson's turkeys. We saw no coyote.

This morning I went with Judge Wilke to Williamsburg to attend court. The business of importance was transacted during the day. Going back this evening I rode with Old Sam Moser of Rock Falls. Besides us there were Sheriff Sweezey, Judge Wilke, Bob and Sam Dale. On the way we encountered a badger. I ran him into a hole and fired two shots from my revolver into his stern while he was digging. This not having the desired effect, I laid hold of his tail and pulled him out, and as he turned around to bite me I fired a shot into his eye that settled him.

Got a copy of the "Phelps County Pioneer" to day. It is much enlarged and quite newsy. My contribution appears under head of "Phelps Centre Items." I also got a letter from Elma Johnson.

June 3rd
Called on Thilda this evening. Found Little Carrie there.

CHAPTER 11

The Black Hills and the Southwest

Kearney, June 4 [1879]

Left home this morning and went to Kearney with the intention of going west for a season. Father and Emil took me in. Thilda also went in to day and I met her this afternoon. She has cried a good deal and begs me to stay, saying that if I go, I will never come back to her.

Sidney, Neb., June 6th

Left Kearney yesterday on the Emigrant train and the last thing I saw was Thilda on the platform with tearful eyes and waving me a last adieu. Passed through Plum Creek and several towns of less importance and stopped at North Platte long enough to take [a] look over town. The residence of "Buffalo Bill" was pointed out to me. It was one of the finest residences in town.[1] Passed last night sleeping as well as I was able in my seat and part of the time in conversation with a young fellow named Bardell, who was on his way to Nevada.

Struck Sidney early this morning and found it to be a town of some 2,000 inhabitants and as lively as a nest of fleas. It is built in a valley walled in by limestone bluffs and through the center of which flows Lodge Pole Creek, a clear, rapid stream by means of which the town is irrigated. Adjoining the town is Fort Sidney, a military post occupied by several companies of cavalry and infantry. It is well laid out, trees planted, and irrigation ditches dug. The officers quarters are quite handsome and the soldiers barracks are also very neat and clean and over all floats the glorious star spangled banner. After breakfast I paid a visit to the fort and saw the soldiers drilling.[2]

Sidney is a hard town. It is the principal outfitting point for the Black Hills and is full of freighters and teams: Soldiers, cowboys, bullwhackers, mule skinners, gamblers, prostitutes, and pimps swarm on the streets, saloon and gambling halls are numerous and a dance hall is in full blast. Nearly everybody carries arms and the sharp crack of the pistol is heard at very short intervals.

This evening I formed the acquaintance of "Ash-hollow Jack" the famous scout, hunter, guide, and champion pistol shot of the plains. He is a young man of slim build about 6 feet tall. His face was goodlooking, his teeth white and regular, a well formed mouth shaded by a long silky mustache; his eyes are a steel blue or gray and very piercing; his hair is worn long and hangs down over his shoulders in long dark ringlets. He wears one of the broadest of broad brimmed hats, fine boots, and a dark suit of clothes.

In the course of conversation he told me that the reason he was called "Ash-hollow Jack" was because he was the only survivor out of eight men who were massacred by the Indians at Ash Hollow. He told me that he had killed seven Indians altogether.

Sidney, June 7th
Visited Joe Lane's Dance Hall last night in company with "Ash-hollow Jack." It was a large wooden structure with smooth floor. One end was taken up by a bar behind which a noted young desperado called Reddy McDonald was dispensing liquid poison to the habitues of the place. At the other end of the room was a raised platform on which was seated the band consisting of two or three fiddlers and a cornet player. Along the sides of the room were benches. On the floor were the dancers: Bullwhackers, cowboys, and soldiers and gamblers with their partners the professional dance girls and prostitutes. Each set danced was wound up with, "Promenade to the bar" and every man would waltz up to the bar with his girl and treat her. This little diversion cost 50 cents. Each girl seemed to be known by some nickname, such as "Mountain Kate," "Red Headed Kit," "Old Logan," etc. I noticed one girl in particular, a pretty, well built little blonde who seemed to be a general favorite and was called "Dolly." She seemed the life of the outfit, bright, and witty; she showed unmistakable signs of culture and refinement.

Lane's dance hall is the most popular resort in the city. It has been the scene of many frontier fights and border brawls, and the crack of the deadly sixshooter has often been heard within its wall[s].

Sidney is a hard town in general and has been the theater of many a bloody frontier drama. Shootings and lynchings are of frequent occurrence, the last one being the shooting of Henry Loomis by Dud Douglas, a Texas outlaw, and the subsequent lynching of Douglas to a telegraph pole in front of the Lockwood House a short time ago.[3]

To day I made the acquaintance of Bill Godkin and Charley Simmons, a couple of travelling photographers who have located here temporarily and are doing a rushing business, especially among the sporting fraternity. I saw several negatives taken by the boys of fast women of the town stark naked.[4]

This afternoon I noticed a crowd on a street corner and winding my way thither, I found the center attraction was a little stubby looking man in a rusty black suit, who was trying to preach to the crowd from a Bible in his hand. It was about the hardest material for a congregation he ever tackled I dare say. Jeers and jokes met him on every hand and when he incidentally remarked that he had "been on the road to heaven seventeen years," "Ash-hollow Jack," who was in the crowd, interrupted him by saying that "if he had been on the road to heaven that long and hadn't got any further than Sidney he had better turn back and try a new route!" The crowd roared so at this sally that the little preacher became disgusted, put his Bible in his grip sack, and started up the railroad track in the direction of Cheyenne.

Saw a sailcar to day. It was a handcar in which a sail had been raised and it sped along the track like a race horse.

I saw a prairie dog town right in front of the Lockwood House and the little animals are so tame they will eat out of a person's hand.

This evening I met Tom Williams, a bullwhacker recently from the Black Hills. He asked me to join him on a trip to the South Platte to-morrow, and I assented.

Lewis Canyon, Sunday, June 8th

Tom Williams and I left Sidney this morning on foot bound for the South Platte. Tom had a bundle of blankets to carry and I had a bag of grub. The sun was pretty hot and we got very tired walking. Our course lay along the Sidney and Sterling stage road through a rough county with sharp peaks and curious knobs jutting out here and there.[5] Thousands of prickly pears in full bloom lined the way and presented a gorgeous appearance. We suffered a good deal from the heat but more from thirst as we had taken only a small bottle of water with us from Lodge-pole Creek. This evening we struck Lewis Canyon, where a cool, clear spring of fresh water bubbled up from among the rocks and we refreshed ourselves and concluded to stay all night, especially as here is a small "shack" or shanty belonging to the stage driver.

Saw quite a number of antelope to day, one this evening close to the spring. I fired several shots at them with my revolver and wounded one but could not get it. I also killed two snakes, a rattler, and a blue racer.

June 9th
The stage driver did not turn up last night so we took possession of the "shack," cooked our supper, slept in the bunk, and this morning cooked our breakfast. "Borrowed" a couple of bottles which we filled with water and started across the divide. Passed through several large prairie dog towns and large herds of long horned Texas cattle and arrived at "Gunn's Ranch" on the South Platte about dinner time.[6] Heard very discouraging reports of the South Platte country and concluded to go back to Sidney. A couple of men with teams loaded with wool started for Sidney after dinner and we decided to accompany them back. They were leading a saddle pony, which I was allowed to ride awhile. Tom got an occasional ride on a wool sack. Camped this evening on the divide without wood or water.

Going down yesterday and coming back to day we passed Riverside post office, which was nothing more nor less than a tin box on top of a pole along side of the road right out in the wilderness. Here the stage driver, as he comes by, deposits mail for the ranchmen and cowboys of the surrounding country and they in turn ride up on their ponies, open the box, and take out such mail as may belong to them, put others back, deposit their letters, and ride away, and no complaints are ever made that anyone takes what does not belong to him. What kind of a show would a post office like this stand in a so called civilized community?

June 10
Got back to Sidney, met "Ash-hollow Jack," and he introduced me to a cowpuncher called "Bill," who was shot through the shoulder, neck, and arm in a row at Joe Lane's dance hall about three weeks ago. He was just out of the military hospital and did not look much the worse for his wounds.

Sidney, June 11
Tom Williams and I have made arrangements to go to the Black Hills with a "bulltrain." The party will consist of St. Leger Beck, a well-

known frontiersman and bullwhacker; Mrs. Beck, his wife, a well preserved lady on the shady side of 40; Crazy Bill Beck, his son, a hopeless lunatic; Capt. Allison Howes; Tom Williams; and I. We had three "lead" wagons and three "trail" wagons drawn by oxen, or bulls, as they are called in this country; the drivers are termed "bullwhackers." We will start for Deadwood in the morning over the Sidney "trail," which is about 300 miles long through a country infested by hostile Indians and road agents.[7]

"Cap" Howes is loaded with lard, hams, and bacon and Beck with flour and grain.

Camp on the Greenwood, Neb., June 13
We left Sidney yesterday morning, made a short drive, and camped last night at Nine Mile Water Holes where there was a stage station. This morning we pulled out early, made a dry camp at noon, and camped this evening near Greenwood ranch on a stream called the Greenwood or Tusler's Creek. Here the Tusler boys have a large cattle ranch[8] and employ quite a number of cowboys, among them being John F. Shafer, Ex-Sheriff of Phelps County. I did not see him this evening as he is absent on a roundup.

This is a pretty rough country, the bold rocky bluffs covered with stunted pine and cedar. The deep canyons and the pretty green valley with the clear stream running through it and the thousand cattle grazing on hill and dale present a picture at once beautiful and animating.

I shot a rattlesnake to day with my sixshooter.

Camp on Pumpkin Seed Creek, June 14
Made short drive to day as we had to "double up" so many times climbing sand hills. We are now camped on Pumpkin Creek within a mile or two of Court House Rock, a noted land mark in the old Overland days. It is about 500 feet high with terraces, pillars, towers, and dome, and bears a striking resemblance to a stupendous pile of ruins; hence its name.

Deputy Sheriff Tom Ryan of Sidney and another fellow armed with six shooters and Winchesters passed by looking for a horse thief.

Sunday, June 15
Laid over to day in the sandhills about half a mile from Pumpkin Creek to give the teams a rest. I amused myself reading "Pickwick Papers,"

varied by an occasional shot at some stray antelope. This afternoon, while lying in the covered wagon being all alone in camp, I heard a noise alongside the wagon and looking out, to my surprise saw a man, tall and well developed, well dressed, with a long linen duster on, a red silk handkerchief knotted about his throat, a cartridge belt and ivory handled sixshooter strapped to his waist standing before me. He saluted me with "Hello, pard! got any water?" I referred him to the water keg and he helped himself. He then sat down on the water keg and wiping the sweat from his face remarked "that it was a hot day," and informed me that he was on the Sidney stage and left it down at the creek, while he went on ahead. Pretty soon the stage coach with it[s] 4 horses hove in sight around a sandhill and my companion arose to meet it, saying that his name was Boone May and that he would probably see me again. I then realized that I had been talking to Boone May, the most noted scout, detective, Indian fighter, and shooting man of the Black Hills. He is at present employed as "shotgun messenger" or guard for the Sidney and Deadwood stage line. He has had more fights with Indians, road agents and desperadoes, captured more stage robbers and horsethiefs, and killed more men than any other man in the Black Hills. He is the man who in company with another messenger named [illegible word] killed the notorious road agent and murderer, Frank Towle, and brought him into Cheyenne.[9]

His eyes were a peculiar feature, being of an indescribable hue between yellow, green, and grey, and had a curious, restless look about them. He was a man I would instinctively fear without knowing who he was.

Mooresville, June 16
Resumed our journey this morning. Crossed the North Platte this afternoon on the toll bridge, at one end of which was the toll station and post office called Camp Clark. At the other end was a ranch and store called Mooresville. On an island near the north end of the bridge is a two-story block house, with the upper story jutting out at right angles with the lower. Both stories are loopholed for riflemen and it was built to protect the bridge from the depredating bands of Sioux and Cheyenne who infest the country.[10]

In full view up the river several miles is Chimney Rock, a celebrated landmark shaped like an inverted funnel.[11]

We camped near Mooresville.

We are having a good time, plenty of good grub, and take things easy. We pass the time in camp in reading, target shooting, and card playing. Mrs. Beck is well versed in the mysteries of Euchre and Cassino and is very fond of playing.

Crazy Bill Beck is also a constant source of amusement. He is always scratching himself, muttering, and holding long conversations with an imaginary enemy whom he calls Bill Price and whom he is continually threatening to knock him down and kill him. He sometimes becomes excited and clubs the ground, imagining it is his enemy and sometimes he pull[s] up whole handsfull of grass. He is not allowed to carry firearms as he has twice shot at his father and once threw an axe at his head. He is a natural snake charmer, and can pick up rattlesnakes and handle them with impunity without being bitten. He is withal a good bullwhacker and can handle the heavy bull whip with the skill and accuracy of an expert.

June 19

Camped night before last at Red Willow Ranch, where we heard that the horse thief whom Tom Ryan was hunting had been in the vicinity. After driving a few miles we were overtaken by one of those terrible hail storms which are so prevalent in the North Platte country and forced to go into camp.

The hailstones fell thick and fast, some of them as large as a hen's egg, and the rain beat through the canvas covering of the wagon soaking everything, including our clothes and blankets. Our cattle were turned loose and stampeded before the storm.

The water was about 6 inches deep on the level prairie.

This morning we hunted up our cattle, which had taken refuge in the breaks of Red Willow Creek, some six or eight miles from camp.

Old Beck, while out hunting the cattle, came, unexpectedly, on the horse thief, whom he found ambushed in a ravine with a Winchester rifle and his horse picketed some distance away. Beck says it was not his funeral, and as he was not hunting horse thieves just then, he went on his way and attended to his own business.

Running Water, Sunday, June 22

We are now camped on the Niobrara at Running Water Station, which is kept by the noted Squawman, Hank Clifford, who's married to a daughter of Red Dog, Chief of the Sioux. He has a swarm of squaws and half breed children about his ranch. The country about here is hilly and covered with a straggling growth of pine.[12]

While bringing up water for cooking Tom Williams and I caught a snake and put it in the water bucket, and when Mrs. Beck undertook to make coffee she poured the snake into the coffee pot from where it wriggled out and crawled away, to the horror and disgust of Mrs. Beck.

Camp on the White Earth River, June 23
Camped for noon on Little White Clay. This afternoon we got into the famous Mauvaises Terres or Bad Lands, which is the natural wonderland of the plains. We drove down a long, crooked, steep, rocky hill called Breakneck Hill and into the beautiful valley of the White Earth river. The country is wild and rocky, some of the rocks being worn by the combined element of wind and water into the most curious and beautiful shapes. We are camped at the old Red Cloud Agency but the agency buildings have been torn down and moved to Pine Ridge, where the Agency is now located. We can see the buildings and flag at Fort Robinson, a mile or so up the river.[13]

Big Cottonwood, June 24
Camped for noon on Little Cottonwood. Met "Sandy's" bull train this afternoon. Among his drivers was "Arkansas Joe," commonly called "Arkenson," a notorious, bullwhacker, fighter, and desperado. He was a perfect specimen of physical manhood. He was a handsome man with clean cut features and long, straw-colored mustache.

June 26
Camped near the Black Banks and I went fossil hunting. Found five specimens of petrified fish, turtles and snakes, and shells.

State Springs, June 28
Camped at noon on Horsehead Creek and I took a bath in its cool, limpid waters. Tom and I paid a visit to the famous underground stables close to the ranch. This ranch used to be the headquarters of Dunk Blackburn's gang of road agents and horse thieves and the stable, which is nothing but a cave dug in the bank of the creek and hidden by a thick growth of underbrush, used to be the rendezvous of the outlaws.

At Horsehead we ran across Boone May and his pard, Scott Davis, also a shotgun messenger and noted footpad exterminator.[14]

For the last three days we have been coming through a prairie dog town which is said to be thirty miles long. Camped at State Springs. Water bitter as gall.

Buffalo Gap, Dak., June 29

Crossed the South Cheyenne this morning on a bridge near Forbes Ranch. After crossing we drove through a canyon full of the remains of a petrified forest. I gathered some beautiful specimens of petrified wood. Camped this evening at Buffalo Gap Ranch.

Beaver Creek, June 30

Camped on Beaver, the scene of the terrible water spout of the 16 of June. The whole valley presents an appearance of desolation. Broken wagon[s], household furniture, and other debris and relics are scattered. In this waterspout 11 persons, emigrants, and freighters who were camped on the creek were drowned. All the bodies but one have been recovered and are buried near Buffalo Gap Ranch. Encountered a hailstorm but it proved of short duration. Killed a rattle snake.[15]

We crossed Dry creek, the scene of the latest stage robbery on the ninth June, in which the driver, Dick Cole, was stopped, the passenger[s] forced to give up their valuables, and the mail robbed by two men, supposed to be Lame Johnny and his pard, Frank Harris.

July 2, 1879

Tom Keating's train caught up with us to day. They informed us that they found a man hanging to a tree on Dry Creek last night. They took him down and buried him at the foot of the tree. The man was recognized as "Lame Johnny," the notorious murderer and desperado.[16]

Rapid City, Dak., July 4

This morning I was roused from sleep by a salutation from Capt. Howe's carbine. I stuck my pistol through a rent in the wagon cover and fired a volley. After breakfast we yoked up and drove into Rapid City, where we spent the greater part of the day. Rapid is a live city and a big crowd was in town and much shooting, yelling, and horse racing. Many hunters, miners, and sports from the neighboring hills were in town. Among other notables was Captain Jack Crawford, known all over the west as "Capt. Jack," the Poet Scout of the Black Hills, a noted scout, plainsman, and newspaper correspondent. He is a fine-looking young fellow with long, dark-brown hair falling in curls over his shoulder.[17] Attended a ball this evening at Lewis Hall at which all the fast women of the hills seemed present and fun ran riot.

We camped this evening just out of town on Rapid Creek, a swift-running stream of clear, cold mountain water.

The scenery around here is grand and beautiful beyond description. Custer's and Harney's peaks lift their rocky battlement[s] high above the pine clad hills and their tops are often hidden above the clouds.

Centennial Prairie, Dak., July 7

Passed through Sturgis City (Scooptown) this morning and made our noon camp on Bear Butte Creek, which takes its name from Bear Butte, a solitary mountain towering above the foothills a few miles distant. Tom and I took a bath in the creek, the waters of which were as clear as crystal and as cool as ice. Soon after leaving "Scooptown" we commenced to climb and our progress was necessarily slow. We passed through Crook City a few miles further on with high, pine covered mountains all around. Crook City is a city of blasted hopes. During the first stages of the Black Hills excitement Crook was a formidable rival of Deadwood but now it is on the decline and about half the buildings are empty. We kept on a few miles further and camped on "Centennial Prairie," a beautiful plateau just in the northern edge of the foothills.

July 8

I nightherded the cattle last night and had a hard time on horseback. We have been ascending and descending mountains all day, but made only a few miles owing to dangerous character of these mountain roads. Camped this evening in a gulch about 2 miles from Deadwood. Woods are all around as the ground is covered with underbrush, grass, and wildflowers of many hues and varieties.

Mrs. Beck and I went picking wild raspberries and strawberries, which were plenty near the camp.

Deadwood, July 9th

Pushed on this morning and crossing the last mountain descended into Whitewood Gulch and the far famed city Deadwood lay spread out below us.

It was an animating scene. The gulch was alive with men and teams, miners' cabins were scattered in the gulch and on the hillsides, sluice boxes and flumes were seen on every hand. Passing on we came through Elizabethstown, Montana City and Fountain City, Chinatown, all suburbs of Deadwood; but it would be hard to tell where one town leaves off and the other commences as there is an unbroken string of buildings all along into Deadwood. We found ourselves at last on the principal street of Deadwood, a narrow street chuck full of bulltrains and mule trains. We stopped nearly opposite the Gem Dance Hall and we unloaded, that is Cap. Howes and I, while Beck and Tom Williams drove on up to Lead City where they were to unload.

Deadwood, Dak., July [10]

Deadwood is built in Whitewood gulch, a narrow defile enclosed by high, pine-covered mountains. On one side rises a cliff 1,700 feet [high] called the "White Rocks." Deadwood has an elevation of 4,640 feet. It is closely built and has two narrow streets running lengthways of the gulch and several smaller cross streets. It has a population of about 4,000. It has several brick buildings, churches, and school houses, and one first class hotel, the Welch House. Second class hotels and restaurants are numerous where meals can be had for 25 c. Saloons, gambling halls, and bagnios are as numerous almost as hair on a dog's back. Three dance halls are in full blast, The Gem, Delmonico's, and Tom Miller's Music Hall. Three theaters are running, the Gem, Metropolitan, and Langrishe.[18] The streets present a lively appearance. Bulltrains and mule outfits, bullwhackers, muleskinners, miners with their pack animals, and cowboys with their bronchos swarm everywhere. Everything is bustle and boom. Whitewood Creek flows through the town, its water almost red as blood from the washings of the sluiceboxes. While unloading yesterday I became acquainted with a typical western boy. He was about 16 years old, small for his age, wore a broad brimmed hat and blue woolen shirt, chewed tobacco, smoked, drank, and swore like a bullwhacker. He had been in the hills about 2 years, and has been a miner, muleskinner, bullwhacker, cowboy song and dance boy in the theaters, and has followed various other occupations. He is sharp as a steel trap, and had not been with me more than two hours till he had told me over a hundred lies and borrowed half a dollar of me. He offered to be my guide about town and took me around to the Gem dance hall, where I met the notorious "Calamity Jane" and "Broncho Moll." "Calamity" is a woman of whom much has been written and I have often seen her name in the papers. Judge Maguire in his work "The Black Hills and American Wonderland" has described her thus:[19]

"After the usual hand-shaking was over the unaffected, 'heart-in-your-hand' kind, peculiar to the mountains, I asked my old Yellowstone friend, Jack Baronett, the first white man to enter the Geyser basins and one of the pioneers of the Black Hills:

'How far is it to Deadwood, Jack?'

'Only a mile and half; that girl on the horse is going there now.'

'Girl! What girl? I don't see anybody on a horse but that dare-devil boy yonder.'

'Why, that's a girl on that bucking cayuse, that's 'Calamity Jane'

"And 'Calamity Jane' she was, as I ascertained in getting some items in regard to her remarkable career of ruin, disgrace, and recklessness. There was nothing in her attire to distinguish her sex as she sat astride the fiery horse she was managing with a cruel Spanish bit in its mouth save her small, neat-fitting gaiters and sweeping raven locks. She wore coat and pantaloons of buckskin, gaily beaded and fringed, fur-trimmed vest of tanned antelope skin, and a broad-brimmed Spanish hat completed her costume. Throwing herself from side to side in the saddle with the daring self-confidence of a California buckaroo in full career, she spurred her horse up the gulch, over ditches, and through reservoirs and mudholes, at each leap of the fractious animal giving as good imitation of a Sioux war whoop as a feminine voice is capable of.

"'Calamity Jane' is a character in the mountains. She has redeeming qualities. Everybody may have. She comes from a Virginia City, Nev. family of respectability and intelligence. The first step of ruin taken, she had not the moral courage to seek retrievement—what encouragement would she have received, had she attempted to do so?—and still there were levels of infamy and degradation to which she could not sink. If she must be a woman of the world she would save at least her independence of character—while following the path of infamy through all its dark windings, she would continue mistress of her own destiny. She sought not the sympathy of kindred associations, but preferred to stand alone, in brave defiance of a frowning world. Donning male attire in the mining regions of Nevada, where no legal restraints were imposed upon such freaks of iniquitous eccentricity, she 'took to the road,' and has ever since been nomadic in her habits—now forming one of a hunting party, then participating in a mining stampede, again attached to and moving with a freight train, and, it is said, she has even rendered good service as a scout in an Indian campaign. She has had experience as a stage driver, and can draw the reins as skillfully over six horses as a veteran John, and handles a revolver with the dexterity and fires it with the accuracy of a Texas Ranger. She is still in early womanhood, and her rough and dissipated career has not yet altogether 'Swept away the lines where beauty lingers.'"

[Rolf's narrative resumes.]

Jane is a hard customer and travels on her muscle. She is very handy with either fists or pistols and it takes a good man to get away with her. In the course of the evening I saw her "stand off" with a beerglass, a big burly bullwhacker called Taylor, who was drunk and tried to impose on her.

The other girl, Broncho Moll, is a plump, handsome girl evidently of Irish extraction. She used to belong to the Black Hills gang of road agents and gained her appellation of "Broncho" from the fact that when she first appeared in Deadwood she was dressed in a suit of men's clothes, had two six shooters in her belt, and was mounted on a stolen broncho pony.

In company with Willie Woodall, my guide, I also took in Tom Miller's music hall, which was under the management of Charlie Utter, known all over the west as "Colorado Charlie," the partner of "Wild Bill."[20] He is a small man apparently about 35 years of age but in reality nearly 50. His long yellow hair falls over his shoulders in ringlets, his yellow mustache was long and the ends waxed, and his goatee was of the most elegant description. His clothes were of the best black broadcloth, his vest white, his shirt collar and necktie were also of immaculate whiteness, his shirt studs were gold nuggets about the size and shape of peanuts, his watch chain was made of various sized gold coin linked together and presented a gorgeous appearance, his well oiled locks were surmounted by an elegant sombrero of marvelous breadth of brim. He was a good specimen of the frontier dandy, and looks as dainty as a girl but his appearance belies his real character, for he is noted for his bravery and endurance, is a noted scout, and has come out first best of many desperate encounters with Indians and frontier desperadoes. At this place I met "Madame Mustache," another famous frontier character. She is known in almost every mining camp from California to the Black Hills. She is here running a "21" game.

We afterwards took in the Langrishe Theater, where a variety troupe were showing their legs to a crowd of miners and freighters, which applauded vigorously.

We also took in "Chinatown," a row of Chinese bagnios and gambling halls facing Whitewood Creek.[21]

Each Chinese house of ill fame was a small frame shanty, with a hole in the wall or the door about 1 foot square at which sat the Chinese courtesans with lips and cheeks painted bright red and eyebrows black, soliciting passers bye in "pidgeon" English. In one corner of their rooms was an ugly little Chinese Idol with incense and "joss" paper burning before it. In the gambling halls were scores of white men drinking and playing Chinese poker, a game much in vogue here. The Chinese are great gamblers and their skill with cards has been well illustrated by Bret Harte in his "Heathen Chinese."

I danced several times with the girls at the Gem last night, particularly with a dashing brunette called Lillie Phelan. She made quite an impression on me but more particularly on my pocket book.

This morning I rambled around town and among other things visited the graveyard up on the side of the mountain in South Deadwood. Here by an old pine stump I found "Wild Bill's" grave.[22] At the head of the grave was a board about 4 feet high, 2 feet wide, and 2 inches thick, painted white, and on it, in black letters, the following curious inscriptions:

J. B. Hickok
"Wild Bill"
Aged 49 Years,
Killed by the Assassin
Jack McCall!
In Deadwood Black Hills
August 2nd 1876.
"Pard we will meet again in the
Happy Hunting Grounds to part

no more, Good bye!"
Colorado Charlie
(C. H. Utter.)

Here rest the bones of the most famous frontiersman of any age. A man before whose exploits those of Daniel Boone, Davy Crockett and Kit Carson, and other border heroes fade into insignificance.

[July 11?]
I slept last night at the Elkhorn Corral where we put up our teams and where a room is fitted up with bunks for the accommodation of customers. There I met Ned North, a young ranchman from the Belle Fourche county and who told me if I would go with him I could get employment on a hay ranch. I decided to go with him and this afternoon we left Deadwood with a hay wagon and 4 yoke of bulls. Ned was a tall, lanky hoosier who had been in the hills about 3 years. He was a clever and entertaining young fellow, and made the time pass pleasantly by telling stories of the early days of the Hills.

Scotney's Ranch, Hay Creek, Dak., July 13 [12?]
We camped last night on False Bottom Creek and three frontiersmen from the Yellowstone camped with us, their names were Hank Bloom, Al Scotney, and Jim McCune. They pushed on this morning to Scotney's ranch.

Ned and I yoked up after breakfast and started for Scotney's Ranch passing through Spearfish, a pretty little town located on a clear beautiful stream of water named Spearfish Creek. We crossed the Red Water, a good sized stream with a valley full of farms and fields of waving grain, ascended the high, rocky pine-covered bluffs and passing through the rocky foothills, descended to the valley of Hay Creek, a beautiful valley with long waving grass and a stream flowing through it, bordered with a luxuriant growth of trees and brush.

Scotney's ranch was a log cabin, a story and a half high, enclosed by a fence and with stables and corral close by. Inside the house was a mongrel assortment of saddles, bridles, rifles, six shooters, bear skins, and deer's antlers and such litter as is usually found in a frontier cabin. John Scotney, the ranchman, was a rough looking, powerful man, yet withal very good natured. His house keeper, Mrs. Sanbolacken, a

Norwegian lady, was very kind and attentive to me. Hank Bloom, Al Scotney, and Jim McCune are stopping at the ranch, Al being a brother of John.

This creek empties into the Belle Fourche a few miles below here, and as its name indicates, is the best hay producing section of the Black Hills. It is about 25 miles northwest of Deadwood and has its rise in the Bear Lodge Mountains, which loom up to the west of here.

All the ranchmen on this creek are engaged in the making of hay from the luxuriant wild grasses which abound and find a ready sale for it in Deadwood at from $25 to $50 per ton.

Hay Creek, Sun., July 14 [13]

Beautiful weather. Amused ourselves playing cards, reading, and target shooting. Al Scotney is the best shot in the outfit, being able to knock a cartridge shell off the fence at a hundred yards every shot. Al has just come down from Montana with a drove of ponies and mules, which he has left in charge of his brother John. He is one of Gen. Terry's most trusted scouts.[23]

Ned North and Jim McCune mounted their horses and went up the creek a couple of miles, hunting. They returned with sixteen prairie chickens and three cottontail rabbits which they had shot with their rifles and revolvers.

This afternoon Ned and I went fishing and caught quite a string of suckers and sunfish in which the creek abounds.

Hay Creek, Sunday, July 20

Life on a hay ranch is not as dull as I at first supposed it would be. We do not work hard, have plenty to eat, and lots of time for hunting the game which abounds in the vicinity. We pass away the evening in card playing, reading, or song and story. Wild fruits are plenty along the creek and in the adjacent hills, such as wild cherries, sand cherries, bull berries, currants, and gooseberries. I see something new every day to interest and amuse. One of the most curious things I have seen is the horned toad, which looks more like a short and squat lizard than a toad. It is covered with sharp horns from an eight[h] of an inch to half inch in length and is so tame it can be picked up in the hand and will make no effort to escape.

Duck Kelly, a noted hunter who supplies the Deadwood market

with game, called on us last week. This is a favorite stomping ground for bands of predatory Indians and only last year they stole 4 head of horses from the ranch and ran Ned North in. They attacked several ranches and committed various depredations in the vicinity. We do not fear them, but we seldom leave the ranch without being armed.

Hay Creek, Sun., July 27

Ned North and I went hunting on several small lakes about half way between here and the Bell Fourche. Ned had his Winchester and I had a Remington rifle. We did not have very good luck and only killed two prairie chickens, one curlew, and one duck.

Bloom, McCune, and Al Scotney left us last week and started for the Powder River country to hunt up a band of about 60 ponies hidden in that part of the country by the Cheyennes last spring at the time of their last raid.

Hay Creek, Aug. 3rd

John Mahon and a young fellow from Deadwood has been staying with us a few days. This morning Ned and John went out hunting and returned with 2 antelope and a lot of rabbits and chickens.

Last week John Scotney sent me in to Spearfish with a horse and buckboard after provisions. I had an eventful and exciting time descending the bluffs on the Red water as the harness broke, the horse started to run away, and it was with the utmost danger and difficulty I succeeded in finally managing to hold it.

At Spearfish I met Jack Cole, a noted hunter, gambler, and desperado, chiefly noted for his fight with Big George, another hunter in the Bear Lodge Mountains in which he shot George three times with a Winchester and killed him.

I first met him when Ned and I were coming from Deadwood, he being an old friend of Ned's. He is a heavy set, dark complexioned man, and is never seen without his cartridge belt and sixshooter.

One day last week as I was alone at the ranch saddling up a horse, a pack of 4 wolves came down from the hills and trotted unconcernedly up to within 50 yards of the house. I started to get my rifle, but in the meantime our dogs, two powerful staghounds and a large ferocious newfoundland dog called Don belonging to Hank Bloom, sighted the wolves and made a break for them running them into the hills.

We have a splendid view of Crow Peak from here. It is just back of Spearfish and about 15 miles distant. It look[s] much closer and presents a grand and striking sight.

Deadwood, Dak., Aug. 10
I left Hay Creek day before yesterday, and walked to "Whiskey Parker's" ranch about 4 miles this side of Spearfish, where I stopped over night and got my supper and breakfast. This place is a sort of frontier tavern and is kept by the noted buffalo hunter, "Whiskey Parker," and his wife. Parker is the author of the famous frontier song entitled "Whiskey Parker's Song" and which I learned on the buffalo range a couple of years ago. He is a tall, raw boned, sandy complexioned fellow about 40 years old and full of quaint stories and songs. Got back to Deadwood yesterday and put up at the Elephant Corral with my friend, Theodore Court, while I get my meals at the "IXL Hotel" or the "Salt Lake House." Received several letters from home in which much anxiety was expressed for my safety.

Among other noted characters in town is a hunter called "Buckskin Shoe," with a head of hair like a lion's mane falling down over his shoulders.

Deadwood, Aug. 12
I met my old pard, Will Woodall, to day. He was all crippled up and walking on crutches, having been run over by a bull train the other day, so he can't go with me to Cheyenne as he had planned.

I have been gambling some since I have been in town, bucking several games such as chuckaluck, Wheel of Fortune, and others and have become initiated into the mysteries of poker. This is a great place for gambling, every one gambles more or less. Won some money from a skin gambler, calling himself Fanshaw, to day. Beat him at his own game.

This afternoon I sauntered into Tom Miller's music hall, where a boxing match with soft glove[s] between Nat Williams and an unknown was in progress. After it was over, a young dance hall rustler named Al Brownell put on the gloves and challenged me to put on the gloves with him. I excused myself, pleading inexperience, but being urged by the bystanders, among them "Colorado Charlie," "Broncho Moll," and "Calamity Jane," I put on the gloves and stepped into the ring, and before I knew it got a welt in the nose that made my eyes water. I soon got the hang of it, fought wary, and hit hard. Brownell was a pretty good boxer but his blows lacked force and he was soon exhausted, while I put in less blows but put them where they would do the most good, and soon had the satisfaction of compelling him to give in to me.

Deadwood, Aug. 14

Al Brownell and I went up the gulch to Central City and visited all the placer diggings en route. Came back in time for dinner.

This afternoon Mitchem['s] bull train from Bismarck pulled into town with doubled teams. When opposite the Chinese Row one of the bullwhackers allowed his team of 18 yoke of oxen to straighten out in a bend and tipped two wagons, loaded with flour and grain, into the Whitewood. "Calamity Jane," who was an eye witness, gave the unlucky bullwhacker a "hell of a cursing" calling him a tender foot and saying if she couldn't do better she would go back to the states and husk pumpkins for a living.

Prairie Spring, Dak., Aug. 16

Last night I left Crook City with Jim Fanshaw and went to "Scooptown." Our object was to strike Red Jim, the muleskinner, and make arrangements to go with him to Cheyenne. It was past midnight when we got to "Scooptown" and as no hotels were open, we curled up in a vacant house and went to sleep, that is, I did. How long I slept I don't know, but I was awakened rather suddenly by some one feeling about in my pockets. In an instant I realized that an attempt was being made to go through me but as I had dropped my pocket book down the back of my neck just before going to sleep, the thief had not found it.

At the same time it dawned on me that my partner, Fanshaw, was the one who was trying to rob me, and all at once I reached up, grasped his throat, and with a desperate effort rolled him over and got on top of him. He tried to release my hold, but I hung on like grim death to a nigger and he soon commenced to choke and gasp and gurgle for breath. All at once I felt a sharp cutting pain in my left side, and reaching my left hand down I ran it against the point of a knife and cut it badly. I, however, grasped his wrist and held him so he couldn't use the knife, and choked him until he dropped the knife. While I was feeling around on the floor for it he, by a supreme effort, broke my hold, scrambled to his feet, and made a break for the opening in the wall which used to be a window. I found the knife and sprang after him, but not getting near enough to reach him, I threw the knife at him with all the force I was capable of just as he sprang through the window and disappeared. I don't know whether I hit him or not, but I am considered pretty good at throwing the bowie knife and I hope I did. I was now bleeding freely from the wounds in my side and hand and didn't know how badly I was hurt, so I went out to a bullwhackers' camp on the prairie, woke up the boys, and told them my story. They were very kind and soon bandaged my wounds. The one in my side was not bad. It had struck for my heart, but glanced on the ribs and cut a gash about 3 inches long. The one in my hand was worse, being a very deep cut in the palm of the hand at the base of the forefinger. I staid in the camp the balance of the night and this morning went out about town with some of the bullwhackers to hunt up Fanshaw, but couldn't see anything of him and as one of the ponies lariated near town was missing, it is fair to presume that Jim and the pony left together. I left Sturgis City after breakfast and walked to "Spring Valley Ranch," where I got a splendid dinner for half a dollar. This is a famous frontier hostelry run by John Adler, who killed his partner a year or two ago. After dinner I walked to Prairie Spring in Red Valley, where I put up for the night with a ranchman named John Bell.

Rapid City, Dak., Aug. 18

Arrived in town yesterday to find the U.S. Court in session and town full of people in attendance.

Among others was a squad of Ogallala Sioux from Pine Ridge Agency including the noted Chiefs Young-Man-Afraid-of-his-Horses, Conquering Bear, Woman's Dress, and the halfbreed interpreter, Bill Garnett. They were all camped out of town on Rapid Creek with their ponies feeding close by. I spent some time in their camp.[24]

In the afternoon I attended the trial of Big Jack McDonald and Fritz Staurck, road agents for the robbery of the stage at Dry Creek on the 9th of June, the same crime for which "Lame Johnny" was lynched. The trial was held up stairs over a store and the furniture of the room was of the simplest description. Judge Moody presided, Col. Parker appeared for the defence, and Mr. Hastie prosecuted. The jury was ranged on a couple of benches at one side of the room and was made up of bullwhackers, miners, and a few well dressed business men.

The prisoners, two villainous-looking fellows, were chained and hand-cuffed. The courtroom was crowded with spectators and witnesses, Indians and bullwhackers in fringed buckskin, and presented a motley appearance.

Witnesses were examined, and Frank Harris, "Lame Johnny's" partner, was brought in on a question of identity and the case was given to the jury at about 11 P.M. I left then and this morning I heard that they found a verdict of guilty.

There seems to be lots of work for the court as about 20 horse thieves, murderers, moonshiners, road agents, and pony boys are in jail here awaiting trial.

Buffalo Gap, Aug. 22

Came here on foot stopping at Spring Creek, Battle Creek, and French Creek on the route. At French Creek I stayed last night with the stock tender, Bob Keenan. While I was there the Black Hills treasure coach came along and stopped while horses were changed. This coach carries no passengers, nothing but gold dust, money, and valuables. With the coach were nine guards or shot-gun messengers as they are called, among them Boone May and Scott Davis, his pard. They are all picked men, noted for their dexterity in the use of firearms and all fighting men who have proved their "sand" in numerous bloody frontier affrays. They are well dressed with six shooters, Winchester rifles, and breechloading shot-guns. Four of them ride in the coach, which is all "ironclad" with loopholes for shooting, 1 rides on top beside the driver, four ride horseback, two some distance ahead and two behind the coach. Thus, it will be seen, it is impossible to surprise the coach, and any foolhardy gang of road agents who would undertake to hold it up would find they had caught a "Tartar."[25]

While they were at French Creek, I saw Boone May make a splendid shot. He drew his sixshooter and fired at a small blackbird that was running along the road over 60 yards away and dropped it dead. Between French Creek and here I passed "Lame Johnny's" grave on Dry Creek. It was only a mound of dirt under the tree on which he was hung with a board stuck up at the head with the following epitaph scrawled on it with lead pencil:

Here lies "Lame Johnny"

> Hung by parties unknown
> July 2nd 1879

The parties are not altogether unknown, being composed of ranchmen and stage station keepers of the vicinity, one of them, no doubt being Bob Keenan of French Creek.

I am now staying at Buffalo Gap Ranch.

White Earth River, Neb., Aug. 24

Struck an outfit of three miners, Bill Noakes, Ike Chandler, and Geo. Eslinger yesterday at North Water hole and have traveled with them since then. They have been mining in the hills but are bound for "fresh fields and pastures now." They are on the way to Arizona. We are now camped on White Earth River alongside of a dance hall tent just put up by Joe Lane of Sidney for the accommodation of the soldiers of Fort Robinson up the river and the cowboys of the surrounding country. A number of girls are here, among them Old Logan and Dolly Lane, whom I had seen at Sidney. The girls went in swimming right before the camp and all hands had a good time.

Sidney, Neb., Aug. 29

Got back to Sidney this evening in company with the three miners and Joe Lane, his son Frank, and Dolly Lane all travelling and camping together. We stopped at Running Water, where we met the famous Sioux Chief Red Dog, and at Halfway Hollow, Snake Creek, Red Willow, Greenwood, and Nine Mile Water holes. At one of our camps Bill Noakes shot a prairie dog which we cooked for dinner, but did not relish much as it tasted too rank.

Cheyenne, Wyoming, Sun. [Sat.] Aug. 30 [1879]

Came up from Sidney last night on the train, arrived here this morning, and found a large, well built town with a stream called Crow Creek flowing close by. This used to be an awful hard town when it was the terminus of the U.P.R.R. and when it was the outfitting point for the Black Hills. It used to be called "Hell on Wheels" and used to "have a man for breakfast" every day and sometimes half a dozen, and it is not the most peaceful spot on earth to day.[26]

A train of cars loaded with troops left here this evening for the west to fight the Utes, who are reported on the war path.[27]

From here we have a magnificent view of the neighboring Rockies.

Loveland, Colorado, Aug. 31

Got a free ride this morning on a freight train to Fort Collins with the conductor, Pete Martin. Fort Collins is a beautiful city built on the banks of the Cache-a-la-Poudre River.

I stopped but a short time in Fort Collins. After getting a lunch I struck out on the track of Colorado Central railway and walked to Loveland, another small but beautiful town on the Big Thompson Creek. It is center of a rich farming country, watered by irrigating canals and ditches. The Big Thompson Valley is one of the finest farming regions in the state. The western horizon is bounded by the snow capped peaks of the Rocky Mountains about 10 or twelve miles distant, while to the east are boundless plains covered with sage brush, cactus, and bunchgrass.[28]

I hired out this evening to Pat Sullivan, section boss, to work on the railroad.

Loveland, Colo., Sept. 14

This a delightful place, well-built, with trees fringing the streets and irrigation full of cold mountain water running everywhere.

Long's Peak, crowned with clouds, overlooks the town, and the Snowy Range. The dark, pine-clad foothills, the yellow prairies, the fields and farmhouses and grainstacks, the stream with its fringe of trees, present a picture full of varied beauty to the eye!

I am now working on the railroad. I board at the section house and live on the fat of the land. My fellow laborers are all Irish and withal a cheerful, goodnatured set of men, full of quaint anecdote and story.

Two section gangs board together and Mrs. Morrisey, the landlady, is a big fat Irishwoman, while her girl, Katie Murray, is a jewel.

Spend my leisure time reading and playing cards with Red Ned at his shack across the railroad track. Last week I attended a greenback meeting in Patron's Hall at which the Hon. Joseph Murray held forth. He was an able speaker but not very convincing, at least to me. He is a big gun among the Irish population and is called the "Dennis Kearney of Colorado."[29]

Saw a tarantula the other day. It was a young one but very fierce and would bite hold of whatever I would point at it. I killed it.

Loveland, Colo., Sept. 28, Sun.

Am still at Loveland. Last night I attended an exhibition at the school house of Prof H. H. Williamson, "Pete Conklin the Clown," in which he exposed all the tricks of ventriloquism, legerdemain, and magic. Had a first rate time. This afternoon I ran an 80 yard foot race with one of our boys, Theodore Gallagher. I beat him midst the plaudits of the rail roaders.

Berthoud, Colo., Sun., Oct. 5th

I quit working for Sullivan last week and went to work for "Black Jack" McCormick at Berthoud on the Little Thompson about 10 miles south of Loveland. Jack is a brother of Mrs. Morrisey and we frequently run up to Loveland on the handcar taking his sister, Bridget, with us. Bridget keeps house for us. Jack has two other men, Thomas O'Hearn alias "Black Tom," and Adam Frybourg alias "Dutchy." To day we took the handcar and ran over to Longmont, seven miles distant, and took dinner with the O'Connors, friends of the McCormicks. Made the acquaintance of two young ladies, Miss Finnerty and Mary O'Connor, had splendid dinner and good time. After dinner we took a stroll around the town, which is a fine, well built, and thriving business place with the adjacent St. Vrain Valley tributary to it. It was located about 10 years ago by a Chicago Colony and named for Long's Peak, a splendid view of which can be had from here.[30]

At present a part of it presents a desolate appearance, having been burnt a couple of weeks ago.

We see fires in the mountains every night and at day the air is murky with smoke and the sun looks like a ball of blood. It is supposed to be caused by the burning of forests by the hostile Utes, who have gone on the war path after murdering the agent and employees at White River and carrying the women and children into captivity.[31]

Berthoud, Colo., Sun., Oct. 19

Last week Dutchy and I caught about a bucket full of fish in a break of an irrigating ditch. We also had a visit from a couple of Sisters of Charity from Denver and one from Father Abel, Catholic priest of Denver, who was a most agreeable companion and played checkers with me in the evening and held Mass the next morning before he went away. The heroes of the Milk River fight passed through here last week. They were a company of the 9th Colored Cavalry under command of Capt. Dodge. They were corralled six days by the Indians and lost all their horses but two. The train stopped long enough for us to have quite a chat with them. They are now on their way to New Mexico to fight the Apaches under Victorio who are on the war path.[32]

Golden, Colorado, Nov. 17

I quit working for McCormick day before yesterday. Yesterday walked to Ni Wot and took the train to Golden, passing through Boulder, Louisville, and other places. Arrived at Golden at about 10 P.M. in the midst of a heavy snow storm. I groped my way up town and put up at the Overland Hotel.

This morning I called on Capt. Reed, the roadmaster of the C. C., to get my time checks cashed. He took me to Denver on the morning train, had my papers signed, and brought me back this afternoon and this evening I got my money.

Denver, Colo., Nov. 20

"Took in" the town of Golden last night, gambled a little, put up at the Overland, which is a pretty good hotel kept by Capt. Lange. Golden is a fine little city built in a hollow in the foothills by which it is almost surrounded. One of the hills has a flat top and is called Table Mountain. Clear Creek runs through the town and a narrow gauge road runs up Clear Creek Cañon to Black Hawk and Central City.

Golden presented a pretty sight this morning nestling among the hills. Everything was covered with a snowy mantle and the smoke which arose from numerous locomotives, railway shop[s], and stampmills, hovered around the tops of the rock-ribbed hills which were glistening like gold in the suns rays!

Went to Denver and put up at a hotel on the corner of Holliday and 19th Streets called the Western Home.

Much has been said and written of Denver and for me to describe it would be a hard job, as I have seen so little of it. It is, however, a fine city with broad streets lined with magnificent blocks of buildings, and contains many many large business houses, churches, school houses, colleges, and elegant private residences.

Trees are planted in rows along all of the streets, and irrigation ditches run down both sides of every street. The streets are crowded with vehicles of every description, and the sidewalks with a throng of pedestrians.

The city has a full system of water work[s], street railways, and is lighted with gas. We might easily imagine we had been transported back to the haunts of civilization if it were not for the glorious view of the Snowy Range about 15 miles distant.

Denver, Nov. 29

I like Denver very well. I am still staying at the Western Home kept by Mr. Moore and have lots of fun flirting with Jennie Chambers and Frankie Van Houghton.

This evening, in company with Walter During, I attended the Palace Theater, a variety show on Blake Street. Among the "steers" who appeared before the footlights were Frankie Barbour, Nellie Hackett, Duncan Sisters, Minnie Farrell, John Richardson, Harry Montague, Perry Bros, Etta LeClair, Lydia Rosa, Blanche Fontainbleau, Alice Dashwood, Millie Christine. The dancing and singing of the girls, who were very liberal in showing their legs and bosoms, was of the most "loud" character.

The place was as hard a one as I ever was in. The afterpiece, "The Mormons," would raise a blush on the cheek of an Indian, it was so dirty.

Denver, Sun. Nov. 30

Last night I attended a free fight in the Red Light Saloon on Fifteenth St. in which beer bottles were the weapons used and bruised heads the result.

This evening I went to hear Josie Meeker lecture at Forrester's Opera House.

Miss Meeker was dressed in a skirt and jacket of yellow blanket cloth with a wide dark border, a suit she wore while a captive among the Utes. She was a blonde, tall and well formed with long golden hair, blue eyes, and fair, clear complexion.[33]

She was introduced by General Chas. Adams, and at once launched forth on the course of her narrative.

She pictured life among the Utes at the White River Agency; told of Douglas, Johnson, Persune, Ute Jack, and Colorow, and other chiefs; told of the massacre of the Indian agent, N. C. Meeker, her father, and the agency employees; of the pillage and burning of the agency building, of the capture of herself, her mother, Mrs. Price and her two children; of Frank Dresser's brave fight for life; of the march from the scene of the massacre to the camp on Grand River; of the hardships and perils of the mountain trails; of the orgies of the savages; of the attachment and fidelity of the Squaw Susan, and of the final rescue by Gen. Adams and Chief Ouray of the Uncompahgre Utes and of everything that was interesting during her captivity of two months.[34]

Denver, Dec. 2

Went to the Opera House this evening to see the Grand Central Theater Combination and enjoyed the songs, dances, jokes, and sallies of Donnely and Drew, Haley and West, Irene Ingersoll, Viola Wray, Frankie Russell, Laura and Maggie Le Clair, Erba Robeson, Estelle Wellington, Little Lillie Tudor, John and Amy Tudor, Lottie Beaumont, Chas W. Young, Wiley Hamilton, and others.[35]

Denver, Dec. 20

Frank Johnson, one of my friends, and I went up town to the post office, where we encountered a Chinese funeral procession, preceded by a brass band and followed by a crowd of curious spectators. We joined the throng and marched out to the Chinese burying ground a couple of miles out of town. First in the procession came the brass band, which was playing "Sweet Bye and Bye," "Babies in our Block" and a great variety of sacred and secular music. Next came about 15 or 20 Chinamen dressed in mourning—white robes and sashes, and carrying burning "joss"-sticks in their hands. They also carried three flags or banners of red and yellow silk—three-cornered with Chinese characters emblazoned thereon. Next came the hearse drawn by six white horses. In the box beside the driver sat a Chinaman with a big bunch of rice paper strips, which he perforated with a punch and scattered along the street. I learned that this was to keep the devil away from the dead man[s] body until he was buried. I secured some of these strips as a memento of the occasion. Next came a carriage containing 4 chinese women dressed in their gaudy costume and with a profusion of jewelry. One of them, a goodlooking woman, wept and mourned and seemed over come by grief and I suppose she was the widow. The other three ladies exhibited the utmost nonchalance, and sustained a very animated conversation, and occasionally laughed outright, showing the utmost indifference to the solemnity of the occasion.

Next to this carriage was another containing a Chinese band, which kept up a continual rattling on a brass gong, occasionally raising their voices in a monotonous chant. Following this came a long line of buggies and carriage[s] filled with Chinese, all dressed in their best, smoking, talking and laughing, and seeming in the best of spirits as if they were going to a wedding instead of a funeral. Judging by their behavior a funeral seems to be an enjoyable affair with them. Arrived at the graveyard, the carriage halted before a new made grave, and they lost no time in dumping the coffin in, end first, and one of them jumped into the grave and straightened it. They then stuck the flags into the grave and filled in the dirt. This done, they brought forth a lot of gilt joss and rice paper and set it afire. The mourners divested themselves of their white sashes and robes, which they piled on the fire. A lot of truck such as bedding, clothes, and an old umbrella which had belonged to the departed heathen during life, was also brought forward and thrown in the flames and made a fearful stink. A lot of "joss sticks" and red candles were stuck into the ground at the head and foot of the grave and lighted, several dishes containing boiled rice cake, raw liver, chickens, and a bottle of liquor were then deposited on the grave to cheer the defunct celestial on his journey to the spirit land. All this being done, one of the Chinamen opened a paper bag and distributed what looked like chocolate candy to the mourners, who then got into their conveyances and started back to town. They had not sooner got well under way until the hoodlums who had followed the crowd fell upon the grave and robbed it of flags, candles, and everything else they wanted. We visited several other graves, of which there was a number. Most of them had a brick with Chinese Letters stamped on them lying on top and some had dishes of food, which seemed to have been recently placed there. Several of the grave[s] had head boards on which were inscribed such names as "Sam Kee," "Lee Hong," "Mong Chin," & c. A lot of broken pottery and glass was scattered about showing the vandalism of the Denver hoodlums.

Went to Bunch and Apples Real Estate Office this afternoon where I met James Lewis, alias "Arizona Bill," a noted scout, hunter, and mountaineer. He wears his hair long, has a heavy black mustache and goatee, and dresses in a fringed buckskin suit and broad brimmed hat. Many stories are told of his exploits among the Indians and desperadoes of the west and southwest.

At Bunch and Apples I also met the Rev. Samuel R. Dimock, pastor of the Congregation Church, and engaged myself to enter his employ as he wants a young man who understands horses to take charge of a pair of wild ponies he has.[36]

Denver, Dec. 26
I am now staying at Mr. Dimock's. He has a fine residence in the suburbs. His family comprises his wife, a handsome graceful lady, his son Frank, a talented but wild young fellow of sixteen who has just graduated from the high school and is now engaged in teaching Greek and Latin to private pupils, and his stepdaughter, Mary Harter, a fascinating young lady of sweet sixteen, who is attending high school.
Dimock is a fine old gentleman, a graduate of Yale College, and of an aristocratic family, one of his ancestors being a celebrated English knight, Sir Charles Dymock, who distinguished himself in a tournament in the sixteenth century. The family is very clever, and Mrs. Dimock is a very fine reader. They have a large and well selected library, play backgammon and other innocent games, and I have a nice time, my duties being very light, being principally the taking care of three ponies and two cows. Two of the ponies, however, are very wild and vicious and I have to use much discretion in handling them. Only this evening one of them, Colonel, kicked me over as I was going into his stall with an armful of hay.

Denver, Colo., Jan. 20, 1880
Dimock's greys are a hard team to manage. A couple of days ago while I was down at Dimock's country place on the Platte, they made a break to run away, throwing me off the spring wagon, and hurting my back some. I, however, managed to get the best of them.
Frank Dimock claims to be a runner and has been bantering me for a long time to run him a foot race. So this afternoon we ran 100 yards for a quarter a side, he being unwilling to wager a larger amount. I beat him easily, to his surprise and chagrin.

Denver, Feb. 4th
Very cold. I got my fingers frostbitten this morning while taking Mary to school in the buggy.
In the Daily Tribune I find a short telegram concerning my old Black

Hills acquaintance, Boone May. It seems that May and Detective Lewellyn had captured Lee Grimes, alias "Curly," a notorious road agent and were taking him to Deadwood and on the 2nd Inst, while in the vicinity of Scooptown, he broke from them and attempted to escape when they fired on him and killed him instantly.[37]

Denver, Colo., Feb. 16

Frank Dimock and I occasionally have a game of poker. He is not much of a player, but he has pluck and stays with it. I win from him right along, but as he makes his money easy, I have no scruples about winning it. One day we were playing poker and the old folks returning unexpectedly from down town, came within an ace of catching us at it. Frank was scared nearly out of his boots.

I had another runaway the other day. I was down in the grove on the Platte. The ponies started away, and it was with the utmost difficulty that I scrambled into the spring wagon. I braced my feet against the dashboard when all at once it flew out on to the horses and I nearly fell on to them myself. As I had now nothing to brace up against I couldn't hold the team and I devoted myself to keeping them in the road and let them go. They ran nearly three miles before they slacked up, but as it was in the direction of home, I was well satisfied and when they showed a disposition to slack up, I commenced to whip them and kept up a breakneck speed to the very gates. I lost the dashboard, lunch pail, and a pair of gloves.

Last night I was introduced to Will Stewart, a friend of Frank's, a student of Cornell University and a member of the University boat crew, who is spending some time here with a friend, Col. Williams. He is something of an athlete and at Frank's suggestion Will and I tried various feats, and found we were about equally matched in strength.

Got a letter from Elma Johnson a couple of days ago enclosing a photograph. She seems to look well and hearty as ever.

Denver, Colo., March 13

While out riding bareback on Shub—one of the ponies—I was thrown, and my coattail torn off but not otherwise injured.

Denver, Colo., March 20

Last night I went to the Adelphia Theater to see "Texas Jack" in his play entitled, "The Trappers Daughter." Enjoyed myself well. Don't think much of Texas Jack as an actor; believe he is better as a scout and trailer.

J. B. Omohundro, (Texas Jack) is a fine looking man, tall and well proportioned, with long black hair falling below his shoulders.[38]

Denver, Mch. 25

Was at a fire on Arapahoe street this evening. The building was a frame dwelling house and burned to the ground in spite of the efforts of the fire department.[39]

Denver, March 31

Went to Bates & Nyes photograph gallery and sat for my picture in broadbrimmed hat, long hair, California suit, and blue woolen shirt with silk necktie. Then I went to a barber's shop and had my hair cut short. It was so long it hung down over my shoulders in true western style.[40]

Denver, April 1st

The morning papers contain an account of the killing of Walter Reed by the cars at Leadville yesterday. He was run over by the engine, his back and neck broken, and left foot and arm cut off. Walter Reed, or Wattie as we called him, was the son of Capt. Reed, the roadmaster of the C. C. R. R. and a brakesman on the road. I knew him well when I worked on the road last fall and he was a good fellow.

Denver, April 5th

While Mr. Dimock and I were down at the grove Dimock's mare, Birdie, ran away with Dimock in the buggy. He was in imminent peril as the trees and stumps were scattered around pretty thick. The preacher, however, was equal to the occasion and finally stopped the mare; but not until she had smashed up the buggy pretty considerable.

Denver, April 22

Was agreeably surprised this evening by a visit from Leander Hallgren of Phelps Co. Neb. He had come out to take a look at the "Queen City of the Plains" and having received my address from my folks, hunted me up. He is now Clerk of Phelps County and Charlie Backman is Deputy.

He told me my folks were well and very anxious about me. Told me lots of news about my friends, said the county was settling up fast, a town called Phelps Center, has been located on section 1 near the Emigrant House and the county seat removed to the town.[41]

Walter Deering, who used to board last fall at the Western Home when I was there, committed suicide by poison at the Lawrence House to day. Cause: financial embarrassment.[42]

Denver, May 4th
I quit working for Dimock on the last day of April and now I am boarding at the New York Hotel on Holliday St. This hotel is kept by Heiser and Rumbeck, the former a German and the latter a Swede. I learned in a conversation with him that he belonged to the Rumbeck family and is a distant relative of my mother.

Holliday street is one of the hardest streets in Denver, it is full of bagnios and saloons and it is unsafe to venture out after dark without arms.

Two blocks away on Wazee street is a row of one-story brick houses occupied exclusively by Chinese courtesans and gamblers.

Denver, May 6th
Saw "Captain Jack [Crawford]," the Poet Scout of the Plains," to day. He is here organizing a theatrical troupe which will be on the road soon.

Denver, May 11th
Went to the Opera House last night in company with George Thorp to see the Jay Rial Combination play, "Uncle Tom's Cabin." I enjoyed the play very much, it being the first time I had seen it.[43]

Denver, May 19th
Dan Costello's Circus is exhibiting close by the hotel. One of the principal attractions is Signor Lowanda, the "Iron Jawed Man." He is a man of tremendous muscular development and his feats of strength and skill are astonishing.[44]

Denver, May 21
Last night about half past seven o'clock George Davis, a young negro employed in Phillips' Livery Stable opposite this Hotel, engaged in

an altercation with a cowboy named Cal McCarthy and called him a "son of a bitch." McCarthy instantly drew a revolver and fired 3 shots into the negro, who ran into the stable and fell on the floor. I came near being arrested for McCarthy as I was about the same size, wore a broadbrimmed hat, and carried a sixshooter and cartridge belt. The police finally got the right man, "got the drop" on him, and took him to jail. Davis is not dead but is not expected to live till morning.[45]

A very large crowd was on the street at the time as Costello's Circus was in full blast.

From the papers I learn that Deffenbach's ranch on the Belle Fourche, a few miles from Scotney's ranch, was recently raided by the Indians. John Deffenbach was killed and eighty seven head of ponies run off. A posse of frontiersmen are out after the redskins.

Denver, June 6th

The mattress factory in West Denver was burned to day. "Dixie" and I were on hand as soon as the fire department. It burned fiercely and all efforts to put the fire out were in vain.

I live at the New York Hotel. A number of the boarders are young fellows and a jollier crowd never got together. Among them are Tom Emmett, a young civil engineer; Harry Lyons, printer and cowboy; Henry Kaufman, alias "Dixie," a young southerner; Jim McSkimming, a blacksmith from Knox Co. Ills.; Tom McCarthy, a "blue nose;" Mike McIntosh, and Tom McManus. We call ourselves the "Owl Club" and play all kinds of practical jokes on newcomers and on each other.

This evening as Tom Emmett, Harry Lyons, and I were sitting at our window we heard three shots in rapid succession in the direction of Chinaman's Row on Wazee street. I went down to investigate and found that Yah-Ho, one of the prettiest of the Chinese girls, and with whom I was well acquainted, had got shot by "Chinaman Joe," a Chinese gambler. Joe was arrested and the girl who is shot in the shoulder will probably recover.

In a recent copy of the Police News I read of the death of "Dolly Lane," the dance girl at Sidney Neb. I traveled with Dolly from Red Cloud Agency to Sidney last summer and found her a pleasant companion. Before she died she gave a history of her life, how she was the child of a wealthy and aristocratic family, and how she was led astray by a professor at a young ladies seminary which she attended.

Tres Piedras, N.M., June 12

Day before yesterday (June 10) Jim McSkimming, "Dixie," and I got a pass from Col. D. C. Dodge over the Rio Grande Railway from Denver to the end of the track about 15 miles northwest of here to work on the railroad. Besides us there were about 50 more young fellows passed down. The scenery along the route was romantic and picturesque. We passed through the towns of Castle Rock, Colorado Springs, Pueblo, Laveta, crossed the Sangre de Christo Mountains through the Veta Pass where the railroad has an altitude of over 8,000 feet and we rode above the clouds. Had a magnificent view of the Spanish Peaks. Passed through several Mexican villages built of adobe or sun dried brick and stopped over night in Alamosa, a new and lively town on the Rio Grande Del Norte. Yesterday we resumed our journey and crossing the mountain-girt San Luis Valley to Antonito, came to the end of [the track] about 15 miles from Tres Piedras, our objective point. We had to walk the entire distance and last night we got to Smith and Mundy's grading camp in the Pataca Mountains about 1 1/2 mile from "Tres Piedras." Here we found about 40 men and about as many spans of mules and horses all engaged in grading for the railroad.[46]

Tres Piedras, June 15

We have been driving scraper teams on the grade the last few days. To day we paid a visit to the town Tres Piedras, which is the headquarters for the graders and tie choppers of the Pataca country.

Tres Piedras—Spanish for Three Rocks, so called from three rocky cliffs in the vicinity, is a small place with about half a dozen rough log and slab shanties, about 6 of them being saloons. It is a lively place and as every one carries a six shooter or two, the sharp crack of the pistol is heard with startling frequency. As we entered the Rio Grande Saloon kept by the notorious desperado "Pistol Johnny," a slim, gaunt, black bearded, wild eyed, long haired fellow waltzed up to us and delivered himself of the following extraordinary introduction:

"Whoop! I'm old Skip the Scout, from the Wild Plains of Wyoming; I'm on the warpath biggern a skinned wolf; I'm the Tarantula of Tres Piedras; I'm Chief and run this town; I'm the Hurricane of the Petaca Hill; I've scouted all over the West from the Yellowstone to the Gila; I've had over 30 balls shot into me and not one of them was put there by no slouch either; I am the Terror of the Territory and can out-run, out-jump, out-shoot, knock down, and drag-out any God d—d galoot in this camp and if you fellows have any doubts about it, just waltz out here and give me room to turn myself loose and I'll give you a square deal with guns, knives, or knuckles! Say pards, is it a go?"

"Nary go," said I, and he walked back and laid down on a counter, looking the picture of disappointment and grumbling about there being "no accommodation about some fellows."

Tres Piedras, N.M., June 16

Last night, as we were at the table in the "grub-tent" eating supper, a Mexican came rushing into camp reporting that a band of hostile Apaches had attacked a "tie camp" about 3 or 4 miles from here, and would undoubtedly come this way. It was also claimed that he saw two captives, two white men from Tres Piedras, in the hands of the Indians. Instantly there was a great commotion in camp. The cook packed up his things and put his wife and family in a wagon and started for Conejos, distant about 30 miles. Soon a fellow came galloping down from Tres Piedras and called for volunteers to join a scouting party at Tres Piedras. Several of us volunteered at once, but when I found that I would have to ride a mule bare back, I concluded I didn't want any scouting [illegible]. After the scouts were gone Dixie and I and several others went over to Tres Piedras and found the scouts gone. We helped the "tie men" make a corral of about a hundred tie wagons, which we ran into a circle three deep and put all the stock inside to prevent a stampede by the Apaches. We could hear a continuous firing two or three miles south in the mountains, and concluded that a timely fight was in progress there. We finally returned to camp and went to bed. During the night one of the mules broke loose and ran against our tent, covered me with sand, and nearly stepping on my head. We jumped up and grasped our arms thinking that the Indians were raiding the camp. We soon found out from the corral boss the cause of the commotion and went to sleep again and were not disturbed any more. To day Knapp, one of the scouts, came in and reported.

He told us it was a false alarm and was caused by a band of friendly Indians who were having a big feast and dance, and that the two whites supposed to be captive were only visitors and were well treated by the Indians. It is quite a relief to hear this, as I aint "stuck" after fighting Indians.

Tres Piedras, June 19

McSkimming, Dixie, Dave Price, and I left Mundy's camp some three days ago and went out to Callahan's tie camp to chop ties. We board with Callahan, and sleep in a hut we have built against a rock with pine poles and brush. The nights here are pretty cool and it takes two or three heavy woolen blankets to keep us comfortable. Several mornings we have found ice on the water about a quarter of an inch thick. "Dixie" and I, who are unused to tie chopping, find it pretty hard work and our hands are full of blisters. We are going to quit and start for Colorado to morrow.

Antonito, Colo., June 21

Yesterday "Dixie" and I started on foot for the end of the track. We got to ride about half way with a freighter. Stopped last night in the tent of "Grey Bill," who has charge of supplies at the end of the track. This morning I walked across the sage plain in to Antonito and "Dixie," who was not very well, came in on the train. Antonito is a hard place for its size. About 2 miles from here is "Conejos" an old Mexican town built of adobe, with a queer church in the middle. To get into town I had to wade the Rio San Antonio, (Conejos Cr.) a cold, swift-running stream.[47]

Fort Garland, Colo., June 23

We walked to Alamosa and staid last night. Came on to this place to day passing Washington Spring, a curious spring on the sage plain, which one might pass close by without knowing of its existence. When about 8 miles from this place we were over taken by a terrible rain storm and had a rough time getting here.

This fort is a government post built, as are most of the forts in this country, of adobes. Close by is Blanca Peak, said to be the highest peak in Colorado. This evening it looks magnificent. A cloud is stretched across the face of the mountain, all above the cloud is gray rock and stretches of snow; all below is green with grass and piñon trees.[48]

Pueblo, Colo., June 25

Staid night before last in the section house at Ft. Garland. Took breakfast yesterday morning with the soldiers at the fort. Here we fell in with a young fellow from Kansas named Richard Carson Burkett. He is a nephew of Richard Owen, a famous frontiersman and companion of Kit Carson. He was just in from the San Antonio Mountains and was bound for Manitou and we agreed to travel together for mutual safety. We left Ft. Garland yesterday morning and soon commenced the ascent of the Sangre de Christo Range. We paid a visit to some gold diggings near Placer but not finding things to suit us we kept on further and stopped over night in a tie choppers' cabin, getting our supper and breakfast there. We had a gay old time, as the tie choppers were a jolly set of fellows, though they nearly scared the wits out of Dick Burkett and "Dixie" by their promiscuous shooting in the cabin. Left them this morning and soon came to Veta Pass, where the railroad makes the celebrated muleshoe curve and the track rises over five hundred feet in a mile. It looks odd to stand on one heel of the curve and look down 500 feet to the other one and know that it is a mile around, though it appears not over 100 yards away.

Passenger trains go very slow over this curve, and they always have two locomotives in ascending. We waited in the pass till the north bound passenger train came down the curve and jumping on the platform of the baggage car rode through Laveta and clear to Cuchara, where the conductor fired us off. We had a ride of 40 miles so we didn't care much. Cuchara was a small place and a half dozen cowboys seemed to be all the population. We wended our way to the only store in the place and bought some crackers and cheese for our dinner. After disposing of these we went over to a coal chute where a freight train was switching. Here we made arrangements with a brakesman to take us to Pueblo at the rate of $1.75 per head. As the train started up we jumped her. I was the last one to get on and being impeded by a big army overcoat, I caught the ladder on the side of the car with one hand only. As we were now passing the coal chute, I couldn't recover myself, but hung by one hand while my body swung back and forth, sometimes striking the coal chute and then again the side of the car. But I hung on for dear life until we got clear of the chute, where I recovered my balance and climbed into the car, whence Dick and "Dixie" had been watching me with blanched faces, expecting every moment to see me drop and be crushed by the wheels and yet were unable to help me. We reached Pueblo all safe and sound.

Pueblo is a lively, bustling city of some 6,000 inhabitants. It has several railroads, large smelting works, and steel rolling mills. It is built on both sides of the Arkansas River and the divisions are known as North and South Pueblo.

Manitou, Colo., June 27

Left Pueblo yesterday morning and walked to Piñon, where we laid over till night, and last night we jumped a freight train and beat our way in to Colorado Springs.

This morning we went out to Manitou and hired out to work on the construction force [for the] Manitou Extension of the Denver & Rio Grande R.R., which is being built between Colorado Springs and Manitou, a distance of about 6 miles. There are between 200 and three hundred men employed and we live in a camp on both sides of the Fontaine qui Bonille or Fountain River. Our camp is in a beautiful grove of elm, hackberry, wild cherry, white oak, pine, and other trees. The cool, clear, rapid waters of the Fountain flows through it, and besides, we have a splendid spring in the middle of it. We are about 1 mile below Manitou, where the celebrated Manitou Mineral Springs are located. I believe this is the loveliest spot in the Rockies. The scenery is grand and beautiful beyond description. The town is built in a magnificent valley surrounded by pine clad foot-hills while over all towers the bald head of the mighty Pikes Peak. [Here are] Several large hotels, the "Manitou," "Cliff House," and others. Groves of trees and shrubbery are every where, and each spring is enclosed by a beautiful rustic arbor. This is the most famous of all western resorts and is surrounded by places of wonder and interest, as the famous "Garden of the Gods," "Crystal Park," "Ute Pass," "Rainbow Falls," "Glen Eyrie," Pikes Peak, & c. all within easy access. Two stages run daily between Colorado Springs and Manitou besides numerous carriages, buggies, & c. all filled with tourists and sight seers.

Manitou, Colo., July 15

Had a terrible storm of rain a few days ago. The mountain streams were roaring torrents and swept everything. Several miles of track were destroyed between Manitou and Colorado Springs and about 25 miles were destroyed between Colorado Springs and Pueblo and several lives lost. Nearly our whole force was ordered out to meet a crew from Denver and repair damages. We did not work half the time but got double wages all the same. Yesterday morning we ran into Pueblo and took breakfast at the different hotels then pulled out to White Meadows, where we lay still all day and last night went into Colorado Springs, from where we were conveyed to camp by teams where a steaming supper awaited us. Incidents of the trip were numerous. The track and embankments was washed entirely away in places, and the rails twisted out of all shape. Several fights occurred, but the most comical thing was a scuffle in Pueblo between "California Bill" and one Holcomb, who rolled all over the street saturating each other with a stream of water from a hose and wallowing in the mud.

Manitou, Colo., July 18

Life in camp is getting monotonous, no fight since yesterday where two fellows chased each other all over camp with knives and axes until stopped by friends. I have a soft snap. I am with the surveyors outfit carrying a pole, and am not on duty more than half the time.

There are several Negroes in camp and every evening they get together and have a concert accompanied by a banjo. They sing their quaint plantation melodies and camp meeting song[s] in a style peculiarly their own.

The principal amusement, though, is gambling. The usual game is "Honest John" dealt by "California Bill," though Spanish Monte, Short faro, "chuckaluck," and poker also has its votaries.

This "California Bill" alias "Nine Miner" [?] is a noted western road agent and desperado and an escaped convict from the California penitentiary. He is employed here as "tool inspector," having charge of all the tools. He however makes most of his money by gambling in which he is proficient. He wears a broad-brimmed sombrero and a pair of beautifully fringed, smoke-tanned, buckskin leggings. He is one of the jolliest fellows in camp always ready with a joke or a laugh and altogether not such a [bad] looking man as one might expect to see in such a desperate border outlaw.

Another character is Dick Dolan, "King of the Bums," a handsome, jolly, reckless, young fellow who a few days ago "stood off" the marshal of Colorado City—a small hamlet between here and Colorado Springs—when he tried to arrest him.

Another celebrity is "Tex," a tall, powerful young man from "Texas," whose exploits with the sixshooter and reckless freaks [?] are the talk of the camp.

Less noted lights are "Smarty," "Cockney," "Terre Haute," and others. A young fellow named Ferguson sometimes comes into camp, gets on a box, and sings a song or recites long poems on the beauty of Pikes Peak and Manitou. The poetry is of his own composition and some of it is grand and sublime. The poor fellow is demented and is always talking of having his poems collected and punished [published?].

We have free access to the different springs at Manitou and we hardly drink anything but soda, magnesia, sulphur, and iron water. It is considered very healthy.

Dick Burkett, "Dixie," Walt Wright, and I with several others occupy a tent together. Dick has been pretty sick with the measles, but is about well now.

One of the fellows in our tent, Harvey Rogers, has just got down from the Black Hills country, where he participated in the pursuit of the Indians who raided Deffenbach's ranch on the Belle Fourche. He says they struck the trail of the Indians and followed it several days finally coming up with them on the Little Missouri. They attacked the camp, routed the Indians after a sharp fight, recovered all the stolen ponies, and also about a hundred head of ponies belonging to the Indians. They had one man killed in the fight.

Manitou, July 20

Dick Burkett, "Dixie," Walt Wright, Tom Douglas, George Coffman, Stephens, and I made a trip to the "Garden of the Gods" and enjoyed ourselves immensely. We visited the cave in the Gate Rocks, the Cathedral Rocks, the Balancing Rock, and other curious and fantastic rocks. It is a sight good for sore eyes to see this picturesque place with its curious shaped rock rising in some instances perpendicularly from the plain, and of every color of the rainbow. The soft, hazy outlines of the foothills and the snowcapped range clearly defined in the blue sky, form a background for the picture that no artist could do justice to.

Manitou, Colo., July 21

Frank Coffman, Jim Coffman, Tom Douglas, and I made a trip to Crystal Park, which lies at the base of Cameron's Cone, thousands of feet above Manitou. On the way up on the trail we were overtaken by a sudden storm of rain, hail, and sleet and obliged to take refuge behind rocky boulders and trees. The storm was over in a short time, but the ground was covered with hail to a depth of two or three inches and we were drenched to the skin and shivering with cold.

We resumed our journey and finally came to the park at the entrance to which was a small cabin, half dug-out and half log cabin. Here we found two mountaineers who keep a toll gate across the trail. We stopped and chatted with them awhile, while we dried our clothes before the blazing fire, and then went out into the park, which was a sort of valley above the clouds with spruce, pine, and other trees and brush growing everywhere.

We spent some time in wandering about the park hunting for Crystals, of which we got several fine specimens.

On the way down we were overtaken by a rain storm and drenched again.

Manitou, July 23

Yesterday just after dinner Dick Burkett, Gideon Mecklem, and I commenced the ascent of Pike's Peak. We entered Ruxton Creek Canon at Manitou and passing the Iron Spring soon struck the new trail, which leads to the summit of the peak. Stopped at Sheltered Falls, Little Minnehaha Falls, and other places of interest. The trail is very serpentine and winds around among trees and rocks and around huge boulders on both sides of the canyon, crossing and recrossing the creek, which falls and leaps, and foams down its rocky bed. The trail is so narrow we had to walk, or rather climb, single file except at a few places where the trail had been widened out to admit the passing of two parties coming from opposite directions. The scenery was of the grandest description, the sides of the mountains being covered with a growth of trees, brush, and grass. The trees, however, become stunted and scarce as we neared "timber line," where it ceased altogether and nothing was before us but the bold naked side of the mountain.

We had occasional glimpses of Manitou and Colorado Springs, far below us.

At sunset we had reached "timberline," where we concluded to halt for the night. So we built a roaring fire of dead cotton wood and pine— of which a vast amount was lying around—and cooked our bacon, this with some bread and a can of strawberries we had brought from Manitou.

The bracing mountain air and our long climb had sharpened our appetites until we could have eaten raw mule if necessary. We had brought no blankets from camp as they were an impediment in travelling and now, as the night grew on, the atmosphere became so chilling we built three rousing big fires in the form of a triangle and laid down on the rocks between them. Even then I was so cold I hardly slept any all night. Got up about 3 o'clock this morning and after regaling ourselves on the remnants of last night's supper we again took to the trail. As we got higher the air became rarer and we had to stop frequently to regain our breath. Spring[s] of ice cold water were not lacking and sometimes the water would run in the trail a distance and soak our feet as we climbed. But at last, just as the sun was rising, we arrived at the summit. The summit is of considerable extent and is covered with huge blocks of rock and boulders.

The U.S. Signal Station here is located in a one story stone house, which is connected by telegraph with Manitou and Colorado Springs. Sergeant O'Keefe, the keeper, also furnishes refreshment for man and beast for tourists. About 100 yards from the house is a grave, merely a cairn of stones, with a headboard with this inscription:

Sacred to the Memory of
Erin O'Keefe
Infant daughter of Sergeant John and Norah O'Keefe, who was
destroyed by mountain rats, on the __ of July 1876.

There is also a piece of poetry but I can't remember the words. This little girl was killed and partly eaten by mountain rats, which are very large and when pressed by hunger, very ferocious. We saw a number of them scampering about among the rocks and sticking up their heads to look at us.[49]

The sunrise was the most glorious I have ever seen, rising, apparently, below us in a blaze of colors. As it grew lighter and the shadows gradually were chased out of the cañons and gulches, we had a magnificent view of the surrounding country. To the east stretched the boundless plains with several towns along the line of the railroad looking for all the world like pictures on a map. The course of the Fountain could be traced across the plain by the fringe of trees along its banks and an occasional silvery glimmer of its waters. To the west nothing but mountains and valleys, hills and hollows, with here and there a lake by way of variety.

Many mountains that when seen from the foothills appeared as high at Pikes Peak, were found to be hundreds of feet below us. Halfway down the side of the mountain was a large cloud. It seemed a mile or two below us and looked like a fleece, shutting out from our view everything beneath it. At one side of the mountain top was a sheer precipice of thousands of feet called the "Crater," and we amused ourselves by rolling huge boulders over the edge of the abyss and watch them go thundering down, leaping from crag to crag and awakening a thousand echoes among the hills and breaking into hundreds of small fragments.

After whiling away a couple of hours on the summit, we took a drink from a clear, cold spring near the house and descended the mountain by the old trail, which took us past "Lake House," a mountain hostelry situated at the edge of a beautiful lake in a splendid park. Here we met a party of tourists ascending the mountain accompanied by a guide accoutered with leather leggings, cartridge belt, Winchester rifle, and sombrero. They were all mounted on Mexican mules and hardy ponies. Several ladies were in this party.

We found descending the mountain much quicker than climbing but not much easier, as we had to hold back all the time to avoid going too fast and falling headlong down some steep declivity.

We got back to camp in time for dinner, having made the quickest time on record in ascending and descending the peak on foot.

Manitou, Colo., July 26

Walt Wright, "Dixie," and myself took a trip up Ute Pass to Rainbow Falls. Ute Pass is a canyon down which the Fountain descends to the plains. It has a good wagon road, though it would go hard with the wagon that should get to near the edge of the precipice and fall into the rocky stream below.

The scenery along the Pass is romantic and picturesque, especially Rainbow Falls, which is a sheet of water about 6 feet wide and 60 feet high.

Manitou, July 28

The track is completed to Manitou and this afternoon Dick Burkett, Walt Wright, and I rode over to Colorado Springs and attended Cole's Circus & Menagerie which was exhibiting there. I purchased tickets for the crowd of us, and we went in and saw all the riding, tumbling and acrobatic performances, the female trapeze performer, saw all the animals and Capt. Bates and wife, the giant and giantess, and Darius Alden the Dwarf, and other things too numerous to mention. We had a good time, and the only drawback was my mortification at being "played for a sucker" by one of the attaches of the show, who by a very slick trick swindled me out of thirty cents in giving me change.

Manitou, Colo., July 31

"Cockney" and "Smarty" quarreled last night over the gambling table and the result was a fight in which "Cockney" got an awful head put on him, and would have fared worse if we hadn't stopped the row.

General U. S. Grant and family have been "doing" Manitou and vicinity. They drove by the camp in an open carriage at dinner time and Grant lifted his hat and bowed to the railroaders while we cheered and not a few called out "Soup," "Hash," and other words of culinary nature, and some went so far as to yell "Come to dinner, you old fraud." Paid a visit this afternoon to Hangman's Gap in search of curiosities. "Hangman's Gap"—so called because two horsethieves were lynched there some years ago—is a narrow cleft in a ledge of red and yellow sandstone rocks, and has a very picturesque appearance.

Leadville, Colo., Aug. 14

On August 10 we were paid off at Colorado Springs. Got our supper at the Empire House and next morning, after breakfast at the Kirk House, we started to Leadville with most of the outfit as the Manitou Extension was complete. My two friends, Dick Burkett and "Dixie," left us at Colorado Springs to go to Denver. I was sorry to part with them as we had been comrades through many trials and hardships. Dixie was a Louisiana Jew, could speak German and French, and was pretty well educated.

Dick Burkett was a jolly, mischievous farmer's boy from Kansas. Both of them generous, openhearted and manly.

About noon the train started and we went to Pueblo, where we stopped long enough to get supper. From Pueblo we went up the Arkansas Valley, travelling all night, and the next morning found ourselves at South Arkansas, a small town on the D. & R. G. R. R.

The scenery was grand and majestic. On every side pine covered hills, bold rocky cliffs, and snow-capped mountain peak[s] bounded the horizon. The Valley of the Arkansas was covered with long grass, with here and there a grove of trees.

We kept on up the valley making sharp curves around rocky headlands, crossing and recrossing the Arkansas which here is a rushing stream of yellow, muddy water, tumbling and leaping over its rocky bed with a continual roar. At 3 P.M. of the same day we reached Malta, three or four miles from Leadville, where we left the train and went into camp about 8 miles from Leadville on the banks of the "Arkansaw." I did not feel very well as I had a touch of the "mountain fever." So as soon as Walt Wright and I had put up our tent I went to bed, i.e. rolled up in my blankets on the ground.

I have been drinking tea made from the mountain sage, which grows in abundance around camp, and I feel a little better to day. This morning Walt Wright, Will Gabriel, "Smarty," and I walked up to Leadville. Staid there nearly all day, visited nearly all places of interest in and about town.

The far famed mountain metropolis is built on Sacramento Flat and on every side are evidences of the miners' industry: holes, shafts, and piles of tailings. It claims a population of about 30,000 though I think it is overestimated. Some fine business blocks have been erected on the principal streets. The sidewalks are crowded with people and the streets with teams but "old timers" tell us that the town is dull at present on account of the recent strike.[50]

I got some Jamaica Ginger and took a dose of it for the fever and I think it has done me some good.

Buena Vista, Colo. Aug. 16

Finding that the high altitude of Leadville—10,200 feet—did not agree with me and that I stood a good show of being numbered among the thousands who have succumbed to mountain fever and pneumonia in this snow bound country, I determined to leave Leadville and seek the plains once more. Walt Wright, my pard, said he'd "stay with me" and so yesterday morning we shipped our blankets and spare baggage from Malta to Pueblo and came down the valley on foot to Granite, a small mountain hamlet, where we put up at Burt's Hotel.

This morning after breakfast we started down the valley and walked to Buena Vista, a place notorious for its hard cases and fast women. Only night before last Deputy Sheriff Fanworth and another man were shot and killed in a saloon fight. We took in the town this evening visiting all places of interest and amusement, including the dance hall. We hunted all over town for my Deadwood friend, "Colorado Charley," who has been running a saloon here called the Black Hills Headquarters, but I found that he had skipped out for New Mexico.

Chalk Creek, Colo., Aug. 17
Arrived here this morning from Buena Vista and had a bang up dinner at the "Chalk Creek House."

Canon City, Colo., Aug. 19
From Chalk Creek to Currant Creek we went by rail, at which place we left the train and came the balance of the way (8 mi.) on foot as we wanted to have plenty of time to study the beauties of the "Royal Gorge" as we came through it. It was a grand and imposing sight—a cleft in the rocks at the bottom of which rolled the "Arkansaw," while on either side the red rock rose perpendicularly to a height of over 2,000 feet.

We arrived here this evening and after having a drink at the Soda Spring and a look at the massive penitentiary, we put up at Boyd's Hotel.

Pueblo, Colo., Aug. 24
We arrived in Pueblo three days ago and put up at the Kansas City House. Our baggage that we shipped from Malta has become lost or missent and we have been waiting for it to turn up. It is quite a loss to us.

Alamosa, Colo., [Aug.] 25
Yesterday Wright and I were passed down with some 50 others to work on the D.&R.G. at Tres Piedras. We arrived here last night and stopped over night.

La Plaza Del Alcalde, N.M., Aug 28
We were passed from Alamosa to Tres Piedras by rail, and 15 miles further by wagon to a grading camp. We stopped there over night and the next morning pulled out for Santa Fe through a country covered with sage brush and stunted piñon. Stopped one night in McCarty's camp and this morning struck the Rio Grande at Lembuda. We crossed the river on McCarty Ferry and struck for the South following the Rio

Grande Valley through Mexican villages, haciendas, rancherias, and vineyards. Got our dinner in a Mexican inn at the Plaza (town) of Lajoya and put up for the night in a Mexican house in a town called La Plaza Del Alcalde (the town of the Judge).

These Mexican towns are built of adobe (sun dried brick) The houses are all one story high, flat roofed, and plastered with mud inside and out. The houses are built in the form of a hollow square with a court-yard or "Placita" in the center. In this "placita" is the well and some-times a garden of flowers, shrubbery, and trees. Many of the houses are whitewashed out side and inside and have a verandah or porch along one or more sides of the house, and many have a railing along the top of the walls.

They present a unique and attractive appearance and remind me of the pictures of Mexican scenes in our old school geographies. In the center of each town is a plaza (square) and on one side of this the Yglesia (church or cathedral) built of adobes and always a massive and picturesque building with one or more towers and steeples sur-mounted by crosses.

To day we saw the Mexican mode of threshing wheat which was by spreading it on the ground and driving a flock of goats round and round over it until the grain is separated from the husk.

Sante Fe, N.M., Aug. 30
Arrived here last night and put up at a place on San Francisco Street called "the Hole in the Wall." On our way here we passed through the Mexican town of Santa Cruz and through the Indian pueblos of San Juan and Tesceque. At San Juan we saw the Indian mode of thresh-ing grain, which differs from that of the Mexicans only in that the Indians use ponies to trample the grain. We also saw several Carettas made entirely of wood with two huge wooden wheels, all very clumsy and heavy and not a nail or piece of iron about the whole vehicle.

The houses in the Indian pueblos were built of adobe, tier upon tier, and some of them several stories high. There were no doors and the inhabitants mode of ingress and egress is by climbing up ladders on the outside and going down through holes in the roof. Their ovens for baking their curious pottery & c. are also on the roof, curious cone-shaped things of mud. In the center of each town is a church built of stone and mud for the natives are nominal Catholics, though they still hold to their old traditions and superstitions.

We left the Rio Grande at Española about 18 miles from here, crossed the Santa Fe Range, and looking down into the valley of the Rio Chiquito, our eyes were gladdened by the sight of the stars and stripes floating from the flagstaff of Fort Marcy.[51]

Adjacent to the fort the oldest town in the United States, Santa Fe, was spread out like a panorama. At that distance it looks for all the world like a vast number of brick kilns, but as we came down the mountain and neared the city, we found it was an oasis in this desert of sand and sage brush It was surrounded by orchards, vineyards, and gardens, all looking particularly green and fresh and attractive to us after our trip across the mountains.

This town, the most ancient in the U.S., is built in the Mexican style of architecture, the houses being mostly 1 story of adobe and plastered with mud on the outside. The windows are deep set and many are protected by iron grating. The panes are small and of the style of 300 years ago. The streets are narrow. The city, like all Mexican towns, is built around a square (plaza).

Taking the entire north side of the "plaza" is the old "palace," which was built previous to 1581. It is a long, one story building with a porch extending along its entire front. Here have lived all the governors of New Mexico, from the early Spanish Governors to Gen. Lew Wallace, the present governor of the territory. It now contains the U.S. and territorial courts and offices.[52]

The "plaza" is the most popular resort in the city. It is well shaded by trees and seats are arranged for the convenience of the public. In the center is the soldier's monument erected in 1867 to the soldiers of New Mexico who had fallen in the Indian wars and in the battles of Glorieta and Apache Cañon during the Civil War.[53]

The "plaza" also contains a stand for musicians, where the Ninth Colored Cavalry band from Fort Marcy plays every Sunday.

Another feature of the "plaza" is the town pump, where are always to be seen a crowd of dark-eyed Mexican senoritas.

The crowd on the "plaza" and streets is always of a heterogeneous character. Dark-eyed senoritas with their "mantilla" thrown over their heads, Mexican caballeros in their gold and silver embroidered sombreros, silk sashes, and jingling spurs, cowboys in their wide hats, leather leggings, and cartridge belts tearing around on their half broken bronchos, long haired hunters and scouts in fringed buckskin, miners in their canvas suits and big boots, Pueblo Indians in their picturesque costumes vending fruit and melons, bullwhackers and muleskinners, soldiers, Mexican dons, gamblers, negroes, and meek-eyed Chinamen jostle each other on the narrow streets.

Other places of interest in and around Santa Fe are the Christian Brothers College; the San Miguel Church, partially destroyed in the Indian war of 1680 and rebuilt by De Vargas; the Convent of the Sisters of Loretto; the Bishop's Cathedral; Guadalupe Chapel; Chapel of the Lady of the Rosary; and Fort Marcy.[54]

Santa Fe was an old city when Columbus discovered America. The Spainards found this a populous Indian pueblo in 1542. Part of the Indian pueblo is still to be seen and is yet inhabited by the descendants of the Indians who lived here in the same houses 400 years ago. We have rambled around town a good deal to day accompanied by Ed Holiday, an intelligent young Canadian. This afternoon we spent several hours on the "plaza" listening to the sweet strains of music from the band—which is justly known as the best band in the West—and in gazing upon the animated crowds that thronged the "plaza" and at troops of burros or "Mexican donkey," with enormous loads of wood tied on their backs.

Albuquerque, N. Mex., Sept. 5

Last Monday Walt Wright, Ed Holiday, and I left Santa Fe and started for the new gold mines in the Sandia Mountains about 50 miles south of Santa Fe. We brought a lot of grub and a frying pan and coffee pot with us from Santa Fe, but they ran short sooner than we had anticipated and we had to forage among the natives for sustenance. The Mexicans were uniformly kind and hospitable and would accept no pay excepting in a Mexican town called Galisteo, where they charged us half a dollar for a loaf of bread and some milk.

We suffered some from thirst as water was very scarce, and we sometimes had to make a dry camp.

The country was mostly wild and uninhabited, the soil sandy and covered with sage brush, mesquite, piñon, and a variety of cactus called "cane cactus," which grows from 4 to 8 feet high and is covered with beautiful flowers. Beautiful canes are made from the stem, hence the name.

After travelling about three days we struck the Tonto Mountains and stopped one night in a Mexican town called San Francisco, where a small stream of water dragged out a miserable existence. There were some rich placer diggings at this place, but they are not worked extensively on account of the scarcity of water. Next day we rambled about in the mountains and visited Gillett's camp, where there are some rich mines. We were unable to get work, so we camped that night in the woods and the next morning started for Albuquerque. Had a good dinner in a Mexican Village called San Antoninio, and in the evening arrived at another village called San Antonio and nestling beside a clear stream of water at the foot of the Sandia Mountains. There we stopped over night in the casa of a Mexican named Patricio Sanchez, who gave us a splendid supper and breakfast of "tortillas," "Carnero," "Caffee," and "Chili Colorado."

This Mexican had served several years as scout under General McKenzie, and could talk pretty good English. He entertained us with numerous yarns of his adventures among the Indians and of the exploits of another noted Mexican scout named Jose Pieda.[55]

Leaving our kind host yesterday morning we passed through Tijeras Cañon, crossed the Sierra Sandia, and emerging on the Rio Grande Valley arrived at Albuquerque last night, on the way falling in with some Mexican bullwhackers from whom we got our dinner of "pan" and coffee.

Albuquerque since the advent of the A.T. & S.F.R.R. is properly two towns. The old town lies about 1 1/2 miles from the railroad near the Rio Grande and is of the Mexican style of architecture. The new town is decidedly American and has sprung up about the railway station in the last six months. Each is practically a distinct town and has its own marshal. The marshal of the new town is Milt Yarberry, a noted frontier desperado and shooting man. He has been a partner of "Billy the Kid," "Mysterious Dave," and other noted outlaws. He is tall and angular and hails from Texas, carries a big sixshooter and cartridge belt, and wears a wide sombrero.[56]

We stopped in the new town last night and this morning went over to the old town, which like all Mexican towns is built of adobe with a "plaza" in the center and surrounded by beautiful orchards and vineyards. On one side of the plaza is a big cathedral and a chime of crazy bells were ringing for Mass this morning when we got there. Although it was Sunday scores of Mexican women and Pueblo Indians were peddling melons ("melonis") grapes ("ovas") and green pepper "chili verde" around the plaza and all the stores ("tinsdas"), [?] saloons, and gambling halls were open and in full blast. "Monte" seemed to be the favorite game, and crowd[s] of eager players surrounded each gaming table. Among the players were several "senoritas," their arms and fingers blazing with jewels, staking their "pesos," (dollars) with as much *sang froid* as the most veteran sports.

This game is dealt with Mexican or Spanish cards, which are smaller, thinner, and altogether different from American cards.

Rio Puerco, New Mex., Sept. 20

On the fifth of this month we left Albuquerque and went out to Luna, 28 miles from Albuquerque, the terminus of the Atlantic and Pacific Railroad, to work on the construction train. We went down to the river 12 miles to Isleta, a large Indian town. Here the road leaves the valley and takes across the divide. The end of the track was at Luna, which is nothing more than a switch near a high hill, or peak, called "Cerro de Las Lunas." Three or four days after our arrival my old partner Walt Wright, alias Harry Clifford, left saying he was going to the panhandle country. I went with him as far as Las Lunas, a pretty Mexican town on the N.M. & S.F. R.R. six miles from Luna. It was the most picturesque town I've seen in New Mexico, surrounded as it was with "rancherias" or farms and orchards shaded by large cottonwoods and with the Manzana Mountains for a background. I left Walt there and went back to camp.[57]

As the tracklaying progresses we move ahead with the construction train until now we are located at Rio Puerco, so called from the Rio Puerco (Muddy River) that flows drowsily along close by. We are thirty-four miles from Albuquerque. We eat, sleep, and have our being on the boarding train which is run off on a "spur" along side the main track. This train consists of some 30 cars comprising dining and sleeping cars, kitchens, store cars, butcher car, bake car, & c. and is under the supervision of the boarding "boss," R. P. Hall, and his steward, Benjamin F. Thompson.

Isleta Indians swarm around camp every day, selling grapes and melons. A band of Apaches passed here last week with a herd of ponies. They were a fierce looking set, all togged up in fringed buckskin and silver buttons and armed with Winchesters and sixshooters.

One evening recently an engine, while switching, ran into the boarding train with such force it broke the cow catcher off the engine and knocked one of the cars off the track. Most of the boys were at supper, and the tables and seats were upset and the grub and boys mixed up in a terrible mess on the floors.

Fortunately no one was seriously injured though some were bruised more or less. I was in my bunk at the time and came near being jarred out of it.

To the south of us a number of mountain ranges bound the horizon. They are the Soccorro range, the Scimitar Mountains, and the Sierra Ladrones (Thieves mountains), out of which rise two peaks, clear cut against the sky, called the Robber's Roost from having been the rendezvous of banditti from time immemorial.

About half a mile from here is a Mexican hamlet called Las Luceros. It is a den of thieves and murderers and on a hill overlooking the town a white man was robbed and murdered a short time ago.

San Jose, N.M., Oct. 10

We are 47 miles from Albuquerque. In the latter part of last month two companies of infantry and a scouting party of the 9th colored cavalry from Ft. Wingate camped here on their way to fight Victorio and his renegade Apaches.[58]

The country around here is covered with flat-topped mountains called "Mesas," with bold precipitous sides. One of them near camp is round, very high, and is called Round Mountain.

Nothing in the shape [of] vegetation grows here but scrub cedar, sage brush, and cane cactus.

El Rito, New Mexico, Oct. 25

Our present location is at the foot of a bold, red sandstone cliff on the Rio San Jose, a shallow stream. Opposite us on the other side of the river is an Indian pueblo called "Mesita Negra" (Little Black Mesa) and about a mile or so down the river is a Mexican village called El Rito and from which this station takes its name. The Pueblos swarm around camp day and night and sometimes pick up articles that may chance to be lying loose. A couple of days ago I had been washing and hanging my clothes up on the side of a car to dry while I went to dinner. Upon returning I missed my best blue woolen shirt, and immediately set about finding out who was the thief. About 15 or 20

Pueblo bucks were sitting on the ground at some distance, and [as] I approached I saw a pile of old overalls, gunny sacks & c. lying on the ground in their midst. I walked up and commenced to kick the old rags right and left. Some of the redskins jumped up to stop me, but just then I found my shirt at the bottom of the pile and holding it up, I gave them to understand as well as my poor Spanish would allow that it was "mi camisa."

"Si senor, muy bueno." "Yes sir, very good" was the answer, accompanied by a bland smile and I walked off in triumph with my shirt.

These Indians have good ponies and are wonderful horsemen. We sometimes get up races among them, the prize usually being a package of tobacco to the winner. They smoke a good deal but only cigarettes. I have not seen one of them use a pipe.

Physically they are small and thin though there are some exceptions. The full dress of a Pueblo buck consists of a red handkerchief, tied turban fashion round the head, a shirt or tunic of white or colored muslin fastened at the waist with a belt in which they carry their knife, white cotton trowsers reach to the knee, and below these are buckskin leggings fastened below the knee with red garters. Their feet are small and encased in moccasins dyed red. Each warrior also carries a small leather pouch suspended by a very broad strap over his shoulder and ornamented with bead work and silver buttons. Each one also carries a heavy striped woolen "serape" or blanket of their own manufacture.

The squaws are smaller than the men and the young ones generally good looking. They wear a loose, black woolen dress reaching to the knee and trimmed with yellow and fastened at the sides with silver pins. These dresses are sleeveless and open from the shoulder to the waist revealing a good part of their plump bodies and swelling bosoms. Around the waist is a red belt. Their legs are encased in buckskin leggings buttoned up the side with silver dollars. Their heads are covered with bright-colored shawl, which hangs down their backs after the style of the Spanish "mantilla." They also wear a lot of jewelry, silver and copper bracelets, and rings of native manufacture.

They wear their hair loose the same as the bucks.

Their toilet is considered complete when they get a colored handkerchief, which they fasten in their belts, and allow it to hang down over their hindquarters.

They are very modest and are said to be the most virtuous of all Indian women. They ride after the "whites style" and not astride like other Indian women.

The Pueblos of New Mexico and Arizona are supposed to be the descendants of the Aztecs of Mexico. They have always been above their neighbors in civilization. They are self supporting and make their living by tilling the soil in the valleys, plowing with a sharp stick and cultivating with a rough hoe. They have orchards and vineyards, raise fruit and melons, cattle and horses, sheep and goats. They have extensive irrigating canals and ditches. They weave some fine blankets, but they are especially famous for their pottery, which they mold into strange and fantastic shapes and paint with curious devices. They are nominally Catholics, though in reality they cling to their old tradition and worship Montezuma.[59]

El Rito, N.M., Nov. 4
This afternoon Jack Kerr, Hathaway, Barney McCabe alias "Tenderfoot Bill," and about a dozen railroaders and telegraph boys went to explore a famous cave about halfway between this place and Laguna. We went out about 3 or 4 miles on the train then turned south and walked about 3/4 of a mile over the lava beds. The entrance to the cavern was a narrow crevice in the lava, about a foot wide. We got through by tight squeezing and went straight down for about eight feet, then stoped to the south east for ten feet more, at which point the opening became large enough to assume an upright position. We had brought several lanterns with us and after becoming some what accustomed to the darkness, we continued our course in the same direction about eight feet over mighty rocks, which had the appearance of having dropped from the roof of the cave, when the opening suddenly widened out into an uneven chamber eight feet in length, fifty feet wide, and thirty feet high. The bottom of the lava bed could be seen here and we observed that it rested on a deposit of small stones, which showed signs of having at one time been exposed to great heat. Below the gravel deposit we turned to the right and climbed over stupendous lumps of lava in a westerly direction about 158 feet, and after creeping under a great ledge of the molten mass, which formed the roof of the chamber, a large well of pure, cold water was found, We had no means of ascertaining the depth of the well but it had a

treacherous look about it. A turn to the left started us down another descent, through another vault about 60 feet long and 30 feet wide. Our progress was impeded by large blocks of lava. On reaching another level and turning into one of the numerous passage ways another pool of water was found—not as large as the first but equally as pure. After quenching our thirst and gathering some thin scales of carbonate of lime, which were strewn thickly over the floor near the water, we turned back and had to do some rough climbing to get out of the cavern.

Throughout, the walls glistened with particles bright as diamonds, which clung to every joint and corner of the rock.

About 150 yards from the mouth of this cave was another opening to which was a yawning hole in the ground like a well or tenaja, about 12 feet wide at the top and gradually widening out as it went down. It could not be entered without ropes but as one had been provided, we let one of the telegraph boys down, and then tied a lantern to the end of the rope and let [it] down to him. He entered several passages branching out from the bottom, and explored them a short distance. We had a hard time pulling him up hand over hand.

This lava country is full of caves. The Indians at El Rito have knowledge of a cave in the vicinity which is said to be six or seven miles long. They, however, refuse to divulge its whereabouts to the whites.

Laguna, N.M., Nov. 11

We are now located at Laguna, an Indian Pueblo on the right side of the Rio San Jose. It is built of sandstone and mud on the bare rocks without regard to regularity. Some of the houses are three stories high. At a distance the town looks like the pictures of cities in the holy land. It has several hundred inhabitants, who have large herds of ponies, cattle, and burros and flocks of sheep, and up the river they have extensive vineyards.

They supply the railroad camps with meat. When we butcher cattle or sheep they are always on hand and take everything we have such as the goats head, & c. They hang this on poles along the walls of their houses to dry and these festoons of guts and offal makes a "tenderfoot" shudder to look at.

A spring near by supplies them with good drinking water and all day long there is a string of Pueblo maidens going to or from the spring with large native jars on their heads carrying water.

Some of these girls are decidedly handsome and well made and I have managed to get up a flirtation with one of them, who often comes to see me. I give her food and fruit and she has given me a silver ring of native manufacture. Our conversation is of course limited, as she don't understand much Spanish or English and I don't know much of the Pueblo tongue.

The Pueblos, I am told, are sun worshippers, and in securing confirmation I notice that every morning at sunrise almost the entire population of the Pueblo are to be seen on the roofs of their houses with faces turned to the east.

The locomotive is a constant source of wonder and delight to these simple folks. They flock around it and examine it, evidently to try and discover the motive power, but the engineer has only to blow a shrill blast on the whistle or to blow off steam when they scatter like sheep, but laugh heartily when they get at what they consider a safe distance.

They are fond of riding on the cars and every train coming or leaving has a crowd of them on top of the cars.

Laguna, Nov. 16

A band of Navajo Indians have been here several days. They are taller and better made than their cousins, the Pueblos. Many of them have mustaches. They are under Cayotanito, a great chief and brother of Manelito, the head chief of the Navajos.[60]

Cayotanito is a splendidly made Indian. He is built from the ground up, straight as an arrow, broad shoulders, tremendous chest and muscular limbs, a proud haughty expression on his face. He wears a very small pointed mustache. He wear[s] his hair Navajo style, tied up in a knot at the back of his head like a door knob. A crimson silk sash is tied around his head, turban fashion. A purple knit woolen jacket covers his body, his legs are encased in black velvet knee breeches with rows of silver buttons up the seams, the lower part of his legs are covered with buckskin leggings dyed black and buttoned up the side with silver buttons, his feet are very small and covered with moccasins of the Navajo style. Around his throat is a heavy necklace of about a dozen strands of beads, conchos, turquoise, and polished stones. It is very valuable and is said to be worth a dozen ponies. Around his wrists are heavy silver bracelets, round his waist is a belt made of large round plates of silver linked together, over all he wears a striped Navajo blanket, thick enough to shed rain. His face, like those of his followers, is painted a bright vermillion color, his arms are a long bow and arrow, which he carries in a quiver of panther skin slung at his side, and a scalping knife. He rides a fine black pony, with silver bridle and saddle decorated with silver and bead work.

He speaks Spanish so I could talk to him a little.

Some of his men have six shooters and cartridge belts in addition to their bows and arrows.

Laguna, N.M., Nov. 18

We had a snow storm night before last and the weather is very cold. About half the men are laying off and we build big fires of railroad ties and crowd around to get warm.

Even the Navajos say it is "mucho frio" and are glad to sit around the blazing ties, wrapped in their heavy blankets. Sometimes I get tired of crowding around the fires, and climb into my bunk, wrap myself up in my blankets, and pass the time reading, watching the squaws carrying water, or playing cards with the boys.

Cubero, N.M., Nov. 25

We are now 5 miles from Laguna in the foothills of the San Mateo Mountains. Mount Taylor, the highest peak in the range, looms up on our right, covered with a mantle of snow.

This station is named from an old Mexican town about 3 miles from here at the foot of Mt. Taylor. This afternoon I went over to Cubero to see the famous Mexican courtesan, "Steamboat," who is running a saloon there with a white man named Harry Harris. She is a lady of ample proportions, weighs over three hundred pounds, but is quick and active, has very small hands and feet, and magnificent black hair and eyes.

She has been proprietress of a number of saloons and dance halls in various frontier towns and is as well known in the south west as "Calamity Jane" is in the north west.

Cubero differs from other Mexican town[s] only in its being rougher and dirtier than any I have yet seen. Around the town are a number of piles of stones, each one surmounted by a cross bearing the names of persons who have been found murdered and buried at these places. These wayside graves are a special feature of most Mexican towns.

Cubero N.M., Nov. 26 [1880]

In a conversation this afternoon with "Captain Jack," the company carpenter, he told me he had news from the north and heard that Boone May had been shot by "Texas Charlie." It seems that May had a warrant for the arrest of Charley for horse stealing. Charlie hearing of it started to hunt for Boone, whom he found at Forbes Ranch on the Cheyenne. He secured the "drop" on May and shot him through the guts.

People Mentioned
in Rolf Johnson's Diaries

Notes

Introduction

1. It has been reported that Rolf continued to keep a diary until sometime in 1882 while he was still in the Southwest, but that only two members of the family read this volume before it was "destroyed." Dan Bloch, "The Saga of a Wandering Swede," *1954 Brand Book*, Denver Posse of the Westerners (Boulder, Colo.: Johnson Publishing Co., 1955) 10: 242.

2. *Holdrege Daily Citizen*, Oct. 11, 1923; Bloch, "The Saga of a Wandering Swede," 241.
John Johnson was born in Sweden in 1831 and came to Chicago in 1854, where he lived with his wife Karen or Carrie for twelve years. During this time he worked in the "car shops" and as a driver of an "express wagon." They then moved to Altona, Illinois, where John worked in a flour mill for four years. After they came to Phelps County, Johnson held a number of public offices, including justice of the peace, county supervisor, and county assessor. *Biographical Souvenir of the Counties of Buffalo, Kearney, Phelps, Harlan, and Franklin, Nebraska* (Chicago: F. A. Battey Company, 1890, Nebraska State Genealogical Society reprint, 1983), 710–11. The Johnsons' children were listed in the *Biographical Souvenir*, but there are some obvious errors. Ralph, a bookkeeper in Gothenburg, was undoubtedly Rolf. Nels Emile was a clerk in Norris's drug store in Holdrege. Hilda was Mrs. Davidson rather than Danielson. George W. lived in Cheyenne, Wyoming. Justus, Ida, and Robert were probably still with their parents. They were all Lutherans. According to the book the Johnsons came to Phelps County in 1872 and spent the Easter storm of 1873 in John M. Dahlstrom's cellar. In his diary Rolf wrote about living in Dahlstrom's cellar during a severe storm in March 1876.

3. George M. Stephenson, *The Religious Aspects of Swedish Immigration: A Study of Immigrant Churches* (Minneapolis: n. p., 1932). During the next eight years emigration dropped to an average of only 750 a year before a second migration began to gather, reaching a peak in 1869 when 32,000 people left for the United States. Harold Runblom and Hans Norman, *From Sweden to America: A History of the Migration* (Minneapolis: University of Minnesota Press, 1976), 117; Theodore C. Blegen, "Leaders in American Immigration," *Transactions of the Illinois State Historical Society* 38 (1931): 152.

4. *Holdrege Daily Citizen*, Oct. 11, 1923. Swedes began settling in the Altona vicinity in the late 1840s, but the major influx came in the 1860s. Ernest W. Olson, ed., *History of the Swedes of Illinois*, 2 vols. (Chicago: Engberg-Holmberg Publishing Co., 1908) 1:181, 234, 323.

5. Sivert Erdahl, "Eric Janson and the Bishop Hill Colony," *Journal of the Illinois State Historical Society* 18 (1925): 503–74. There were a few Swedish settlements farther west at this time. Peter Cassel founded New Sweden, a settlement near Fairfield, Iowa,

in 1845. It has been characterized as the first permanent, nineteenth-century Swedish settlement in America. Blegen, "Leaders in American Immigration," 152; Olson, *History of the Swedes of Illinois*, 1:354. Bloch concluded that the Johnsons moved first to Altona, then to Henderson Grove, and then in about 1874 to North Prairie. Bloch, "The Saga of a Wandering Swede," 241. This last move conflicts with Rolf's diary entry for January 10, 1876, where he notes that he was only staying at a friend's house in North Prairie, and on February 17 he again mentions visiting the community. On January 20, 1876, Rolf specifically refers to "my house in Henderson Grove." Then on March 5 Rolf wrote, "We left Henderson Grove to day . . . my forest home that has sheltered me nearly six years." Thus the Johnsons would have moved to Henderson Grove in the spring of 1870, which agrees with Bloch's date for that move.

6. Ernest Ludlow Bogart and Charles Manfred Thompson, *The Centennial History of Illinois*, 4 vols. (Springfield: Illinois Centennial Commission, 1920), 1:234.

7. A. T. Andreas, *History of the State of Nebraska* (Chicago: Western Historical Co., 1882), 169. The estimate was probably low. By the end of 1875 there were 105 homesteads and timber claims in the county. *Tract Books*, United States General Land Office, vols. 123–26, RG508, Nebraska State Historical Society (hereafter cited as *Tract Books*).

8. Addison E. Sheldon, "Land Systems and Land Policies in Nebraska," *Publications of the Nebraska State Historical Society* 22 (1936): 25, 75, 94, 97, 98.

9. Ralph H. Brown, *Historical Geography of the United States* (New York: Harcourt, Brace and Company, 1948), 418–19; *Platte Valley Independent*, June 22, 1878.

Advice to timber claimants was published in newspapers. It was claimed that a cottonwood cutting would be sixteen feet tall in only three years. The advice assumed ideal conditions. It was never mentioned that cottonwood cuttings thrive only in moist ground, and even a short dry period will kill them. If the cuttings do take root, severe damage can still be caused by rabbits, antelope, and cattle who all enjoy the tender leaves and bark. *Daily State Journal*, (Lincoln, Nebr.) Mar. 15, 1876.

10. *Tract Books*, vols. 123–26.

11. Brown, *Historical Geography of the United States*, 42.

12. "Rocky Mountain Locust, or Grasshopper of the West," *Report of the Commissioner of Agriculture, 1877* (Washington, D. C.: GPO, 1878); Everett Dick, *Conquering the Great American Desert* (Lincoln: Nebraska State Historical Society, 1975), 209.

13. Charles Valentine Riley was largely self-taught. He served as Missouri's entomologist from 1868 to 1877. Dr. David L. Keith, personal communication, August 13, 1999. *Platte Valley Independent*, Mar. 4, 1876; *Central Nebraska Press*, Sept. 14, 1876.

The issue of the *Platte Valley Independent* on Feb. 10, 1877, offered its readers a solution. During a warm spell in February, a Hall County farmer harrowed a field and uncovered countless locust eggs. It was reported that birds ate most of the eggs and a frost killed the rest. The *Independent* urged farmers to follow this practice and assured them the locust would not be a problem if this precaution were taken.

14. *Grand Island Times*, Oct. 4, 1877.

15. B. E. Bengston, *Pen Pictures of Pioneers* (n. p., 1926), 18.

16. Page T. Francis, "Reminiscences of Page T. Francis," *Publications of the Nebraska State Historical Society* 19 (1919): 49.

17. Everett Dick, "Water, a Frontier Problem," *Nebraska History* 49 (1968): 215–45. John Unruh loosely quoted Mennonite settlers of about this time and wrote the "wonderful American machinery" obviated the problem of hand-digging deep wells. Drilling was apparently expensive. John D. Unruh, Jr., "The Burlington and Missouri River Railroad Brings the Mennonites to Nebraska," *Nebraska History* 45 (1964): 197, 203.

18. Bengston, *Pen Pictures of Pioneers*, 16. Olson's description suggests he was using a machine sold by the Jilz Well Auger Company. Their illustrated advertisements claimed an owner of an auger could earn twenty-five dollars a day. *Central Nebraska Press*, Nov. 30, 1876. Other brands were Morgan's well auger and the Palmer auger. *Platte Valley Independent*, Mar. 25, 1876; *Grand Island Times*, May 12, 1875.

19. A. Clyde Eide, "Free as the Wind," *Nebraska History* 51 (1970): 25–47.

20. *Columbus Journal*, July 15, 1877; Bengston, *Pen Pictures of Pioneers*, 46. Funk paid twelve cents a pound for wire.

21. James C. Olson and Ronald C. Naugle, *History of Nebraska* (Lincoln: University of Nebraska Press, 1997), 153–54, 181.

22. The total number is an estimate based upon Rolf's entry for March 6, 1876. On March 15 he says there were "over 30."

23. Blegen, "Leaders in American Immigration," 152; Ruth Billdt, *Pioneer Swedish-American Culture in Central Kansas* (Lindsborg, Kan.: Lindsborg News-Record, 1965), 12. The first Galesburg Colonization Committee settlers located about twenty-five miles southwest of Salina. Ibid., 35; Joseph Alexis, "Swedes in Nebraska," *Publications of the Nebraska State Historical Society* 19 (1919): 81–84.

24. Olaf Hedlund was born in Sweden in 1827. In 1857 he emigrated to the United States with his wife, Frita Person, and his brother, Matthias, settling at Wautauga, Illinois, about five miles east of Henderson Grove. Olaf was a blacksmith and lay minister. In the spring of 1875 he accompanied a group of landseekers to Nebraska led by F. A. Beiyon, who was selling Union Pacific Railroad land. The party went south from Kearney to Franklin County and then to Phelps County, where Olaf homesteaded. It was called Blacksmith Ranch on the Kearney-Orleans mail route. Olaf was elected county treasurer and his son, P. O. Hedlund, was elected surveyor. Olaf was a founder of the Swedish Lutheran Bethel congregation in Phelps County. Services were first held in peoples' homes and then in a church built three miles east of where Holdrege now stands. *Biographical Souvenir*, 696–97; Bengston, *Pen Pictures of Pioneers*, 3–5.

25. James Iverne Dowie, "Prairie Grass Dividing," *Augustana Historical Society Publications* 18 (1959): 17, 36. By 1880 there was a Swedish Lutheran Church, businesses, and a post office at Seva. Ibid. Charles Perky, *Past and Present of Saunders County, Nebraska*, 2 vols. (Chicago: S. J. Clark Publishing Company, 1915), 1:44; Andreas, *History of the State of Nebraska*, 729.

26. Merrill Mattes and Paul Henderson, "The Pony Express: Across Nebraska From St. Joseph to Fort Laramie," *Nebraska History* 41 (1960): 101; Colton's Map of the Land Grant to the Union Pacific Rail Road, 1873. M782, 1872 C72, Nebraska State Historical Society, Lincoln. Garden Station was also called Craig and Shakespear.

27. Plum Creek, Nebr., Report of Post Office Site Locations (National Archives Microfilm Publication M1126, roll 78). Record Group 28, Records of the U.S. Post Office

Department, National Archives and Records Administration (hereafter cited as Report of Site Locations, and the roll number).

28. *Holdrege Progress*, Oct. 22, 1925; *Tract Books*, 126:243–50.

29. *Tract Books*, vols. 123–26.

30. Robert C. Ostergren, "Cultural Homogeneity and Population Stability among Swedish Immigrants in Chisago County," *Minnesota History* 43 (1973): 255; Helge Nelson, *The Swedes and the Swedish Settlements in North America* (Lund, Sweden: 1943), 63–65; John S. Lindberg, *The Background of Swedish Emigration to the United States* (Minneapolis: 1930), 49–50.

31. Eighty-nine claims were filed in the county in 1876 and twenty were filed the next year. In 1878 the number of Swedish immigrants declined to 40 percent. *Tract Books*, vols. 123–26.
    The population of Phelps County was conservatively estimated at 110 at the end of 1875. Andreas, *History of the State of Nebraska*, 169. The estimate for 1876 was 151. *Daily State Journal*, July 7, 1876. The estimate seems low because the Johnsons and their friends arrived in 1876 and increased the population by thirty to forty people and they were not the only immigrants. In that year nearly ninety claims were filed on government land, although certainly some were absentee claimants.
    Olson has reported that from 1874 through 1877 immigration "fell off considerably, and only one large group settled on Union Pacific lands—348 families of Swedes from Illinois, who occupied a large tract in Phelps and Kearney counties." Unfortunately Olson did not provide a source for this interesting statistic. Olson, *History of Nebraska*, 173. In his discussion of the settlement of Phelps County Andreas wrote, "Early in the year 1873, quite a heavy immigration commenced, and a large number of settlers entered claims during the year." Andreas, *History of the State of Nebraska*, 1261. Fourteen claims were entered that year.

32. Unruh, "The Burlington and Missouri River Railroad Brings the Mennonites to Nebraska," 23, 192; *Tract Books*, vols. 113–16.

33. *Tract Books*, vols. 123–26.

34. Howard Ruede, *Sod-House Days, Letters from a Kansas Homesteader 1877–78*, John Ise, ed. (Lawrence: University Press of Kansas, 1983), 20–21.

35. *Tract Books*, vols. 123–26.

36. Ibid.; Olson, *History of Nebraska*, 160.

37. Andreas, *History of the State of Nebraska*, 1261–62. Rolf has more to say about the ring in Chapter 5. The presence of a county ring was recalled as late as 1909. W. H. Arnold, *Arnold's Complete Directory of Phelps County, Nebraska* (Kearney, Nebr.: W. H. Arnold, 1909), 9.

38. *Compendium of the Tenth Census, June 1, 1880*, Part II, (Washington, D. C.: GPO, 1888), 1618; *Nebraska Nugget*, Aug. 22, 1883.

39. Andreas, *History of the State of Nebraska*, 1261–62.

40. *Tract Books*, 123:73–83.

41. H. Arnold Barton, *Letters from the Promised Land: Swedes in America, 1840–1914*

(Minneapolis: University of Minnesota Press, 1975), 171. Mission Friends were part of the Waldenstrom movement that swept over Nebraska in the 1870s. They were considered heretics by orthodox Lutherans. James Iverne Dowie, "Sven Gustaf Larson, Pioneer Pastor to the Swedes of Nebraska," *Nebraska History* 40 (1959): 220.

42. Phelps County Historical Society, comp., *History of Phelps County, Nebraska* (Dallas, Tex.: Taylor Publishing Co., 1981), 11.

43. Ruede, *Sod-House Days*, 49, 158.

44. John Johnson's timber claim was filed on June 28, 1876, for NW24 T7N R19W and the homestead was filed on September 29, 1879, on the southwest quarter of the section. He ultimately received a title or "proved up" on both parcels. *Tract Books*, 124:16.

45. Rolf's homestead was the SE18 T7N R18W. *Tract Books*, 126:256. Aaron's homestead was the SE24 T7N R19W. John Johnson's land was the western half of the section, but no one filed on the remaining quarter section until May 1880. *Tract Books*, 124:16.

46. Bloch, "The Saga of a Wandering Swede," 243. Rolf's homestead application was canceled on December 12, 1879, while he was living in Denver. *Tract Books*, 126:256.

47. Thilda married N. P. Holm on October 21, 1879. She was twenty-one and he was twenty-three years old. Marriage Records, Phelps County, Nebraska, 1887–98, p. 40, RG255, Nebraska State Historical Society, Lincoln. Thilda died in childbirth on October 2, 1884. *Holdrege Republican*, Oct. 8, 1884. Nels Peter Holm filed for a homestead on December 8, 1879, on SE8 T7N R18W and received title in 1888. *Tract Books*, 124:9, 19. The similarity of the names and the lack of any alternatives suggests that N. P. and Nels Peter were the same person. He may also be the Peter Holm mentioned in the diary.

48. Phelps Center, Nebraska, Record of Appointment of Postmasters (National Archives Microfilm Publication M841, roll 79). Record Group 28, Records of the U.S. Post Office Department, National Archives and Records Administration (hereafter cited as Appointment of Postmasters and the roll number). *Tract Books*, 124:16. The claim was for SW10 T7N R18W filed on July 17, 1884. Rolf also purchased NE23 T7N R18W from the Union Pacific Railroad at a later date. *Holdrege Daily Citizen*, July 1, 1976.

49. *Holdrege Daily Citizen*, May 12, 1945; *Nebraska Nugget*, Sept. 10, 1884; 1885 State Census, Phelps County, Nebraska.

50. Bloch, "The Saga of a Wandering Swede," 243; *Tract Books*, 124:16. Prior to this, West owned the Pioneer Lumber Company in Gothenburg. *Gothenburg Independent*, May 9, 1885.

51. *Gothenburg Independent*, June 15 and July 27, 1892, Feb. 4, 1893; Bloch, "The Saga of a Wandering Swede," 243–44; *Kearney Daily Hub*, July 25, 1892.

52. *Gothenburg Independent*, Feb. 4, 1893; Bloch, "The Saga of a Wandering Swede," 243–44.

53. *Gothenburg Independent* Jan. 25, 1896. At this time Rolf's former employer, E. G. West, was selling Hecla Lump Coal. By 1900 Rolf listed his occupation as a bookkeeper. 1900 and 1910 U. S. Census, Dawson County; *Gothenburg Times*, Nov. 8, 1912.

54. 1900 and 1910 U. S. Census, Dawson County; *Holdrege Daily Citizen*, May 12, 1945; *Gothenburg Independent*, Sept. 4, 1920; Bloch, "The Saga of a Wandering Swede," 244; *Holdrege Weekly Progress*, Feb. 2, 1922. Rolf's wife Ellen died in 1945 at age eighty-four. *Gothenburg Times*, May 17, 1945.

1. Illinois Homeland

1. Rolf's friends and relatives were from a small area north of Galesburg, Illinois.

2. Rolf discusses Rev. Jacob Danielson later after Danielson moved to Phelps County. Leander Hallgren and his brother, Frank, were land agents for the Union Pacific Railroad. They targeted Swedish communities, especially in Illinois, with their sales pitches. Leander also made trips to Sweden. *Holdrege Daily Citizen*, June 18, 1958. He continued in various land promotion schemes until he contracted malaria in Texas in 1892, forcing him to return to his home in Kearney, where he died on July 23. *Gothenburg Independent*, July 27, 1892.

3. In the 1850s immigrants came from rural Sweden and settled in the vicinity of Soperville. Coal mining was the major business. Carl V. Hallberg, "Soperville: An Immigrant Community in Knox County," *Journal of the Illinois State Historical Society* 74 (1981): 51, 54.

4. Fridolf W. Stenfelt, his wife Carrie, and two children, were farming in Phelps County in 1880. Apparently Vendla had left home by this time. 1880 U.S. Census, Phelps County.

5. Mrs. Hawkinson was John Johnson's sister. *Biographical Souvenir*, 710.

6. August Bragg moved to Phelps County in March 1877. He came with John P. Bragg and family. In 1880 he was a twenty-two-year-old resident of Prairie Precinct. 1880 U.S. Census, Phelps County.

2. The Trip to Nebraska

1. The Chicago, Burlington, and Quincy Railroad went from Galesburg about twenty miles to the northeast to Galva, where the emigrants would have boarded the Chicago, Rock Island, and Pacific Railroad. They crossed the Mississippi River from Rock Island, Illinois, to Davenport, Iowa, and then traveled west through Iowa City, Des Moines, and ending at Council Bluffs. In 1876 a sleeping car ticket from Chicago to Omaha was three dollars. Henry T. Williams, ed., *Williams' Illustrated Trans-Continental Guide of Travel from the Atlantic to the Pacific Ocean* (New York: Henry T. Williams Publisher, 1877), 13.

George Davenport served in the army from 1804 to 1814. Later he purchased government land and platted the Iowa town named for him. He was robbed and murdered on July 4, 1845. Three men were executed for the crime. Benjamin F. Gue, *History of Iowa*, 4 vols. (New York: Century History Co., 1903), 4:67–68.

2. Entries in the *Tract Books* show that all of the men filed for timber claims or homesteads. All but three received title to the land.

3. The explorers Lewis and Clark first used the term Council Bluffs in reference to a landmark on the west side of the Missouri River about twenty miles north of Council Bluffs, Iowa. The founders of the community borrowed the well-known name.

4. Although the Union Pacific Railroad began building track westward from Omaha in 1865, a bridge over the Missouri River was not completed until March 25, 1873. Harrison Johnson, *Johnson's History of Nebraska* (Omaha: Herald Printing, 1880), 120.

5. At the time of Rolf's brief visit there was a small Swedish community in Omaha. A Swedish Lutheran Church had been organized in 1868, but the chapel was over a mile from the railroad depot. Andreas, *History of the State of Nebraska*, 729.

When Rolf passed through Fremont, Columbus, and Grand Island, each community had a population in excess of 1,000. Smaller villages were located about every ten miles along the railroad.

6. The Pawnee had a reservation centered around Genoa, twenty miles west of the Loup River crossing, but the last contingent of the tribe was relocated on a reservation in present Oklahoma in the fall of 1875. George Hyde, *The Pawnee Indians* (Norman: University of Oklahoma Press, 1974), 332–33. It is possible that a few Pawnee mixed-bloods remained behind. The Santee, Omaha, and Ponca lived on reservations in northeastern Nebraska and segments of these tribes still hunted buffalo in central and western Kansas. Rolf may have seen one of these groups returning from a winter hunt, but his "whole village of wigwams" must have been an exaggeration resulting from what was probably his first glimpse of Native Americans.

The Platte River is a broad, braided river with many channels and long sloughs. It would have been unlike anything Rolf had ever seen.

7. A week after the Johnsons and their friends arrived in Kearney "seven car loads of Swedes" disembarked from a train. Their destination was not mentioned. *Grand Island Times*, Mar. 15, 1876.

A journalist visited Kearney about this same time and described it as "a lively enterprising town" with "four church edifices, two daily newspapers, the *Times* and the *Press*, two brick bank buildings and other brick blocks, with hotels, numerous stores, school house, court-house, etc." The Union Pacific coming from Omaha and the Burlington and Missouri River Railroad coming from Hastings converged at Kearney. Williams, *Williams' Illustrated Trans-Continental Guide*, 32–33. The Union Pacific was the first railroad to reach Kearney, arriving in August 1866. Olson, *History of Nebraska*, 115.

8. Cattle drives from Texas to Kearney began in a small way in 1871. The town was a primary destination for the drovers for the next three years until the influx of farmers forced the cattlemen westward, shifting the trail's end to Ogallala, Nebraska. Norbert R. Mahnken, "Early Nebraska Markets for Texas Cattle," *Nebraska History*, 26 (1945): 100. There were large ranching operations in the area before the farmers arrived. Their herds were free-roaming, but by 1874 farmers had arrived in sufficient numbers to demand that the cattle either be herded or the ranchers must pay for crop damage.

Milton M. Collins, the son of a minister, farmed on the south edge of Kearney. On September 17, 1875, he discovered a herd of forty horses had ruined his cornfield and he penned the animals in a corral. The animals belonged to Jordon P. Smith and when he came to get them, Collins asked for compensation for his crop losses. An argument ensued and Smith shot and killed the young farmer. Some people claimed Smith was intoxicated at the time. A deputy U. S. marshal and a posse of twenty finally succeeded in capturing Smith, who was tried and convicted of manslaughter. The following summer a man claiming to be Smith's brother rode into town, vowing revenge on those responsible for Smith's capture. City Marshal Stimpson attempted to arrest the stranger, but he resisted and the marshal shot him. It was later discovered the dead man was not Smith's brother, but a local cowboy from Plum Creek. Andreas, *History of the State of Nebraska*, 424–25. If the cowboy was from Plum Creek it is likely he worked on the Dilworth ranch. It is probable he was the Ed Smith mentioned by Rolf. The city marshal was Charles R. "Dick" Stimpson. *Biographical Souvenir*, 458.

9. Rolf's mention of a bridge "wide enough for trains to pass each other" probably refers to wagons and not railroad trains. The wagon bridge was less than a mile due south of Kearney and was in place by 1874. The Burlington and Missouri Railroad laid track and built a bridge across the Platte in the fall of 1872. This bridge was nearly four miles southeast of Kearney. Andreas, *History of the State of Nebraska*, 416; *Official State Atlas of Nebraska* (Philadelphia: Everts and Kirk, 1885), 170.

10. John M. Dahlstrom was born in Sweden in 1844 and came to the Cambridge, Illinois, vicinity in 1868. In 1873 he purchased land from the Union Pacific Railroad in Phelps County. He was one of the more fortunate newcomers, with assets of $2,000 in cash and personal possessions. *Biographical Souvenir*, 711. He was married to Annie and by 1880 they had four children. 1880 U.S. Census, Phelps County.

3. Phelps County, Nebraska

1. Williamsburg was the first county seat after Phelps County was formed in 1873. A post office was established there on July 18, 1874. Report of Site Locations, frame 159, roll 366.

An emigrant house was a hotel where new arrivals could stay at no charge until they found land to homestead or purchase and establish living quarters there. Emigrant houses were provided by railroads or speculators who had acquired large tracts of land they hoped to sell at a profit. Rex German and Russ Czaplewski, *Battle of the Bridges* (Lexington, Nebr.: Dawson County Historical Society, 1988), 20. The emigrant house in Phelps County was a frame structure about twenty by thirty feet and occasionally as many as six families lived there. Joseph Clark Mitchell, *An Early History of Phelps County, Nebraska* (Masters thesis, University of Nebraska, 1927), 53.

2. Caleb James Dilworth fought in the Battle of Atlanta in the Civil War and attained the rank of brevet brigadier general. He died in 1900. Francis B. Heitman *Historical Register and Dictionary of the United States Army* (Washington, D. C.: GPO, 1903), 373–74. Dilworth owned a ranch on Plum Creek in the northwest corner of the county and was an early settler. He was Nebraska's attorney general from 1879 to 1883. *Nebraska Blue Book 1994–95* (Lincoln: Joe Christensen, Inc., n.d.), 392. Phelps County was named for William Phelps, the father of Dilworth's wife. Mitchell, *An Early History of Phelps County*, 22. Dilworth was a leader of what Rolf calls "the ring," a group opposed to the political aspirations of the Swedes. A. S. Baldwin opened his law practice in Williamsburg in the fall of 1873. He served as a county commissioner for five years and in 1879 he moved to Lexington, Nebraska. Andreas, *History of the State of Nebraska*, 621. Albert Hansen and his wife Mary had two children and lived on a timber claim near Williamsburg. 1880 U.S. Census, Phelps County. He became the Williamsburg postmaster on August 28, 1878. Appointment of Postmasters, roll 79. John F. Shafer served as the first Phelps County judge. Andreas, *History of the State of Nebraska*, 1261.

3. Basement-like dwellings called slattorps were built by Swedish settlers in Phelps County. One built in the 1880s was twenty-four by twenty-eight by nine feet deep.

Ralph Arthur Larson, *Three Brothers from Nebraska* (Alexandria, Minn.: Echo Printing, 1978), 7.

4. In December the Johnsons picked up buffalo bones and sold them in Kearney for $6.00 a ton. Earlier in the year the price had been $5.00 and the trade was reported as "lively." *Platte Valley Independent*, Mar. 11, 1876. Christian Jensen came to Phelps County in the spring of 1874 and a decade later he recalled that "so hard were the times, and so difficult was it to get money" that he also collected buffalo bones and sold them in Kearney for $5.00 a ton. *Biographical Souvenir*, 625.

5. Kearney businessmen were making a concerted effort to convince travelers bound for the Black Hills gold fields that the road from the city to the Hills was the shortest route and that Kearney was the best outfitting point. Maps published in the local newspaper conveniently omitted Sidney, Nebraska, and the shorter trail from that point. *Central Nebraska Press*, Apr. 19, 1877.

6. The little "bug eater" was Atle, son of Charles and Johana Nelson who immigrated from Sweden to Chicago in about 1870. The Nelsons had three other children, two of whom were born in Sweden and one in Illinois. 1880 U.S. Census, Phelps County. The nickname probably had its origin during the grasshopper infestations in 1874–76.

7. There were U.S. government land offices in Bloomington, Grand Island, and North Platte, but none in Kearney. Johnson must have gone to a "locator," an individual who for a fee would guide a settler through the bureaucracy, fill out the proper forms, and deliver the paperwork to a government land agent. Johnson's timber claim was not filed until June 28, 1876. *Tract Books*, 124:16. He could have applied for a preemption on March 21, but no record could be found.

8. At this time hand-dug wells cost about sixty cents a foot. Unruh, "The Burlington and Missouri River Railroad," 6. Later Rolf mentioned the completed well was 110 feet deep.

9. William Lee opened the first grocery store in Williamsburg in September 1877. *Central Nebraska Press*, Sept. 6, 1877.

10. Samuel Moser was fifty-seven years old. 1880 U. S. Census, Phelps County.

11. By the end of 1876 twenty people had claimed government land along Spring Creek in Phelps County. *Tract Books*, 123. Rolf's comment that the valley was "settled nearly its entire length" suggests there were a number of squatters.

12. It seems sod houses are invariably described as cool in summer, warm in winter, and generally comfortable. Howard Ruede, a northern Kansas homesteader about this time, had more experience with sod buildings. He wrote, "The people who live in sod houses, and, in fact, all who live under a dirt roof, are pestered with swarms of bed bugs. . . . if you wish to measure them in a spoon, you can gather them up in that way from between the sods in the wall." Ruede, *Sod-House Days*, 91–92. About this same time the roof of one sod house in Hall county collapsed killing two children. *Grand Island Independent*, June 21, 1877. It would have been necessary to strip the sod from an acre of land to build Johnson's house and it would have weighed about ninety tons. Joanna L. Stratton, *Pioneer Women, Voices from the Kansas Frontier* (New York: Simon and Schuster, 1981), 54.

13. Henry Ward Beecher (1813–87) was an extremely influential Congregational

minister, orator, and newspaper editor. His trial for adultery in 1875, which ended with a hung jury, created a public sensation. Clifford Edward Clark, *Henry Ward Beecher: Spokesman for a Middle Class America* (Urbana: University of Illinois Press, 1978), 209. Rolf may have seen pictures of Beecher in the newspapers.

14. The Williamsburg post office was opened in July 1874. The first postmistress was Eva M. Baldwin. Report of Site Locations, roll 366, frame 159. William A. Dilworth, son of Caleb James Dilworth, took over on June 15, 1876. Appointment of Postmasters, roll 79.

15. The prairie rattlesnake occasionally reached a length of five feet. They are extremely venomous and were soon hunted to near extinction in the area. A report that one nine feet long with twenty-seven rattles was killed about this time in Buffalo County must have been an exaggeration. *Central Nebraska Press*, Sept. 14, 1876.

16. The family is not listed in the 1880 census of Phelps County. In October 1878 Rolf described the heavy losses suffered by Carlson in a prairie fire and this may have led to his decision to leave Phelps County.

17. Buckwheat (*F. esculentum*) had been cultivated in Europe since the Middle Ages. The small seeds could be ground into flour for human consumption or could be used for poultry and livestock feed. *Columbia Encyclopedia*, 386.

4. Summer Rambles in Eastern Nebraska

1. Andrew J. "Andy" Johnson was the fifteen-year-old son of Gustaf and Stina Johnson. 1880 U.S. Census, Phelps County.

The Burlington and Missouri River Railroad reached Juniata in June 1872 and a month later trains were running through Hastings. By September Hastings was also the terminus of the St. Joseph and Denver City Railroad. This combination assured the town's growth. Andreas, *History of the State of Nebraska*, 358 and 337.

2. Robbins' Great American and Rentz's German Allied Shows featuring 1,500 "living wild animals" and 1,000 performers were advertised to appear in Lincoln on July 25. *Daily State Journal*, July 16, 1876.

3. Rolf's host may have been Willime Mertens, who owned a farm near Plattsmouth since coming to Nebraska in 1866. Andreas, *History of the State of Nebraska*, 499.

4. Both Mennonites and Germans from Russia had settled in this general area. Newspapers often confused the two and perhaps Rolf did also. The Germans from Russia were in the immediate Sutton vicinity, while Mennonites were farther north in Hamilton County. Unruh, "The Burlington and Missouri River Railroad," 191.

5. A neighbor of the Johnsons later recalled that when the grasshoppers were first seen on August 5, 1876, they appeared like "a thin brownish colored cloud or haze over the Platte River." Bengston, *Pen Pictures of Pioneers*, 18.

6. In 1864 Elim Jones was in charge and was killed while trying to prevent some Indians from stealing his horses. Margaret (Jones) Estey, "Pioneer Sketch" manuscript, letter from Louise W. Lynch to librarian, July 27, 1976, Paul D. Riley Collection, Nebraska State Historical Society. Stories of a "hare brained youth" wantonly killing an Indian abound in the folklore of the West. Unlike Rolf's story the youth is killed and skinned by Indians, thus giving the name rawhide to a butte or stream.

Rolf never mentioned Fort Kearny. It was on the south side of the Platte River only a few miles east of the Kearney bridge. This large army outpost on the Overland Trail was abandoned in 1871. Francis Paul Prucha, *Guide to the Military Posts of the United States* (Madison: State Historical Society of Wisconsin, 1964), 82.

5. Back to Phelps County

1. Plastering a sod house would eliminate most of the dirt that continually crumbled from the walls. Bedbugs and fleas were a problem in sod houses and plastering eliminated the pests' hiding places. A Kansas pioneer noted, "Where the sod houses are plastered the bed bugs are not such a nuisance." Ruede, *Sod-House Days*, 92.

2. Rev. Jacob Danielson was a Lutheran minister. He and his wife Christena and their three oldest children, Thilda, Alexander, and John, were born in Sweden. Esther, age three, was their youngest and was born in Illinois. 1880 U.S. Census, Phelps County.

3. The first settlers in Harlan County spent the winter of 1870–71 in a rude stockade at the Melrose townsite. In the spring F. A. Bieyon built a store there. Andreas, *History of the State of Nebraska*, 966. Royal Buck visited the Melrose site in November 1871 and "found a few Swedish settlers in an adobe stockade where they had the previous winter fortified against Indians." Albert Watkins, "The Beginnings of Red Willow County," *Publications of the Nebraska State Historical Society* 19 (1919): 31.

In the spring of 1875 Bieyon was selling Union Pacific land and brought a group of settlers to Phelps County and some of them homesteaded in the southeast corner of the county. Bengston, *Pen Pictures of Pioneers*, 4.

Orleans was a more successful town. By 1873 it had a school, post office, and a hotel. Andreas, *History of the State of Nebraska*, 964. Only a few early issues of the *Republican Valley Sentinel* have survived.

4. Although Alma was the county seat it could hardly be considered a town. The courthouse was a small building moved in from a neighboring farm. Republican City could boast a school, store, and a newspaper. Andreas, *History of the State of Nebraska*, 962, 966.

According to Andreas's *History of the State of Nebraska*, 875, the Walther and Gallard grist mill at Naponee was built in 1874. The next spring high water damaged the building and it was sold to J. D. Gage, who operated it when the Johnsons were there. An item in the *Republican Valley Sentinel* on January 1, 1876, briefly reported that the mill was under construction.

5. The Swedish settlement would have been in northeastern Harlan County centered around the now defunct community of Garber, where a post office was established in October 1874. Settlement originated around the mouth of Turkey Creek in 1871. Andreas, *History of the State of Nebraska*, 866.

6. Plum Creek flows into the Platte River in the extreme northwest corner of Phelps County. There was also a small town called Plum Creek on the Union Pacific Railroad about twelve miles to the northwest, where Lexington now stands.

In 1868 the Utes agreed to a reservation in western Colorado. For a few years they continued to hunt buffalo on the east side of the Rocky Mountains and an agency was opened in Denver in 1871. By 1876 the buffalo were gone from the east slope and the white residents complained that the Indians, with no robes to sell, were becoming troublesome. Wilson Rockwell, *The Utes: A Forgotten People* (Denver: Sage Books, 1956), 81–82. Rolf's buffalo hunt was postponed for one year.

7. Andrew E. Harvey was born in Indiana in 1847. He attended Oberlin College in Ohio and studied law in Iowa. In 1873 he came to Arapahoe, Nebraska, where he practiced law and homesteaded nearby. He was elected to the state legislature in 1876 representing Phelps, Furnas, and Gosper counties. In later years he formed a partnership with George W. Burton in the banking business. *Biographical Souvenir*, 799–801. Henry V. Hoagland was the first person to file for a homestead in Phelps County on August 13, 1872, on NW24 T8N R17W. He proved up in 1875. *Tract Books*, 126:246.

8. Historian A. T. Andreas concluded, "there is no county property of any value, and that its indebtedness is about $25,000, it would appear that there was mismanagement on the part of some of the early county officials, and a gross careless extravagance on the part of the early settlers in voting bonds which resulted in no benefit to the county." Andreas, *History of the State of Nebraska*, 1262.

9. Silas Garber settled in Webster County in May 1870. He served two terms as governor of Nebraska from 1875 to 1879. Andreas, *History of the State of Nebraska*, 1483.

10. Joseph A. Harron had a general merchandise store in Kearney. *Central Nebraska Press*, Apr. 19, 1877.
A felon is a suppurative inflammation usually around a finger or toenail. In the 1870s the best remedy was a compress made of the pulp of prickly pear cacti. *Platte Valley Independent*, Apr. 2, 1878.

11. Rolf discusses "Crazy Miller" in more detail in his entry for July 20, 1877.

12. Sherwood Post Office was opened in February 1875. Robert M. Hindman was the postmaster. Report of Site Locations, roll 366, frame 159. He later became the first treasurer of Phelps County. Andreas, *History of the State of Nebraska*, 1261.

13. Unfortunately only a few issues of the Swedish paper *Vart Nya Hem*, published in 1877, have survived. Microfilm 078.4 K21w, Nebraska State Historical Society.

14. At this time the average salary for a teacher in Nebraska was $37.00 a month. *Central Nebraska Press*, Sept. 6, 1877.

15. The new graveyard is present day Moses Hill Cemetery located in the center of the county.

16. In 1862 W. H. Knaggs, his wife, and four-year-old son William H. Knaggs, Jr., came to Dobytown, the civilian community on the west edge of the Fort Kearny reserve. Later they homesteaded about twelve miles to the west. Their son moved to Kearney in 1881 and years later was elected mayor. Mrs. Clifford Zehr, "William H. Knaggs," *Where the Buffalo Roamed* (Shenandoah, Iowa: World Publishing Co., 1967), 255–56. The senior Mr. Knaggs and his wife, Ann, were from England. In 1880 they had two adult sons and a daughter living with them. 1880 U.S. Census, Phelps County.

17. Ida would marry a Mr. Gray. They were "engaged in missionary work" in Garnett, Kansas, when she died of pleurisy on January 16, 1902. She was buried at Moses Hill Cemetery. The couple had three small children. *Holdrege Weekly Progress*, Jan. 31, 1902.

18. Newspaper reports of the incidents are similar to Rolf's account. *Daily State Journal*, July 29, 1877; *Republican Valley Sentinel*, Nov. 27, 1880.
Nine Millers are listed in *Tract Books*, but neither William C. "Crazy" Miller nor his brother Elton are among them. Robert Dale, Samuel Dale, and John Daggett all had homesteads in the southeast corner of the county at that time. *Tract Books* 123:206–16.

The Dales were from England. 1880 U.S. Census, Phelps County. On September 20, 1877, Elton P. Miller, the brother of the slain ex-sheriff, wrote a letter to the editor of the *Central Nebraska Press*. He admitted his brother had been insane for the past four years and held no one responsible for his brother's death. He asked people to stop discussing the incident. *Central Nebraska Press*, Sept. 27, 1877.

Rolf discusses the killing of the three Sioux chiefs in more detail in his entry for October 23, 1877.

19. Unfortunately local newspapers failed to report the crime or issues are missing for this time period. David Anderson, the Buffalo County sheriff, gave a similar report of the incident. The sheriff worried that the perpetrator was a well known local individual because two "cross" dogs in the store did not bark when he entered through an unlocked window. The sheriff also admitted, "We have no idea [and] not the least thing to identify the murder[er] by." No one was ever charged with the crime. David Anderson to L. E. Cropsey. Aug. 29, 1877, Silas Garber Papers, RG1 SG11, Nebraska State Historical Society, Lincoln. Thomas C. Roberts opened his general merchandise store on April 1, 1873. Andreas, *History of the State of Nebraska*, 436.

20. There is no record of the land hunters. Either they decided against Phelps County and moved elsewhere, or they purchased railroad land.

21. The Red Cloud Agency for the Oglala Sioux was established in August 1873 on the White River near the northwestern corner of Nebraska.

22. Broomcorn was not only a rugged and adaptable plant, but one with a ready market. Varieties had been developed with a very long panicle that was cut off just before the seeds formed. The panicles were placed in a drying barn for a time and then a horse-powered scraping machine removed husks and chaff. The panicles were then baled and sent to broom-manufacturing companies. *Grand Island Times*, Mar. 29, 1877. Farmers also planted broomcorn because grasshoppers would not eat the plant. Dick, *Conquering the Great American Desert*, 195. Brooms made of broomcorn are still produced, but have been largely replaced by synthetic fibers.

23. Rolf will have more to say about "Indian John" in later entries.

24. In the fall of 1877 wheat was seventy-five cents a bushel, barley was thirty-two cents, and rye was twenty-five cents. The Johnsons would have received $114.05 for their crop. *Grand Island Times*, Oct. 25, 1877.

25. On July 25, 1864, soldiers temporarily stationed at Plum Creek found the scalped body of Garrett eight miles south of the garrison. He had gone in search of a mule. *History of Phelps County, Nebraska*, 9.

26. Andrew Ruben was born in Sweden in 1842 and came to Des Moines, Iowa, in 1868. *Biographical Souvenir*, 796. Two years later he went to Harlan County with a party of forty men to select homesites. Andreas, *History of the State of Nebraska*, 959.

6. The Buffalo Hunt

1. The buffalo hunt was an attempt to earn money and Rolf and his friends probably would have denied it was sport or a vacation. About this time a dealer at Plum Creek Station, Nebraska, was paying $2.50 for a buffalo hide. German and Czaplewski, *Battle of the Bridges*, 14.

2. The Watson Post Office was established in May 1872. Fred Switzer took over as postmaster a year later. Appointment of Postmasters, roll 79.

3. Jonas Clarin was born in Sweden and was a dealer in furs after emigrating to Chicago. In 1872 he and his wife homesteaded west of Watson in Furnas County. His son was also named Jonas. Selma Clarine Culver, "Jonas Clarine," Furnas County Historical Society, comp. *Furnas County, Nebraska* (Dallas, Tex.: Curtis Media Corp., 1987), 227.

4. Arapahoe was founded in 1871 by the Arapahoe Town Company of Plattsmouth, Nebraska. It lost its bid to be the county seat and grew very slowly. It was incorporated in 1878. Jennie Cox, "Arapahoe," *Furnas County, Nebraska*, 14.

5. I. B. Burton built a trading post at Burton's Bend near the mouth of Deer Creek in 1870. Shirley I. McCoy, "Ben Burton," *Furnas County, Nebraska*, 215.

6. Rolf's story is generally consistent with contemporary accounts. These earlier versions had the Indian stealing food from a breadbox rather than coffee. Newspaper accounts in 1873 accused Mortimer N. "Wild Bill" Kress and John C. "Jack" Ralston of the crime. The incident occurred in December 1872. Paul D. Riley, "The Battle of Massacre Canyon," *Nebraska History* 54 (1973): 228; *Omaha Daily Herald*, Feb. 19, 1873. Kress came to Nebraska in 1865 and "led a migratory life on the frontier, experiencing many thrilling encounters with both the Indians and border ruffians." When Rolf wrote about him he was living on a farm southeast of Hastings. Andreas, *History of the State of Nebraska*, 329.
The Sioux did not set out on a mission of revenge, but found the Pawnee by accident near present Atwood, Rawlins County, Kansas, many miles from Frenchman Creek. The Sioux stole most of the Pawnee horses and killed one young man. The attackers were never positively identified but were probably Whistler's Cut-off Oglalas. Riley, "The Battle of Massacre Canyon," 229–30.

7. A post office at Indianola was established in June 1873. Appointment of Postmasters, roll 79.

8. Smoky Hill Ranch would have been a few miles west of Culbertson, Nebraska.

9. A company of cavalry from Fort McPherson on the Platte River east of North Platte, Nebraska, was on patrol and camped near the mouth of Blackwood Creek on the night of May 31–June 1, 1873. Torrential rains at the upper reaches of the creek caused a sudden and dramatic flood downstream. Flood waters rose at an incredible rate, perhaps as the result of the bursting of a natural brush dam. A fifteen-foot wall of water engulfed the men and six drowned. Twenty-five horses were also lost. Settlers in a cabin nearer the mouth of the creek survived. *Trenton Torpedo*, June 11, 1886.

10. Culbertson, Nebraska, was named for Alexander Culbertson, a famous fur trader in the upper Missouri River country until his retirement in 1862. At the time Rolf wrote about him he was living with his daughter and son-in-law in Orleans. Charles E. Hanson, Jr., "Marking the Grave of Alexander Culbertson," *Nebraska History* 32 (1951): 120–29.

11. An 1885 atlas of Nebraska places Camp Creek about three miles above Dry Creek. *Official State Atlas of Nebraska*, 108. Today it is called Hay Canyon.
Three days later Rolf learned that the rumor was exaggerated. No one was killed, but "some ponies and a pack mule" were stolen. On November 12 Rolf was again told

there were Cheyenne Indians in the vicinity, but it is more likely they were Lakotas from the Sioux Indian Reservation in Dakota. During the summer of 1877 over 900 Cheyennes had been taken from the Sioux Reservation in Dakota and transferred to the Southern Cheyenne reservation in present-day Oklahoma, where they arrived on August 5. Approximately 100 Cheyennes remained in the north. Both groups were carefully watched by the army and government employees. It is unlikely they would have had an opportunity to go on a horse-stealing expedition so far from their respective agencies. James Irwin, "Red Cloud Agency," *Annual Report of the Commissioner of Indian Affairs* (Washington, D.C.: GPO, 1877), 62; J. M. Hayworth, "Cheyenne and Arapahoe Agency," *Annual Report of the Commissioner of Indian Affairs* (Washington, D.C.: GPO, 1877), 85.

12. Battle Canyon is about seven miles above the Frenchman rather than twelve. It is known today as Massacre Canyon and a monument commemorates the tragic event. Although Rolf said they passed the canyon on the morning of October 26, earlier diary entries make it clear they passed it on the morning of October 25.

13. Rolf tells a very garbled version of the incident. On August 5, 1873, about 350 Pawnees were moving along the divide between the Frenchman and the Republican west of Culbertson. Buffalo were sighted and the men rode forward to begin a surround, only to be attacked by a combined force of about 1,000 Oglalas and Brulés. The Pawnees retreated into a little valley, where 60 to 80 Pawnees were killed. The Pawnees retreated down the canyon, but were not pursued by the Sioux who were content with the number they had killed and all of the meat, hides, and equipment abandoned by the Pawnees in their flight to safety. John William Williamson was the white agent who accompanied the Pawnees on the trail. Antoine Janis and Stephen F. Estes were with the Sioux. Capt. Charles Meinhold commanded an army scouting party camped east of Culbertson and was unaware of the battle until the Pawnees began straggling into his camp. By the time the soldiers arrived at Massacre Canyon the Sioux were gone. Riley, "The Battle of Massacre Canyon," 235–39; Paul D. Riley, "Red Willow County Letters of Royal Buck, 1872–1873," *Nebraska History* 47 (1966): 390–91; *Nebraska City News*, Sept. 6, 1873.

14. Rolf and his companions left the mouth of Indian Creek on the morning of October 27 and reached the Frenchman on the twenty-eighth and after spending some time at a ranch, proceeded up the valley in the afternoon. In a day and one-half of travel it would have been possible for them to cover the thirty-five miles to a ranch shown in the *Official State Atlas of Nebraska*, 108. This is probably the site of the Rock Bluffs ranch. The atlas locates Webster Ranch on the south side of Spring Creek six miles north of Imperial.

15. The head of Frenchman's Fork is nearly thirty miles west of the Nebraska-Colorado state line. Rolf found a state line marker on November 1 so the camp was not a great distance west of Rock Bluffs.

16. Dr. John S. Hoyt studied medicine in Iowa. He came to Nebraska in 1872, first to Melrose, and then in 1875 to Orleans. Andreas, *History of the State of Nebraska*, 965.

17. The Henry rifle, although a repeater, was woefully inadequate as a buffalo gun. Its .44 caliber rimfire cartridge contained only twenty-eight grains of black powder and lacked the velocity and energy needed for big- game hunting. Clarence Peterson's "Big 44" Sharps rifle, by contrast, was probably chambered for the .44/90 cartridge,

which contained ninety grains of black powder and which was more than adequate as a buffalo killer.

18. Samuel McNeece was born in Indiana in 1831. He moved to Iowa in 1862, served in the Civil War, and then returned to his Iowa farm until 1872 when he and his wife moved to a farm in Harlan County. Samuel was an avid hunter throughout his life. William was his son. *Biographical Souvenir*, 794–95.

7. Home Again, Politics and Romances

1. Phelps Post Office was authorized in September 1877. Carl J. Anderson was the postmaster. Report of Site Locations, roll 366, frame 132.

2. Christian Jensen was born in Denmark in 1836 and in 1867 migrated to Omaha, Nebraska, and worked for the Union Pacific Railroad. *Biographical Souvenir*, 624–25.

3. John H. Irvin lived in Illinois, where he was engaged in the manufacture of brooms prior to coming to Nebraska in 1874. He purchased the Grand Central Hotel in Kearney. The two-story, twenty-six-room building could accommodate fifty guests. Andreas, *History of the State of Nebraska*, 434.

4. Devil's Gap would have been about ten miles northwest of Rock Falls.

5. Earlier Rolf mentioned that he helped "dig" a well. His comment here that he "commenced to drill a well" may refer to a well auger rather than a hand-dug well. Augers were available by this time. *Platte Valley Independent*, Mar. 25, 1876; *Grand Island Times*, May 12, 1875.

6. Manlius Lucas was born in Kentucky in 1849 and came with his parents to central Illinois in 1852. He moved to Phelps County in the fall of 1872 and started a cattle ranch. *Biographical Souvenir*, 638.

7. Samuel L. Savidge advertised his law practice in the *Central Nebraska Press*, Nov. 30, 1876. Guy A. Brown was named clerk of the Nebraska Supreme Court in 1868. Andreas, *History of the State of Nebraska*, 161.

8. Simon C. Ayer located in Gibbon, Nebraska, in 1871 and held a variety of jobs. He was elected Buffalo County clerk in 1875 and in 1880 he was chosen a representative to the state legislature. *Central Nebraska Press*, Sept. 14, 1876. Andreas, *History of the State of Nebraska*, 442.

9. Ex-President Grant and his family sailed for England on May 17, 1877, beginning a two-year tour around the world. Jesse Root Grant was born in 1858 and was the youngest of the Grants' four children. W. E. Woodward, *Meet General Grant* (New York: Horace Liveright, 1928), 123, 458–59.

10. Rolf's entry on March 8, 1876, discusses the murder of Milton Collins. City Marshal Charles R. "Dick" Stimpson arrived in Kearney in 1872. He was a Civil War veteran and was a professional carpenter. *Biographical Souvenir*, 458. In Andreas, *History of the State of Nebraska*, 425, the city marshal is identified as Robert Stimpson. The Harrold House was touted as one of the best hotels in the West. *Central Nebraska Press*, Oct. 25, 1877. In the summer of 1874 cowboys were galloping through the streets, shooting and generally creating a potentially dangerous nuisance. When the city marshal tried to put a stop to it, one of the cowboys shot at him and then a cowboy named Peeler was

shot in the neck and presumably killed. If this occurred in front of a bagnio it was not noted. Shortly thereafter, Texas Spence shot up a saloon and created a larger disturbance when the marshal made an unsuccessful attempt to arrest him. Two days later a gang of cowboys came looking for the marshal, but the citizens of Kearney had had enough. They banded together, forming a vigilante committee called the Kearney Guard, and ran the cowboys out of town, killing Texas Spence in the fray. Andreas, *History of the State of Nebraska*, 423–24; Mahnken, "Early Nebraska Markets for Texas Cattle," 101.

11. On September 19, 1877, six men robbed a train of $60,000 in gold coins at Big Springs, Nebraska. Shortly thereafter three of the men were killed resisting arrest. Tom Nixon, a gang member, fled to Canada, while the remaining two bandits, Sam Bass and Jack Davis, went to Texas. Bass and Davis met their old friend Henry Underwood in Texas and a few days later they robbed a stagecoach. When Underwood was captured on December 24 the arresting officers were convinced he was Tom Nixon. Because of the misidentification Underwood was sent to jail in Kearney, Nebraska, to await trial for the more serious Big Springs robbery. He was placed in a cell with a man variously known as Huckstron, McKeen, or Arkansas Johnson, a petty thief charged with stealing lumber. Underwood paid a discharged inmate to bring him a file and Huckstron's wife smuggled hacksaw blades into the jail in a bucket of butter. On March 14, 1878, the two men sawed through the bars and escaped. They stole horses and fled to Underwood's home near Fort Worth and again met with Sam Bass. By this time the police were closing in and on June 13 the three outlaws were ambushed by a posse not far from Fort Worth. Huckstron was killed but the others escaped. Bass was killed in a shootout four months later. Underwood disappeared and only rumors tell of his fate. Wayne Gard, *Sam Bass* (Boston: Houghton Mifflin Company, 1936), 99–230.

There can be little doubt that the man Huckstron, in the Kearney jail for stealing lumber, was really Jasper Haralson, Rolf's "bridge lumber thief." The jail break by Haralson and Underwood is also mentioned in the S. D. Richards' confession that Rolf later copied in his diary. In the confession Richards twice referred to "Underwood, alias Nixon" and identified him as a Big Springs robber, so Richards seems to have had the same misconception as did Underwood's arresting officers. Richards also claimed to have provided some "instruments" that helped them escape. Rolf never mentions Nixon and refers only to Underwood.

A reward of $50 was offered in September 1877 for the conviction of the thief who stole a plank from the bridge over the Platte River. *Central Nebraska Press*, Sept. 6, 1877.

12. A. L. Webb's Hardware and Agricultural Implements Store was located on the corner of Wyoming Avenue and Tenth Street. Construction began in October 1873. J. M. Frantz operated the New Drug Store on South Wyoming Avenue. *Central Nebraska Press*, Sept. 14, 1876. Rolf mentioned John P. Nelson in passing in the entry for January 13. Nelson was working in Kramer's mercantile store in Kearney at the time and fought the blaze. By 1884 he managed one of Kramer's stores in Holdrege. Nelson was born in Sweden in 1855 and moved to Minnesota in 1868 with his parents. *Biographical Souvenir*, 680.

13. The fire was set by John "Indian John" Nelson who was caught, tried, and sentenced to twenty years in the state penitentiary in Lincoln. He was released after fourteen years for good behavior. Nebraska Board of Pardons and Parole, RG034, Nebraska State Historical Society, Lincoln.

Shortly before the fire Eugene Hall was arrested for his involvement in a "disturbance" in a house of ill repute in Kearney. Bail was set at $300, suggesting the charge was serious, but apparently he was found innocent. *Central Nebraska Press*, May 13, 1877.

14. David Anderson was born in Indiana in 1839 and served in the Civil War before settling near Elm Creek, Buffalo County, in 1871. He was elected sheriff of the county in 1874 and held office for six years. He then returned to farming. Andreas, *History of the State of Nebraska*, 429.

15. Edward R. S. Canby was an army officer who served in the Mexican War and the Union army in the Civil War. Heitman, *Historical Register*, 279.

16. Rolf made a small error. His father's land was on NW24 T7N R19E not T6N. *Tract Books*, 124:16. Rolf would have to pay $400 one year from the date of his preemption application to receive title to the land. If he had the money or thought he could acquire it, there are no hints in his diary. Apparently Rolf did make some improvements. In his diary for April 22, 1879, he mentions selling his preemption to Aaron Blomquist for $100. On May 5 Blomquist filed for a homestead on NE24 T7N R19E. *Tract Books*, 124:16.

John H. Roe was a real estate agent who assisted customers in filling out the proper forms and then delivered them to the U. S. land offices. He was also a sales agent for the Union Pacific, selling railroad land for $2 to $4 an acre. *Central Nebraska Press*, Nov. 30, 1876.

17. Rolf does not explain his business at the land office, but he may have been delivering the preemption papers. The government land office at Bloomington was managed by George W. Dorsey. *Central Nebraska Press*, Sept. 27, 1877.

18. John Lindbloom was born in Sweden in 1842 and moved to northeastern Illinois in 1864. He lived in Minnesota for a short time where he met and married Maggie Swanson. *Biographical Souvenir*, 700. The county seat would be moved from Williamsburg in the northwest corner of the county to Phelps Center, where it was more accessible to the Swedish residents.

8. The Harvest Circuit

1. Shelton could scarcely be considered a village at the time of Rolf's visit. Although it was on the railroad there was no depot. Gibbon was founded in 1871 by a colony made up largely of Civil War veterans from Ohio. Samuel C. Bassett, "Free Homestead Colony of Buffalo County, Nebraska" (mimeographed, n.d.), 29–30. Irish immigrants settled along Wood River. The village of Wood River was founded in 1868. In 1874 the town was moved two miles to the east. Andreas, *History of the State of Nebraska*, 943–44.

2. Martin Schimmer opened the Sand Krog in 1875. By the end of the century it would grow into Hall County's finest resort before it began to decline. Tom Allen, "Once-Lively Harmony Hall Now Abandoned And Forgotten," *Stuhr Museum News* 31 (1997): 3–4.

Rolf is probably referring to Emory Peck. He was forty-two years old, lived near Wood River, was married, and had five children. *Biographical Souvenir*, 322–23.

3. William B. Hollister was a telegrapher when he went to work for the Union

Pacific Railroad in North Platte in 1868. A year later he became the station agent at Wood River. He acquired a 450-acre farm one mile south of Wood River and another 240 acres one mile to the east. Andreas, *History of the State of Nebraska*, 944.

4. Luther L. Holbrook, Herman Allen, and brothers William F. and Jacob A. Sutton set out on a hunting and trapping expedition in mid-February and camped on the Dismal River about thirty miles above its mouth. Nothing was heard from them and by late April their friends around Kearney organized a search party. The bodies of Holbrook and one of the Suttons were found in the camp. Both had been shot in the head. The bodies of the other two were not immediately found and it was suspected they were in the Dismal River. The search party thought the hunters were killed about March 1 because Allen had been keeping a diary and the last entry was on February 28. The searchers found wagon tracks leading from the scene and thought the killers were headed for the Black Hills. The investigation continued and warrants were later issued for Henry Hargrave, John Kinney, and Tip Larue. Investigators speculated that the motive for the killings was a quarrel of some kind. Because Holbrook had been a member of the state legislature in the late 1860s the investigation of the crime was probably more vigorous than if the slain men had been itinerant hunters. Nevertheless it is not known if the killers were apprehended. *Daily State Journal*, May 3, May 8, and June 5, 1878; *Cheyenne Daily Leader*, June 7, 1878; Andreas, *History of the State of Nebraska*, 130–35.

5. John E. Swanson was born in Sweden in 1847 and came to Minnesota with his parents in 1867. Ten years later he moved to Phelps County and soon thereafter married Cristina Swanson from Furnas County. *Biographical Souvenir*, 632–33.

9. More Politics and Romances at Home

1. Rev. J. N. Allen of the Congregational Church accompanied the Soldiers' Free Homestead Temperance Colony from Ohio in the spring of 1871. Allen may have been a home missionary, since he is credited with preaching at the founding of Wood River in 1874 and Minden in 1878. Andreas, *History of the State of Nebraska*, 440, 444, 944, 1023.

The losses in the prairie fire suggest the blaze burned an area between Sacramento and Rock Falls and then turned northward toward Phelps Center. Prairie fires were widespread. Several deaths were reported in northeastern Nebraska and in Howard and Valley counties there was a "terrible loss of property." It was feared that Kearney would have to be evacuated due to nearby prairie fires. *Fremont Daily Herald*, Oct. 23, 1878.

2. The "recent Indian massacres" refers to stories about the Cheyennes under Dull Knife and Little Wolf, who had fled from the reservation in Oklahoma on September 9 in an attempt to return to their homeland in Montana. The Cheyennes may have crossed the headwaters of Beaver and Sappa creeks, but went no farther east. George Bird Grinnell, *The Fighting Cheyennes* (Norman: University of Oklahoma Press, 1956), 405ff. There were depredations and some whites were killed, but newspapers exaggerated many stories about Cheyennes. *Sidney Telegraph*, Sept. 28, 1878.

3. George Armstrong Custer's Seventh Cavalry protected surveyors mapping the line of the proposed Northern Pacific Railroad across present North Dakota and Montana in 1873. Paul Andrew Hutton, ed., *The Custer Reader* (Lincoln: University of Nebraska Press, 1992), 180–81.

4. The Johnsons raised more than two and a half times as much grain in 1878 as they did the previous year. Due to a sharp drop in the price of wheat, however, the crop was worth only $200. *Grand Island Times*, Oct. 31, 1878.

5. John D. Seaman opened a grain and agricultural implement business in Kearney in 1874. He served in the Nebraska senate in 1879–80. Andreas, *History of the State of Nebraska*, 437.

6. The expression "ground hog case" refers to a situation with no alternative.

7. The Dilworth stock ranch was along Plum Creek in the extreme northwest corner of Phelps County. By 1880 the Dilworth family owned over one thousand acres. 1880 U. S. Census, Phelps County, Nebraska, Schedule 2, Products of Agriculture.

8. In the summer of 1872 Charles Walker built a house and outbuildings near the southwest corner of Kearney County. A store was added later. Roy T. Bang, *Heroes Without Medals: A Pioneer History of Kearney County* (Minden Nebr.: Warp Publishing Co., 1952), 68. Walker stayed there only a few months and the ranch was taken over by Daniel B. Ball. *Holdrege Daily Citizen*, June 18, 1958.

9. The burial place of Mrs. Haralson and her children has not been determined to be in any nearby cemeteries. If they were buried at the farmstead it is likely the graves were marked only in a temporary manner and are now lost. James E. Potter, personal communication, March 24, 1999.

10. Stephen D. Richards is discussed in more detail later. A similar report of the brutal slayings is in Andreas, *History of the State of Nebraska*, 1022.

11. Andreas noted the marriage of Rosa Jessup to Fred Risland, but erred when he wrote it was in August 1876, and the first in Hall County. Andreas, *History of the State of Nebraska*, 944.

12. *Julatta* was a church service held at 5 A.M. on Christmas morning. Elenor Trott, *Svenska Nebraska* (York, Nebr.: Gillen Inc., 1967), 27. A crown or *ljusa crona* consisting of white candles and colored paper streamers on a wire frame was suspended from the church ceiling. *Holdrege Daily Citizen*, June 18, 1958.

13. It was reported in Sidney, Nebraska, that two young sons of W. H. [*sic*] Shafer were shot and killed by a band of twenty Cheyennes while the boys were searching for cattle on the Shafers' ranch twenty-eight miles north of Sidney. The boys' names were not mentioned. *Sidney Plaindealer*, Oct. 24, 1878.

14. Wilson's office was a sod building and the newspaper was printed on a homemade press. Arnold, *Arnold's Complete Directory of Phelps County*, 9.

15. Frank L. Gibbs, an Ohio native, came to Kearney in the spring of 1877 and was a clerk in Moore's Bank. Andreas, *History of the State of Nebraska*, 432.

10. The Execution of Stephen D. Richards

1. Minden was unbroken prairie when it was chosen as the site for the new county seat in the fall of 1876, but because of an injunction brought by the residents of Lowell the county records were not moved until May 1878. At that time Minden had a school and one store. Andreas, *History of the State of Nebraska*, 1023.

2. John B. Peterson was born in Sweden in 1846. He came to the United States in 1867, going first to Iowa, then to the Cambridge, Illinois, vicinity, and to Phelps County in 1879. *Biographical Souvenir*, 617–18.

3. Indian Territory is present day Oklahoma. The colonel was probably Richard Irving Dodge. Camp Supply was an army outpost in northwestern Oklahoma and Fort Reno was in the center of the territory. Prucha, *Guide to Military Posts*, 101, 110.

4. The wooden enclosure was sixteen feet square and fourteen feet high. *Daily State Journal*, Apr. 24, 1879.

5. Rev. W. Sanford Gee was pastor of a Baptist church in Lincoln, Nebraska. *Daily State Journal*, May 4, 1879. Lewis A. Kent was born in Illinois in 1847. He and his wife came to Nebraska in 1871 and homesteaded in the northeast corner of Kearney County. He helped organize the county and served as the county clerk for five terms. *Biographical Souvenir*, 590–93.

6. Rolf's description of the execution and Richards's remarks prior to it are similar to the report in the *Daily State Journal*, Apr. 27, 1879.

7. Rolf must have copied Richards's confession from a newspaper. The *Daily State Journal* paid Richards "a liberal price" for it and published it on April 27, 1879.

8. The Haralsons are not listed in the U.S. land records nor in the real estate tax records of Kearney County. Jasper Haralson is named in the county's personal property tax list for 1877. Kearney County Tax Lists, County Treasurer's Office, Minden, Nebraska.

9. William Gaslin, Jr. was elected judge to the Fifth Judicial District of Nebraska in 1875 and reelected in 1879. John Haskell, *Judge William Gaslin, Nebraska Jurist* (Omaha: n. p., 1983), 28, 33. He had a reputation for rendering maximum sentences. Norbert R. Mahnken, "Ogallala—Nebraska's Cowboy Capital," *Nebraska History* 28 (1947): 102.

Peter Anderson was buried in Bethany Cemetery, southeast of Axtell, Nebraska. His estate papers are in the Albinus Nance Papers, RG1, SG12, Nebraska State Historical Society, Lincoln.

10. The county debt was approaching $36,000 at this time. *Compendium of the Tenth Census, June 1, 1880*, Part II, (Washington, D. C.: GPO, 1888), 1618. The bond was for $35,000. Arnold, *Arnold's Complete Directory of Phelps County*, 9. The voters of the county rejected the issuance of bonds until 1883, when they approved the $35,000 bond issue. *Nebraska Nugget*, Aug. 22, 1883.

11. The Republican Valley Railroad Company was organized on March 28, 1878, by officers from the Burlington and Missouri and the Chicago, Burlington, and Quincy companies. They built a railroad south from Hastings to the Republican River and then west up the valley. By the end of May 1880 the line had reached Indianola. Richard C. Overton, "Why Did The C. B. & Q. Build to Denver?" *Nebraska History* 40 (1959): 189, 193.

12. Rolf Johnson filed a homestead claim on SE18 T7N R18W on May 5, 1879. It was canceled on Dec. 12, 1879, when Rolf was in Denver. *Tract Books*, 126:256. On July 17, 1884, he filed a timber claim on SW10 T7N R18W, but canceled two years later. *Tract Books*, 126:251–62.

13. Orleans began as a stockade built in the fall of 1870 to protect the first settlers in the county. It was not until 1873 that a village grew up around the abandoned stronghold. Carl Boehl built the gristmill. Andreas, *History of the State of Nebraska*, 964. James Lukecart was born in Ohio in 1827. He and his wife moved to Phelps County in 1878. Their assets consisted of "some live stock" and $2.40. *Biographical Souvenir*, 668–69.

11. The Black Hills and the Southwest

1. William F. "Buffalo Bill" Cody was a well-known showman by this time. He had toured the United States with his troupe performing in dramas about the early West. The house Rolf saw was completed in May 1878. The more palatial Scout's Rest was built eight years later. Don Russell, *The Lives and Legends of Buffalo Bill* (Norman: University of Oklahoma Press, 1960), 260, 422.

2. By the time Rolf arrived Sidney had established itself as the principal jumping off place for travelers going to the Black Hills. William E. Lass, *From the Missouri To the Great Salt Lake* (Lincoln: Nebraska State Historical Society, 1972), 193. Fort Sidney was established in 1867 to protect workers building the Union Pacific Railroad. Troops were withdrawn in 1894. Prucha, *Guide to the Military Posts*, 107.

3. Rolf garbled the story slightly. Charles Reed, not Dug Douglas, had been in Sidney for a few months living with Mollie Wardner in a bagnio. Harry Looomis was walking past her house about eleven o'clock one evening and she invited him to come in. Loomis rejected the invitation and added an insult. Ms. Wardner complained to Reed, who ran after Loomis, struck him, and shot him in the leg. Loomis was taken to the army hospital at Fort Sidney, where the doctors amputated the shattered limb. He died the next day. Reed was arrested and jailed shortly after the attack. An angry mob dragged him from the jail and hung him from a telegraph pole on Front Street. *Sidney Telegraph*, May 17, 1879.

4. A newspaper article titled "Hanging Too Good For Him" told of an old man named Godkin in Rapid City, who was "perusing the devilish practice of inducing little girls to let him take their pictures with their clothing arranged in the same manner and in similar positions to those assumed by the lowest class of prostitutes." He was arrested and the report left little doubt that he would go to prison. *Black Hills Daily News*, Dec. 5, 1890.

5. Sidney Propst began operating a stage and mail route from Sidney to Sterling and Greeley, Colorado, about 1877. Harriet Persinger Searcy Murphy, "A. B. Persinger, Nebraska Panhandle Pioneer," *Nebraska History* 54 (1973): 273.

6. This may have been George Gunn, who came west about 1875. In 1881 he was temporarily in charge of a ranch on the South Platte River south of Sidney. Ibid.

7. It was about 270 miles from Sidney to Deadwood. White bandits were a more serious threat on the trail than Indians. By 1878 robberies were so common that one sarcastic article in a Sidney newspaper began, "The usual weekly stage robbery of the Cheyenne mail coach occurred Thursday afternoon." *Sidney Telegraph*, Sept. 26, 1878. The stage lines owners retaliated and by the time of Rolf's visit the trail was less dangerous. Norbert R. Mahnken, "The Sidney-Black Hills Trail," *Nebraska History* 30 (1949): 217, 222–23.

8. The Tusler brothers began ranching on Greenwood Creek in the early 1870s and

by the summer of 1876 they owned 3,500 cattle. Aubrey J. Buhrdorf, compiler, *History of Cheyenne County, Nebraska* (Dallas, Tex.: Curtis Media Corp., 1987), 27.

9. Frank Towle was a member of a gang that was robbing stagecoaches in the Black Hills area in the summer of 1877. Boone May was a guard on one of these coaches and killed Towle during a foiled robbery attempt. A substantial reward had been posted in Wyoming for the bandit, so May cut off the dead man's head and carried it to Cheyenne to claim the dead-or-alive reward. Officials there said the reward had been withdrawn. Gard, *Sam Bass*, 72. Boone May was also mentioned as a guard for the Gilmer and Salisbury stage company. Mahnken, "The Sidney-Black Hills Trail," 221.

10. The North Platte toll bridge was built by Henry T. Clarke and opened on May 10, 1876. Clarke charged two dollars for each wagon crossing the bridge. Rolf's Mooresville was Clarke's store and a post office at the south end of the bridge. The U. S. Army established Camp Clarke at the north end as protection against brigands both red and white. The blockhouse was thirty-two feet square. Mahnken, "The Sidney-Black Hills Trail," 211–13.

11. Chimney Rock was about twelve miles west of the bridge. Virtually every diary written by travelers on the old Oregon-California and Mormon trails mentioned this remarkable landmark. It is a major tourist attraction today with a museum operated by the Nebraska State Historical Society.

12. Henry C. Clifford came to Nebraska in 1860 and about five years later married a Lakota woman. Eli S. Ricker Collection, MS8, Tablet 8: 79, Nebraska State Historical Society, Lincoln. O. C. Marsh, a Yale University paleontologist, hired Clifford as a guide. James H. Cook, *Fifty Years on the Old Frontier* (Norman: University of Oklahoma Press, 1957), 277. When Rolf met him, Clifford had been running the station for only a short time. Clarence Schnurr, "Edgar Beecher Bronson," *Sioux County, Memoirs of its Pioneers*, Ruth Van Ackeren, ed. (Harrison, Nebr.: Harrison Ladies' Community Club, 1967). About this time Clifford, his brother Mortimer, and John Y. Nelson became involved in a nefarious business trading whiskey to the Lakota for horses the Indians had stolen from the whites, and then selling the animals back to the settlers. Harrington O'Reilly, *Fifty Years on the Trail: A True Story of Western Life* (Norman: University of Oklahoma Press, 1963), 244–245. Red Dog was a member of the Oglala Loafer band and, unlike Red Cloud, was in favor of an agency on the White River. J. E. Smith to assistant adjutant general, Sept. 27, 1872, Letters Received by the Office of Indian Affairs, 1824–81, Red Cloud Agency (National Archives Microfilm Publication M 234, roll 715), Record Group 75, Records of the Office of Indian Affairs, National Archives and Records Administration. Although Red Dog was certainly an influential leader of the Oglalas, Rolf has elevated his status somewhat. James C. Olson, *Red Cloud and the Sioux Problem* (Lincoln: University of Nebraska Press Bison Book, 1975), 273, 292–93.

13. Rolf's Little White Clay Creek may be the upper end of the White River that flows past Fort Robinson. His Mauvaises Terres or Bad Lands should not be confused with the present National Park in South Dakota. The White Earth River is today the White River. The old Red Cloud Agency was founded in the latter part of 1873. It was moved to the Missouri River in 1877 and moved again in the in the fall of 1878 to southwestern South Dakota and renamed the Pine Ridge Agency. On March 5, 1874, a temporary military post was established near the Red Cloud Agency. At first it was called Camp At Red Cloud Agency, but on March 29 it was officially christened Camp Robinson in honor of Lt. Levi H. Robinson, who had been killed by a party of Miniconjous and Hunkpapas the previous month. In May the camp was moved about

one and one-half miles up the river to a site that is today's Fort Robinson. Thomas R. Buecker, *Fort Robinson and the American West, 1874 - 1899* (Lincoln: Nebraska State Historical Society, 1999), 21, 26, 30.

14. Duncan Blackburn and his compatriots had successfully robbed several stagecoaches prior to the gang's capture in the Black Hills by Scott Davis on January 17, 1879. Davis was the captain of the guards or shotgun messengers hired by the Gilmer and Salisbury stage company. The Blackburn gang was tried, found guilty, and sentenced to ten years in the penitentiary. Robert J. Casey, *The Black Hills and Their Incredible Characters* (New York: Bobbs-Merrill Company, 1949), 233, 241–45; Mahnken, "The Sidney-Black Hills Trail," 221.

15. The tragedy occurred on June 12. Newspapers reported somewhat conflicting stories. Four men, two women, and three children were said to have perished. The women, children, and probably some of the men were from Mills County, Iowa, on their way to the Black Hills. Some of the men were muleskinners hauling mining machinery to the Hills. *Cheyenne Daily Leader*, June 15, 1879. Other papers reported that six men, two women, and two children died. *Sidney Telegraph*, Sept. 26, 1879.

There was a stage station and post office at Buffalo Gap managed by George Boland. A decade later it would be the terminus of the Fremont, Elkhorn, and Missouri Valley Railroad, the first line to reach the Black Hills. Casey, *The Black Hills*, 86–87.

16. Historian Robert J. Casey recounted the incident, but was misinformed concerning the date, which he said was October 1878. According to Casey, Cornelius "Lame Johnny" Donahue came to the Black Hills in 1877 from Philadelphia by way of Texas. For a time he served as a Custer County, South Dakota, peace officer, but rumors that he stole horses forced an early retirement. Then he was accused of robbing a stagecoach and was arrested on the Pine Ridge Reservation by detective Frank Smith. Smith and Lame Johnny set out for Deadwood on a stagecoach. Boone May went along on horseback as a guard, but rode some distance to the side of the coach and was sometimes out of sight. About four miles north of Buffalo Gap a masked gunman stopped the coach and allowed all the passengers to flee except Lame Johnny. When the passengers were out of sight of the coach they heard shots and when they returned Lame Johnny was gone. The next day Pete Oslund, boss of a bull train, happened upon Johnny's body hanging from a tree. The bullwhackers buried him by the tree. Jesse Brown and A. M. Willard, *The Black Hills Trails* (Rapid City, S. Dak.: Rapid City Journal Co., 1924), 298–301. Brown and Willard did not mention the stage driver or Tom Keating, but the latter may have been a member of Pete Oslund's train.

17. Crawford's poetry was mediocre and his assignments as a scout were few, but he was an exceptional self-promoter and became extremely popular, first appearing in Buffalo Bill Cody's show and then on his own. Darlis A. Miller, *Captain Jack Crawford: Buckskin Poet, Scout, and Showman* (Albuquerque: University of New Mexico Press, 1993). Tallent also described Jack Crawford as a poet-scout and to prove it quoted his eleven-verse poem about Custer's defeat at the Little Big Horn. Annie D. Tallent, *The Black Hills: or, The Last Hunting Ground of the Dakotas* (Sioux Falls, S. Dak.: Brevet Press, 1974), 165–68.

18. Jack Langrishe, from Dublin, Ireland, has been described as an actor of considerable talent. The Gem Theater was "the most raucous dive" in Deadwood. Casey, *The Black Hills*, 142.

19. Rolf mentions Martha "Calamity Jane" Canary in Deadwood again on August 11.

He may have met her, but so much fiction has crept into her life story it is difficult to find the truth. It has been reported that she was on a Missouri River steamboat bound for Fort Pierre on May 29, 1879. When she arrived she was probably hired as a bullwhacker on a train to Rapid City. The twenty-one-day trip would have allowed enough time for her to continue on to Deadwood. Roberta Beed Sollid, *Calamity Jane: A Study in Historical Criticism* (Helena: Montana Historical Society Press, 1995), 69–71. In a pamphlet entitled *Calamity Jane, Written by Herself* she says that in 1879 she drove freight wagons between Fort Pierre and Rapid City. Casey, *The Black Hills*, 358. The book Rolf quotes is II. N. Maguire, *The Black Hills and American Wonderland*, Vol. 4, No. 82 of the Lakeside Library (Chicago: Donnelly, Lloyd and Co., 1877).

20. "Colorado Charlie" was C. H. Utter, who arrived in Deadwood with his friend, James Butler Hickok, in mid-April 1876. After Wild Bill was shot Utter prepared his grave. Casey, *The Black Hills*, 161, 165.

21. Most western mining towns had a Chinese colony. They made a living by gleaning the tailings in the streams for gold the miners had missed. Other colonists operated small stores and businesses. Casey, *The Black Hills*, 348–39.

22. Tallent recounted a conversation she had with James Butler Hickok and portrayed him as a very refined and chivalrous gentleman. She concluded, "Wild Bill was by no means all bad. It is hard to tell what environments may have conspired to mould his life into the desperate character he is said to have been." Tallent, *The Black Hills*, 73. Wild Bill was playing poker when Jack McCall shot him in the back. Casey, *The Black Hills*, 164.

23. Alfred Howe Terry served in the Civil War and in the 1870s in the upper Missouri River country. He retired a major general in 1888. Heitman, *Historical Register*, 951.

24. William Garnett was employed as an interpreter at the Red Cloud Agency in 1874. List of Employees, Sept. 21, 1874, Red Cloud Agency, roll 718. Garnett was the son of Richard Brooke Garnett who was commander of Fort Laramie from 1852 to 1854. His mother was Looks At Him, a Lakota. When William was young he went to work for Jules Ecoffey, a road ranche operator near Fort Laramie. Donald F. Danker, "The Violent Deaths of Yellow Bear and John Richard Jr.," *Nebraska History* 63 (1982): 136–49. Rolf correctly identifies three Oglala Lakota leaders.

25. Stagecoaches were heavily guarded in an attempt to thwart thieves. In 1878 the *Sidney Plaindealer* described an "iron-clad treasure coach" with "arms-bristling messengers." The article ended with the comment, "Take warning road agents." *Sidney Plaindealer*, Nov. 28, 1878.

26. Rolf's description of Cheyenne is accurate. The town was founded in 1867, grew rapidly, and had a population of about 5,000 by 1879. Robert E. Strahorn, *The Handbook of Wyoming and Guide to the Black Hills and Big Horn Mountains* (Cheyenne, Wy.: Western Press, 1877), 142

27. The first hint of trouble with the Utes was noticed near present Meeker, Colorado. On November 30 Rolf would have more to write about the fight with the Utes.

28. Fort Collins was an army post established in 1863 to protect the overland stagecoaches. The military left four years later, but the civilian community remained. Prucha, *Guide to the Military Posts*, 66.

29. The Greenback political party advocated inflated money. This appealed to farmers and ranchers in the West and South as a way to reduce debts incurred in the early 1870s. Denis Kearney led a branch of the party in California. Irwin Unger, *The Greenback Era: A Social and Political History of American Finance, 1865–79* (Princeton: Princeton University Press, 1965) 385, n60.

30. The colony was organized in Chicago in November 1870 as a commercial enterprise. Within two months trustees of the association secured approximately 70,000 acres of railroad and government land along St. Vrain Creek and Boulder Creek to the south. Longmont was platted to be the colony's business center. Alonzo H. Allen, "Early Days in Longmont," *The Colorado Magazine* 14 (1937): 191–92.

31. The Utes did battle the army at this time and they were accused of setting fire to the forests outside of their reservation. This occurred about 150 miles to the west and across the continental divide so it is unlikely Rolf saw these fires, but the smoke could have drifted across the mountains. Robert Emmitt, *The Last War Trail: The Utes and the Settlement of Colorado* (Norman: University Oklahoma Press, 1954), 159.

32. Maj. Thomas Tipton Thornburgh with a command of 175 soldiers of the Fourth Cavalry was sent to rescue government employees of the White River Ute agency located west of Meeker, Colorado. On September 29 the command was trapped and forced to take a defensive position. Thornburgh was killed in the attack. The Ninth Cavalry went to their rescue and were also "corralled." Fortunately the Utes decided a truce was in their best interest and the soldiers were freed. Thomas R. Buecker, "One Soldier's Service: Caleb Benson in the Ninth and Tenth Cavalry, 1875–1908," *Nebraska History* 74 (1993): 55–56. Beginning in October, Colorado newspapers described the conflict in detail and followed its aftermath for weeks. *Denver Daily Times*, Oct. 1, 1879.
   Victorio's Apaches were beginning to cause trouble in the vicinity of the agency west of present Roswell, New Mexico. Bruce J. Dinges, "Benjamin H. Grierson," *Soldiers West: Biographies from the Military Frontier*, Paul Andrew Hutton, ed. (Lincoln: University of Nebraska Press, 1987), 165–66.

33. It was reported that Josephine Meeker was dressed in "Indian costume." Admission was fifty cents. *Denver Daily Times*, Nov. 29, 1879.

34. Nathan C. Meeker was in charge of the White River Ute agency. The immediate cause of the Ute offensive was Agent Meeker's insistence that a certain plot of land should be plowed. Canàvish or Johnson, the Ute headman, was equally determined that it would not be plowed. The argument escalated until the agent panicked and called in the U. S. Army. When the soldiers arrived the Utes led by Colorow fought off the troops. Agent Meeker and agency employees Frank Dresser, Frank Price, and others were killed and the agency buildings were burned on September 29, 1879. The agent's wife Arvella, daughter Josephine or Josie, and Mrs. Frank Price and her children were captured. The Meeker women were held prisoner by Douglas or Quinkent, a Ute leader opposed to the whites. Persune was with the kidnappers, but showed kindness to Josephine. Ouray was the head of the Utes in the Uncompahgre River country to the south. He sent a message to the White River people imploring them to surrender and an uneasy truce ended the fighting on October 10. Charles Adams was formerly a general in the Colorado militia and for a time agent at the White River agency. Because he knew these Indians the army sent him to Quinkent's camp, where he successfully negotiated for the release of the hostages. Emmitt, *The Last War Trail*, 151ff.

35. The actors and their acts were advertised in the *Denver Daily Times*, Dec. 2, 1879.

36. Reverend Dimock would give a sermon titled "The Pilgrim Fathers" at the First Congregational Church on the following Sunday. *Denver Daily Times*, Dec. 27, 1879.

37. The *Denver Republican*, Feb. 4, 1880, reported the same information, adding that Grimes was a member of the Doc Middleton gang.

38. The *Denver Republican*, Mar. 20, 1880, carried a brief note that Texas Jack appeared "in his border drama" in a matinee performance at Forrester's Opera House. Texas Jack was John Burwell Omohundro, a seasoned frontiersman, who was the trail agent with the Pawnee in 1872 on their last successful buffalo hunt. Riley, "The Battle of Massacre Canyon," 225. He died in Leadville, Colorado, on June 28, 1880. Russell, *Buffalo Bill*, 253.

39. On March 25, 1880, the *Denver Republican* reported the fire on Arapaho Street, but said the fire department arrived in minutes and no serious damage was done. The building was a dwelling and laundry.

40. In the fall of 1879 Bates and Nye installed new backgrounds for their photographs, but promised to keep the same low prices. *Denver Daily Times*, Oct. 7, 1879.

41. An election was held in November 1879 to determine the location of the county seat. The Swedes prevailed over "the ring" and Phelps Center became the new location. The courthouse was moved from Williamsburg during the winter. A short time later it was destroyed by fire and several years would pass before a new one was built. Andreas, *History of the State of Nebraska*, 1261–62. The post office was opened nearby on November 4, 1881. Appointment of Postmasters, roll 79.

42. Walter D. Deering invested heavily in real estate and had moved into an elegant house in Denver. In the afternoon of April 21 he checked into the Lawrence House, where he died within a few hours. Authorities first thought his death was the result of convulsions, but when they learned he had purchased a quantity of strychnine at a local drugstore they decided Deering had committed suicide. *Denver Republican*, Apr. 22–23, 1880.

43. The play was at Forrester's Opera House. Ticket prices ranged from twenty-five to fifty cents. *Denver Republican* May 4, 1880.

44. The Dan Costello and Company show placed large advertisements in the *Denver Republican* from May 17 to May 22, 1880, but the top billing went to "educated horses and performing goats." Signor Lowanda was not mentioned.

45. The incident happened on Holliday Street. It was reported that McCarthy was intoxicated when he fired three shots at Davis, hitting him twice. The police arrived almost immediately and arrested McCarthy. Davis was also taken to the city jail, but only to be treated for wounds in his chest. He may not have been allowed in the city hospital because he was a black man. Davis died three days later. *Denver Republican*, May 21, 24, 25, 1880.

46. The Denver and Rio Grande Railroad planned to build a line from Denver to Mexico City, Mexico. The narrow gauge line was completed to near Trinidad, Colorado, by 1876 but financial and other problems stalled the project. A branch line was built west of Cuchairas, Colorado, and then curved southward to Tres Piedras, New

Mexico. William S. Greever, "Railway Development in the Southwest," *New Mexico Historical Review* 32 (1957): 160.

47. Newspapers were reporting that Conejos was a boomtown. The railroad was only ten miles away and in the spring three new stores opened and there were eight additional saloons. *Denver Republican*, Mar. 22, 1880.

48. Fort Garland was garrisoned in 1858 to protect whites from the Utes and Apaches. It was abandoned in 1883. Prucha, *Guide to the Military Posts*, 75. Blanca Peak is probably present Mount Lindsey, north of Fort Garland, Colorado.

49. Sgt. John T. O'Keefe of the U.S. Army Signal Corps was stationed on Pikes Peak to record climatic data. In May 1876 Colorado newspapers reported the terrible attack by mountain rats on the sergeant, his wife, and their daughter. When hundreds of rats invaded their cabin O'Keefe and his wife wrapped themselves in zinc sheathing left from the construction of the cabin's roof. They finally fought off the rats, but were badly bitten and for a time it was thought the sergeant would lose an arm. Their two-month-old daughter was in a high crib and wrapped in blankets, but the animals found the baby and ate her, leaving only fragments of the infant's skull. The baby's rock-covered grave became a popular tourist attraction and contemporary photographs show visitors standing with hats in their hands somberly viewing the cairn. For several years almost everyone believed the story including Rolf, who even saw the rats "sticking up their heads to look at us." O'Keefe told other tall tales, including one about digging a well to a depth of 628 feet. In time people realized it was all a hoax. There was no well and there were no rats or any other animals on top of Pikes Peak capable of an attack on humans. Levette Jay Davidson, "The Pikes Peak Prevaricator," *The Colorado Magazine* 20 (1943): 216–25.

50. Rich silver deposits were discovered in the area early in 1879 and Leadville sprang up almost overnight. The railroad to Malta was completed in July 1880. The recent strike mentioned by Rolf may have been the war between the Denver and Rio Grande Railroad and the Santa Fe line over control of the right-of-way along the Arkansas River through Royal Gorge. The Denver and Rio Grande gained the upper hand in March. Ralph C. Taylor, *Colorado, South of the Border* (Denver: Sage Books, 1963), 338–45.

51. Rolf would have crossed only some foothills of the Santa Fe mountains between Espanola and Santa Fe. Fort Marcy was built in 1846 by United States troops during the Mexican War. The fort was abandoned in 1894. Prucha, *Guide to the Military Posts*, 90.

52. Lewis Wallace had served in the Mexican War and the Civil War. He was governor of the territory of New Mexico from 1878 to 1881 and author of the popular novel, *Ben Hur*. *Columbia Encyclopedia*, 2917.

53. Glorieta Pass was often called Apache Canyon. The battle occurred in March 1862. The victory by Union troops foiled a plan by the Confederacy to expand into the far West. J. F. Santee, "The Battle of La Glorieta Pass," *New Mexico Historical Review* 6 (1931): 66.

54. The Catholic Church at Santa Fe was razed to the ground and Spanish settlers were driven out of Pueblo country during the revolt of 1680. The territory was reoccupied in 1697 and Diego de Vargas was appointed governor. Construction of a new church did not begin until late in 1697, a few months after de Vargas was removed

from office. Fray Angelico Chavez, "Santa Fe Church and Convent Sites in the Seventeenth and Eighteenth Centuries," *New Mexico Historical Review* 24 (1949): 90.

55. Scouts Jose Pieda and Patricio Sanchez have disappeared from history. Ranald S. Mackenzie was a young colonel when he arrived in Texas in 1867 and served in the Southwest until 1876. J'Nell L. Pate, "Ranald S. Mackenzie," *Soldiers West: Biographies from the Military Frontier*, Paul Andrew Hutton, ed. (Lincoln: University of Nebraska Press, 1987), 178–84.

56. The Atchinson, Topeka, and Santa Fe Railroad reached Albuquerque in April 1880, and a depot was built about two miles from the old townsite. Greever, "Railway Development in the Southwest," 162.

57. The Atlantic and Pacific Railroad was a subsidiary of the Atchinson, Topeka, and Santa Fe. Ibid., 164.

58. Fort Wingate was founded in 1868 near Gallup in western New Mexico. Prucha, *Guide to the Military Posts*, 117.
Rolf's scouting party was probably just that and no more. The Ninth Cavalry was made up of black enlisted men and white officers. In April 1880 they disarmed some of Victorio's Apaches, but many of the band escaped into Mexico. During the summer Victorio returned, but was out-maneuvered by the Tenth Cavalry and forced back to Mexico, where he was killed by Mexican soldiers. Bruce J. Dinges, "Benjamin H. Grierson," 166.

59. El Rito was in Laguna County, although the several different groups in central New Mexico did not observe specific boundaries. Many religious ceremonies diffused into the Southwest from Mexico at different times, but worshiping Montezuma was not among them. James Seavey Griffith, "Kachinas and Masking," *Handbook of North American Indians*, William C. Sturtevant, ed. (Washington, D.C.: Smithsonian Institution, 1983), 10:765.

60. The Navajo reservation was established in northeastern Arizona in 1868, but many Navajos lived outside the reserve. Rolf correctly identified the head chief, but his name was usually spelled Manuelito. Frank D. Reeve, "The Government and the Navaho, 1878–1883," *New Mexico Historical Review* 16 (1941): 281.

Bibliography

Alexis, Joseph. "Swedes in Nebraska." *Publications of the Nebraska State Historical Society* 19 (1919): 78–85.

Allen, Alonzo H. "Early Days in Longmont." *The Colorado Magazine* 14 (1937): 191–98.

Allen, Tom. "Once-Lively Harmony Hall Now Abandoned And Forgotten." *Stuhr Museum News* 31 (1997): 3–4.

Andreas, A. T. *History of the State of Nebraska*. Chicago: Western Historical Company, 1882. Nebraska State Genealogical Society reprint, 1983.

Arnold, W. H. *Arnold's Complete Directory of Phelps County, Nebraska*. Kearney, Nebr.: W. H. Arnold, 1909.

Bang, Roy T. *Heroes Without Medals: A Pioneer History of Kearney County*. Minden Nebr.: Warp Publishing Co., 1952.

Barton, H. Arnold. *Letters from the Promised Land: Swedes in America, 1840–1914*. Minneapolis: University of Minnesota Press, 1975.

Bassett, Samuel C. "Free Homestead Colony of Buffalo County, Nebraska." N.p, n.d. Nebraska State Historical Society, Lincoln.

Bengston, B. E. *Pen Pictures of Pioneers*. Vol. 1, N. p., 1926. Vol. 2, Holdrege, Nebr.: Progress Printing Co., 1931.

Billdt, Ruth. *Pioneer Swedish-American Culture in Central Kansas*. Lindsborg, Kan.: Lindsborg News-Record, 1965.

Biographical Souvenir of the Counties of Buffalo, Kearney, Phelps, Harlan and Franklin, Nebraska. Chicago: F. A. Battey, 1890. Nebraska State Genealogical Society Reprint, 1983.

Blegen, Theodore C. "Leaders in American Immigration." *Transactions of the Illinois State Historical Society* 38 (1931): 144–55.

Bloch, Dan. "The Saga of a Wandering Swede." *1954 Brand Book* 10 (1955): 237–93. Denver Posse of the Westerners. Boulder, Colo.: Johnson Publishing Co.

Bogart, Ernest Ludlow and Charles Manfred Thompson. *The Centennial History of Illinois*. 4 vols. Springfield: Illinois Centennial Commission, 1920.

Brown, Jesse and A. M. Willard. *The Black Hills Trails*. Rapid City, S. Dak.: Rapid City Journal Co., 1924.

Brown, Ralph H. *Historical Geography of the United States*. New York: Harcourt, Brace and Company, 1948.

Buecker, Thomas R. "One Soldier's Service: Caleb Benson in the Ninth and Tenth Cavalry, 1875–1908," *Nebraska History* 74 (1993): 54–62.

———. *Fort Robinson and the American West, 1874–1899*. Lincoln: Nebraska State Historical Society, 1999.

Buhrdorf, Aubrey J., comp. *History of Cheyenne County, Nebraska*. Dallas, Tex.: Curtis Media Corp., 1987.

Casey, Robert J. *The Black Hills and Their Incredible Characters*. New York: Bobbs-Merrill Company, 1949.

Chavez, Fray Angelico. "Santa Fe Church and Convent Sites in the Seventeenth and Eighteenth Centuries." *New Mexico Historical Review* 24 (1949): 85–94.

Clark, Clifford Edward. *Henry Ward Beecher: Spokesman for a Middle Class America*. Urbana: University of Illinois Press, 1978

Compendium of the Tenth Census, June 1, 1880, Part II. Washington, D. C.: GPO, 1888.

Cook, James H. *Fifty Years on the Old Frontier*. Norman: University of Oklahoma Press, 1957.

Colton's Map of the Land Grant to the Union Pacific Rail Road, 1873. M782, 1872, C72. Nebraska State Historical Society, Lincoln.

Columbia Encyclopedia. New York: Columbia University Press, 1993.

Cox, Jennie. "Arapahoe." Furnas County Historical Society, comp. *Furnas County, Nebraska*. Dallas, Tex.: Curtis Media Corp., 1987.

Culver, Selma Clarine. "Jonas Clarine." Furnas County Historical Society, comp. *Furnas County Nebraska*. Dallas, Tex.: Curtis Media Corp., 1987.

Danker, Donald F. "The Violent Deaths of Yellow Bear and John Richard Jr." *Nebraska History* 63 (1982): 136–49.

Davidson, Levette Jay. "The Pikes Peak Prevaricator." *The Colorado Magazine* 20 (1943): 216–25.

Dick, Everett. *Conquering the Great American Desert*. Lincoln: Nebraska State Historical Society, 1975.

———. "Water a Frontier Problem." *Nebraska History*, 49 (1968): 215–45.

Dinges, Bruce J. "Benjamin H. Grierson." *Soldiers West: Biographies from the Military Frontier*, Paul Andrew Hutton, ed. Lincoln: University of Nebraska Press, 1987, 157–76.

Dowie, James Iverne. "Prairie Grass Dividing." *Augustana Historical Society Publications* 18 (1959).

———. "Sven Gustaf Larson, Pioneer Pastor to the Swedes of Nebraska." *Nebraska History* 40 (1959): 207–21.

Eide, A. Clyde. "Free as the Wind." *Nebraska History* 51 (1970): 25–47.

Emmitt, Robert. *The Last War Trail: The Utes and the Settlement of Colorado*. Norman: University Oklahoma Press, 1954.

Erdahl, Sivert. "Eric Janson and the Bishop Hill Colony." *Journal of the Illinois State Historical Society* 18 (1925): 503–74.

Estey, Margaret (Jones). "Pioneer Sketch." Paul D. Riley. Collection. Nebraska State Historical Society, Lincoln.

Francis, Page T. "Reminiscences of Page T. Francis." *Publications of the Nebraska State Historical Society* 19 (1919): 46–52.

Garber, Silas. Papers. RG1 SG11. Nebraska State Historical Society, Lincoln.

Gard, Wayne. *Sam Bass*. Boston: Houghton Mifflin Company, 1936.

German, Rex and Russ Czaplewski. *Battle of the Bridges*. Lexington, Nebr.: Dawson County Historical Society, 1988.

Greever, William S. "Railway Development in the Southwest," *New Mexico Historical Review* 32 (1957): 151–203.

Griffith, James Seavey. "Kachinas and Masking." *Handbook of North American Indians*. 20 vols. William C. Sturtevant, ed. Washington, D.C.: Smithsonian Institution, 1983, 10:764–77.

Grinnell, George Bird. *The Fighting Cheyennes*. Norman: University of Oklahoma Press, 1956.

Gue, Benjamin F. *History of Iowa*. 4 vols. New York: Century History Co., 1903.

Hallberg, Carl V. "Soperville: An Immigrant Community in Knox County." *Journal of the Illinois State Historical Society* 74 (1981): 51–57.

Hanson, Charles E., Jr. "Marking the Grave of Alexander Culbertson." *Nebraska History* 32 (1951): 120–29.

Haskell, John. *Judge William Gaslin, Nebraska Jurist*. Omaha, N.p., 1983.

Hayworth, J. M. "Cheyenne and Arapahoe Agency." *Annual Report of the Commissioner of Indian Affairs*. Washington, D.C.: GPO, 1877: 81–90.

Heitman, Francis B. *Historical Register and Dictionary of the United States Army*. Washington, D. C.: GPO, 1903.

Hutton, Paul Andrew, ed. *The Custer Reader*. Lincoln: University of Nebraska Press, 1992.

Hyde, George. *The Pawnee Indians*. Norman: University of Oklahoma Press, 1974.

Irwin, James. "Red Cloud Agency." *Annual Report of the Commissioner of Indian Affairs*. Washington, D.C: GPO, 1877: 62–63.

Johnson, Harrison. *Johnson's History of Nebraska*. Omaha: Herald Printing, 1880.

Kearney County, Nebraska. Tax Lists. County Treasurer's Office, Minden, Nebraska.

Larson, Ralph Arthur. *Three Brothers from Nebraska*. Alexandria, Minn.: Echo Printing, 1978.

Lass, William E. *From The Missouri to the Great Salt Lake*. Lincoln: Nebraska State Historical Society, 1972.

Lindberg, John S. *The Background of Swedish Emigration to the United States*. (Minneapolis: 1930).

Lindquist, Emory. "The Swedes in Kansas Before the Civil War." *Kansas Historical Quarterly* 19 (1951): 254–68.

Mahnken, Norbert. "Early Nebraska Markets for Texas Cattle." *Nebraska History* 26 (1945): 91–103.

———. "Ogallala—Nebraska's Cowboy Capital." *Nebraska History* 28 (1947): 85–109.

———. "The Sidney-Black Hills Trail." *Nebraska History* 30 (1949): 203–25.

Mattes, Merrill and Paul Henderson. "The Pony Express: Across Nebraska From St. Joseph to Fort Laramie." *Nebraska History* 41 (1960): 83–122

McCoy, Shirley I. "Ben Burton." Furnas County Historical Society, comp. *Furnas County, Nebraska*. Dallas, Tex.: Curtis Media Corp., 1987.

McGillycuddy, V. T. "Red Cloud Agency, 1879." *Annual Report of the Commissioner of Indian Affairs*. Washington, D.C.: GPO, 1879: 37–40.

Miller, Darlis A. *Captain Jack Crawford: Buckskin Poet, Scout, and Showman*. Albuquerque: University of New Mexico Press, 1993.

Mitchell, Joseph Clark. *An Early History of Phelps County, Nebraska*. Masters thesis, University of Nebraska, 1927.

Murphy, Harriet Persinger Searcy. "A. B. Persinger, Nebraska Panhandle Pioneer," *Nebraska History* 54 (1973): 251–306.

Nance, Albinus. Papers. RG1 SG12. Nebraska State Historical Society, Lincoln.

National Archives and Records Administration. Letters Received by the Office of Indian Affairs, 1824–81, Red Cloud Agency (National Archives Microfilm Publication M234). Record Group 75. Records of the Office of Indian Affairs.

———. Report of Post Office Site Locations (National Archives Microfilm Publication M1126). Record Group 28. Records of the U.S. Post Office Department.

———. Record of Appointment of Postmasters. (National Archives Microfilm Publication M841). Record Group 28. Records of the U.S. Post Office Department.

Nebraska Blue Book 1994–95. Lincoln: Joe Christensen, Inc., N.d.

Nebraska Board of Pardons and Parole. RG034. Nebraska State Historical Society, Lincoln.

Nebraska State Census of 1885. National Archives Microcopy 352, roll 42. Schedule of the State of Nebraska.

Nelson, Helge. *The Swedes and Swedish Settlements in North America*. Lund, Sweden: 1943.

Official State Atlas of Nebraska. Philadelphia: Everts and Kirk, 1885.

Olson, Ernest W., ed. *History of the Swedes of Illinois*. 2 vols. Chicago: Engberg-Holmberg Publishing Co., 1908.

Olson, James C. and Ronald C. Naugle. *History of Nebraska*. Lincoln: University of Nebraska Press, 1997.

Olson, James C. *Red Cloud and the Sioux Problem*. Lincoln: University of Nebraska Press Bison Book, 1975.

O'Reilly, Harrington. *Fifty Years on the Trail: A True Story of Western Life*. Norman: University of Oklahoma Press, 1963.

Ostergren, Robert C. "Cultural Homogeneity and Population Stability Among Swedish Immigrants in Chisago County." *Minnesota History* 43 (1973): 255–69.

Overton, Richard C. "Why Did The C. B. & Q. Build to Denver?" *Nebraska History* 40 (1959): 177–206.

Pate, J'Nell L. "Ranald S. Mackenzie." *Soldiers West: Biographies from the Military Frontier*. Paul Andrew Hutton, ed. Lincoln: University of Nebraska Press, 1987, 177–92.

Perky, Charles. *Past and Present of Saunders County, Nebraska*. 2 vols. Chicago: S. J. Clark Publishing Company, 1915.

Phelps County, Nebraska. Marriage Records, 1887–98. RG255. Nebraska State Historical Society, Lincoln.

Phelps County Historical Society, comp. *History of Phelps County, Nebraska*. Dallas, Tex.: Taylor Publishing Co., 1981.

Prucha, Francis Paul. *Guide to the Military Posts of the United States*. Madison: State Historical Society of Wisconsin, 1964.

Reeve, Frank D. "The Government and the Navaho, 1878–1883." *New Mexico Historical Review* 16 (1941): 275–312.

Ricker, Eli S. Collection. MS8, Interviews. Nebraska State Historical Society, Lincoln.

Riley, Paul D. "Red Willow County Letters of Royal Buck, 1872–1873." *Nebraska History* 47 (1966): 371–97.

———. "The Battle of Massacre Canyon." *Nebraska History* 54 (1973): 221–49.

——— Collection. Nebraska State Historical Society.

Rockwell, Wilson. *The Utes: A Forgotten People*. Denver: Sage Books, 1956.

"Rocky Mountain Locust, or Grasshopper of the West." *Report of the Commissioner of Agriculture, 1877*. Washington, D. C.: GPO, 1878.

Ruede, Howard. *Sod-House Days: Letters from a Kansas Homesteader, 1877–78*. John Ise, ed. Lawrence: University Press of Kansas, 1983.

Runblom, Harold and Hans Norman. *From Sweden to America: A History of the Migration*. Minneapolis: University of Minnesota Press, 1976.

Russell, Don. *The Lives and Legends of Buffalo Bill*. Norman: University of Oklahoma Press, 1960.

Santee, J. F. "The Battle of La Glorieta Pass." *New Mexico Historical Review* 6 (1931): 66–75.

Schnurr, Clarence. "Edgar Beecher Bronson." *Sioux County: Memoirs of its Pioneers*. Ruth Van Ackeren, ed. Harrison, Nebr.: Harrison Ladies' Community Club, 1967.

Sheldon, Addison E. "Land Systems and Land Policies in Nebraska." *Publications of the Nebraska State Historical Society*, 22 (1936).

Sollid, Roberta Beed. *Calamity Jane: A Study in Historical Criticism*. Helena: Montana Historical Society Press, 1995.

Stephenson, George M. *The Religious Aspects of Swedish Immigration: A Study of Immigrant Churches.* Minneapolis: n.p., 1932.

Strahorn, Robert E. *The Handbook of Wyoming and Guide to the Black Hills and Big Horn Mountains.* Cheyenne, Wy.: Western Press, 1877.

Stratton, Joanna L. *Pioneer Women: Voices from the Kansas Frontier.* New York: Simon and Schuster, 1981.

Tallent, Annie D. *The Black Hills: or The Last Hunting Ground of the Dakotas.* Sioux Falls, S. Dak.: Brevet Press, 1974.

Taylor, Ralph C. *Colorado, South of the Border.* Denver: Sage Books, 1963.

Trott, Elenor. *Svenska Nebraska.* York, Nebr.: Gillen Inc., 1967.

Unger, Irwin. *The Greenback Era: A Social and Political History of American Finance, 1865–79.* Princeton: Princeton University Press, 1965.

United States Census of 1880, Phelps County Nebraska.

United States Census of 1880, Phelps County Nebraska. Schedule 2, Products of Agriculture.

United States General Land Office. *Tract Books.* vols. 123–26. RG508. Nebraska State Historical Society, Lincoln.

Unruh, John D., Jr. "The Burlington and Missouri River Railroad Brings the Mennonites to Nebraska." *Nebraska History* 45 (1964): 3–30, 177–206.

Watkins, Albert. "The Beginnings of Red Willow County." *Publications of the Nebraska State Historical Society* 19 (1919): 29–63.

Williams, Henry T., ed. *Williams' Illustrated Trans-Continental Guide of Travel from the Atlantic to the Pacific Ocean.* New York: Henry T. Williams Publisher, 1877.

Woodward, W. E. *Meet General Grant.* New York: Horace Liveright, 1928.

Zehr, Mrs. Clifford. "William H. Knaggs." *Where the Buffalo Roamed.* Shenandoah, Iowa: World Publishing Co., 1967, 255–56.

Newspapers

Black Hills Daily News, Deadwood, South Dakota.

Central Nebraska Press, Kearney, Nebraska.

Cheyenne Daily Leader, Cheyenne, Wyoming.

Columbus Journal, Columbus, Nebraska.

Daily State Journal, Lincoln, Nebraska.

Denver Daily Times, Denver, Colorado.

Denver Republican, Denver, Colorado.

Fremont Daily Herald, Fremont, Nebraska.

Gothenburg Independent, Gothenburg, Nebraska.

Gothenburg Times, Gothenburg, Nebraska.

Grand Island Independent, Grand Island, Nebraska.

Grand Island Times, Grand Island, Nebraska.

Holdrege Citizen, Holdrege, Nebraska.

Holdrege Daily Citizen, Holdrege, Nebraska.

Holdrege Republican, Holdrege, Nebraska.

Holdrege Weekly Progress, Holdrege, Nebraska.

Kearney Daily Hub, Kearney, Nebraska.

Nebraska City News, Nebraska City, Nebraska.

Nebraska Nugget, Holdrege, Nebraska.

Omaha Daily Herald, Omaha, Nebraska.

Platte Valley Independent, Grand Island, Nebraska.

Republican Valley Sentinel, Orleans, Nebraska.

Sidney Plaindealer. Sidney, Nebraska.

Sidney Telegraph. Sidney, Nebraska.

Trenton Torpedo, Trenton, Nebraska.

Index